90 Days to C.E.O

A GUIDE TO AVOID BUSINESS PITFALLS AND UNLOCK THE SECRETS OF ENTREPRENEURSHIP

Rochelle Graham-Campbell

Printed in the United States of America

First Printing, 2019

ISBN: 978-0-578-56547-7

Book Design by
www.roushellereign.com

Published by RG Legacy Enterprises LLC

FOREWORD

Rochelle's destiny was written in her name. Her name means Little Rock, and it would be easy to say she has lived up to that title and more.

Rochelle was destined to be an entrepreneur from a very early age. I can remember when she decided to sell candy in middle school. Rochelle talked me into taking her to Sam's Club and we would get bags and bags of candy that she would take to school and sell to her classmates. She would easily make four times more money than what she had spent, proving her early entrepreneurial prowess. Soon after, her teacher got wind of what was going on and shut down Rochelle's business. To her dismay, that same teacher initiated a candy-selling business of her own the very next week in the same classroom that my daughter had been servicing. Rochelle was so annoyed. The event upset her so much that she decided this was never going to happen to her again. But what she wasn't aware of at twelve years old was that this was the beginning of a good thing.

People say that imitation is the sincerest form of flattery, and that has proven to be a theme in Rochelle's life and career. Today, she continues to be a guiding light to others, and a model of excellence within her industry. Her business style and approach have been emulated by many but duplicated by none. Some might call it motherly bias, but I know it to be a fact – my daughter was born for business.

Rochelle is special and I am truly honored to be her mother. I vividly remember when she was about five years old and did something wrong – as children do. What's more is that Rochelle was well aware that what she did was wrong. She confessed to my Aunt Veda and actually advocated for her own punishment. She told Aunt Veda that she should not "spare the rod and spoil the child," a proverb well beyond my daughter's years at the time. It's hard to say where she got that from because I never spanked her growing up. It could be that she heard it from church, but when I asked her how she came up with that, she told me that God had written it on her heart. And so, at just five years old, this incident confirmed for me that my child was special. Rochelle was a light to be reckoned with and she was going to make an indelible mark on this planet. I knew she would contribute to society in ways that I could not even imagine. Even decades later, I know that she has only just gotten started. I know her journey will be a challenge, but I'm not worried. When you talk about brilliant, smart, energetic, and lovely – you're talking about Rochelle.

Rochelle and I have such a strong bond as mother and daughter. As I grow older, she's more like my little sister and best friend. We are more alike than different, and the older I get, the more I realize that she's so much like me in so many ways. Every day I am so grateful for the relationship I have with her, and to bear witness to her ups and downs in life and business. My little rock has grown into a woman, mother, wife, and entrepreneur I am proud to know.

– Marlene Moulton

TABLE OF CONTENTS

INTRODUCTION

BREADSTICKS TO BREADWINNING

"Welcome! My name is Rochelle and I'll be your server this evening. How may I help you?"

Like many broke college students working shifts at insert-restaurant-chain-here, these words were embedded in my brain like a song. Night after night, after a full day of classes, I'd put on my apron, throw my hair in a bun, and rush over to my night shift waiting tables at the Olive Garden in Tampa, Florida. After hours of endless breadsticks, I'd then head off to my second job chucking newspapers with my husband from 11 pm to 2 or 3 o'clock in the morning — Every. Damn. Day. Clearly committed to my own demise, my third job — yes, third — was working as a CNA at the nursing home down the block from my apartment. Between three jobs and four to six classes a day at the University of Southern Florida, I was seriously tapped out.

One day I decided to work an extra night at Olive Garden. I traded shifts with my coworker Tiffany and ended up making an extra $100 in tips. Little did I know, that $100 would change my life forever. Fast-forward to today and I am now the co-founder and C.E.O of Alikay Naturals, an internationally distributed natural hair, skin, and body care brand with organic ingredients at affordable prices. I make all my own formulas, operate my own manufacturing facility, and run the company with my husband and business partner of twelve years, Demond. I've been self-employed as an entrepreneur from the age of twenty-two, and have built my business from the ground up, completely debt-free. The best part? It all started from that one shift at Olive Garden and that same hundred bucks. Thanks, Tiffany!

That pocket change allowed me to purchase the ingredients, bottles, and labels for my very first homemade hair products. By investing that money into my kitchen concoctions, I've been able to build a successful bootstrapped business and go from selling my products on Etsy, to lining the shelves of Target, Walmart, CVS, Rite Aid, JCPenney, Bed Bath & Beyond, and Kroger, in twenty-two countries. Through hustle, hard work, and a hell of a lot of faith, I've been able to survive and thrive through my first decade of entrepreneurship. This is my story: from server to C.E.O, breadsticks to breadwinning.

But enough about me. Let's talk about you.

Let's talk about that idea you've been brewing in the back of your head for months. Let's talk about that product or service that everyone and their mother have been telling you to sell for years. Let's talk about those dreams of running your own business collecting dust in your heart. Did I strike a nerve? Good.

If you picked up this book it must be for a reason, and that reason is that you're ready. You're past the idea phase; you're no longer brainstorming, hoping, or wishing upon a star. You're in the action phase: branding, marketing, pitching, licensing, hiring, and making real, honest-to-goodness revenue off of your side-hustle. Maybe you're tired of splitting focus between your nine to five and your passion. Maybe you're itching to leave and get out there on your own, full-time! Well, I'm here to tell you that you can absolutely do it. That beauty salon, restaurant, consulting business, event planning agency, tech startup — whatever it is, you can do it. It's possible. And not in three, five, or ten years. It's possible. *Now.*

IMPOSSIBLE?...PSSH!

But the world is full of zanies and fools

Who don't believe in sensible rules

And don't believe what sensible people say

And because these daft and dewy-eyed dopes keep building up impossible hopes

Impossible, things are happening every day

> *- Whitney Houston, Rodgers & Hammerstein's Cinderella (1997 production)*

In the words of the late, great Whitney Houston, impossible things are happening every day — but they don't happen to just anyone. The Fairy Godmother doesn't swoop in and grant the wishes of any old girl walking down the street. No. It's the woman who is on her grind —Cinderella style — putting in her work, day after day. That's the woman whose visions become reality. I know how it feels to hustle hard; I know the work it takes to go from prayer to profit because I've done it myself. Now, I want to help you do the same. Just call me Fairy Business Godmother Rochelle, only instead of a gown and horse-drawn carriage, I'm giving you my personal rules to entrepreneurship. Poof!

For too many of us, starting and running a successful business is like losing those last 10 pounds. It would be nice, but it never seems to happen. Why? We're scared. Why are we scared? We don't know what the hell we're doing! When you know better, you do better, right? Well, what I've realized is that most of us don't know enough about entrepreneurship. Allow me to fill in the blanks, give you the cheat codes, and the answers in the back of the book.

WHAT THIS IS...

A no-nonsense guide to business - for both men and women. I'll give you the tea on everything from getting started to daily operations, hiring and building a team, pivoting after failures, time and money management, staying focused, and more. We'll also get into self-care, affirmations, knowing your worth, and juggling family and relationships with work. Why? Because there are two sides to being a successful entrepreneur: the business side and the human side. Nuggets of my journey will hopefully inspire you on your own path, but most importantly, this book is meant to give you the tools and the innovation behind the inspiration. The first eight chapters will give you the blueprint of my own professional journey as well as the key takeaways I've picked up along the way. In the last two chapters, I will break down the specifics of starting up and running your business in 90 days — a business Bible, if you will. There, you'll find a three-month checklist designed to get you to your goals. No secrets, full transparency. I want you to win.

WHAT THIS IS NOT...

Sugar, spice, and everything nice. In other words, if you want fluff and fantasy, this is not the book for you. If your business ideas only exist as Instagram inspo, this is not the book for you. If your side-biz is more hobby and less hustle, you guessed it, this is not the book for you. I'm not here to convince you to quit your day job or entice you with glamorous stories of the self-made woman. I'm also not here to add to the pile of untouched books on your coffee table — although I'm sure this book will look fabulous on your coffee table as well! I'm here to teach you how to become a C.E.O. I want to share with you all the things that I wish someone would have told me. This book is the real deal as to what to expect on your entrepreneurship journey — the heads-up that I didn't receive. I'm getting straight to the point; exactly what you need to know to get your business off the ground in 90 days.

This is a get-your-hands-dirty type of read. By the end, it should be dogeared, war-torn, and committed to memory. Okay, I may be exaggerating a bit, but you get the picture. Now break out that highlighter and let's get down to business — literally!

PART I.

NOURISH TO FLOURISH

"There is a season to sow and a season to reap."

In the beginning, keep your head down and do the work. Plant the seeds of your ideas firmly in your mind, tend and water your roots with patience, and nourish your business until it blossoms with life.

CHAPTER 1

KNOW YOUR ROOTS

If your business is a tree, your "why" is the roots. Your why is the reason behind your company; it's what keeps you and your business firmly planted while weathering the storms of entrepreneurship. Be warned — there will be many storms: failure, rejection, mistakes, trial and error, doubt, and the list goes on and on. I myself had three failed businesses before "making it" – whatever that means – with Alikay. We'll dive into those failures more in depth later on, but for now, know that what kept me going through all the uncertainty was sticking steadfastly to my roots, my why.

WHAT'S YOUR WHY?

If your answer is money, try again. Believe it or not, money is not the greatest motivator – not on its own, at least. I mean, think about it. People go to work every day for a paycheck. Does it keep them showing up? Sure. But does it get them there on time? Does it push them to produce their very best work? Does it keep them from calling out sick? Does it stop them from taking long lunches or secretly binging Netflix while on the clock? Of course not. That's because money, in and of itself, does nothing to incentivize the spirit. That's why your why has got to be bigger than dollars.

Don't get me wrong. Money may not buy happiness, but it sure as hell doesn't hurt, either. I'm not here to demonize money. As a business owner, profit should definitely be your goal. However, if you can attach a bigger reason, a goal beyond the green, *that* is what will keep you going when the going gets tough. Money is not the why, but the means to a larger purpose. My larger purpose? My loved ones.

ALL IN THE FAMILY

For me, family has always been my reason – the generations before me and the ones after. When I look at the level of sacrifice that my mother made, that my grandparents made, I know that my work is far from done. Thankfully, my grandparents have been able to watch me attain a level of success that none of us could have fathomed, but they're getting older every day. I'm watching the people who molded me age right in front of my eyes, and it's literally a ticking clock hanging over my head. Sure, they see my success, but I want them around to actually *experience* it, to reap the benefits. In my eyes, until granny is living it up, it's still grind-time.

Obviously, my kids are another huge motivation. As a mother, you literally make a choice to bring your children into the world. That comes with the responsibility to provide for them — not only financially, but emotionally and spiritually, as well. That means that momma has work to do, college funds to create, and an example to set. At seven and one and a half, respectively, my son, Landon Levi, and daughter, Serenity Sapphire may not understand exactly what mommy does, or why she has to leave them sometimes. Still, I bust my butt to make sure that they don't have to experience the same hardships that I have. On my hardest days, when I'm exhausted and want to throw my hands up and quit, I think of my family and I know that failure is not an option.

When it comes to my most successful company, Alikay Naturals, the family roots run deep. They're more than the why, they're the how my business came to be in the first place. Picture a young Rochelle, seven or eight-years-old, growing up in Jamaica under the watchful eyes of her mom and grandparents, including her Yaya. A sickly child, or pickney, as YaYa would say, I spent much of my childhood choking down mysterious herbal concoctions of my grandmother's design. An herbalist with a green thumb and a my-way-or-the-highway attitude, YaYa would single-handedly evaluate, diagnose, and treat any sneeze or sniffle that dared to escape from my body. My least favorite prescription of YaYa's was a God-awful salt water nasal wash she made me do every single morning. As tortuous as her methods and tense as our relationship might have been, my YaYa's methods introduced me to the power of nature and holistic healing.

She also taught me the power of serving your community. A devout Seventh Day Adventist, YaYa would take me to church with her every week. As we walked to church on Saturday mornings, neighbors would fly down their front steps for her seasoned diagnoses. After listening to descriptions of various illnesses and ailments, my YaYa would return the following week with vials and bottles of homemade medicines for her loyal customers. Back home, we would sit in her bedroom and read countless health books from her church sisters. Her favorite? *Back to Eden: The Classic Guide to Herbal Medicine, Natural Foods, and Home Remedies since 1939* by Jethro Kloss. A cult classic among Adventists, this book was her Bible, and together we'd read about all the amazing remedies that exist on God's green earth. Handing out her mixtures, YaYa would order, "drink this," "swish that around three times and spit," "rub this on your forehead." She was direct in her instructions and resolute in her purpose, and eight-year-old Rochelle watched in awe at the authority and respect she commanded from the entire neighborhood. More than anything, I remember the love she had for serving others.

If YaYa taught me about holistic healing and service, my Aunty Veda taught me the meaning of creativity and chasing joy. Aunty Veda is the grandmother who took my mother in and helped to raise me. To this day, she is my heartbeat and my inspiration; it was from Aunty Veda that I inherited my creative spirit. Together, we would collect plastic forks and spoons and weave crochet fabric through them to fashion beautiful placemats. We would take paper towel rolls and design them to look like lamps. There was no shortage to Aunty Veda's innovation and craftsmanship, and what I remember most was the joy she received from her creations. We would present them to my mother and she would laugh at our makeshift valuables, but still, Aunty Veda carried on with a smile. She truly loved to work with her hands and create something out of nothing.

It was her example that led me to start my very first business, Nyamani Chic. As I sat down making my handcrafted jewelry, I would think back on childhood days of whimsy and imagination with my aunt. My crafting eventually turned from jewelry to hair products, but Aunty Veda remains at the center of it all. I owe my creative spark to her.

Last but not least, my mom planted the seeds of grit, determination, and the entrepreneurial spirit. My mother is the epitome of a go-getter; the type to just jump and build a parachute on the way down. When I was just seven-years-old, she sat me down and told me that she had an opportunity to leave Jamaica and go to school in the states. To this very day, I know that my mom would have stayed right by my side had I asked her to, but instead, I gave her my blessing to go and follow her dreams for the both of us.

After immigrating to the United States on a scholarship to Howard University, my mother — formerly a lab technician in Jamaica — decided to go to medical school. When I finally came to the states two years later, she took me from my father's house, rescued me from an abusive stepmother, packed our bags, and moved us to Nashville where she attended medical school for four years. From there, we moved to Minnesota so that she could do her residency program at the prestigious Mayo Clinic. Unwilling to trust my care to anyone else, she brought me along to her classes where I literally watched as she cut open cadavers. Just three years ago, she opened up her own medical clinic, again, without a parachute, and has been learning the ropes of business every day since. Without a doubt, the fire in my belly comes straight from her.

Between my YaYa, my Aunty Veda, and my mother, the raw materials for entrepreneurship, creativity, innovation, and self-sufficiency are woven into the fabric of my DNA. It's why I named my company Alikay Naturals. It keeps me tied to my family, my roots, my why. Alikay is my middle name, meaning "impact on destiny and luck," two things that have definitely steered my life and career. Add to that a ridiculous Jamaican work ethic, and *voilà*!

So again, I ask you, what is *your* why? Whatever it is, keep it central in your life. Hold it close. Journal about it, stick post-its all over your home and office, create affirmations if you must. Tattoo it into your brain. Visualization is everything and the more you keep your why top of mind, the more likely that you and your business will thrive.

BRANCH OUT

Now that we've put down our roots, let's talk branches. Your branches are the effects your business will have on others; the larger reach that your company will provide. Ask yourself, what comes out of me starting this business? Whose lives will be touched? Why *this* business? Why *this* demographic? Why am *I* qualified to be a leader in this space? Alikay allows me to pursue financial freedom, feel fulfilled, exercise my creativity, and solve problems for my tribe of amazing supporters, Alikay

Nation. All of these things have an impact that branches out and exists beyond me and my needs as an individual.

Financial freedom allows me to provide for myself, yes, but it also allows me to care for my family. It enables me to secure money for my children's futures, to give my parents and grandparents the option to retire, and to give back and invest in my community. My financial freedom trickles down even further. Money allows me to employ more and more people and give *them* the means to provide for their own families as well.

Feeling fulfilled makes me happy, of course. It also makes me a better wife, mother, friend, and boss. It enriches my relationships, thus creating a better return for the people around me. Doing work that I actually enjoy also benefits anyone I conduct business with. Be they suppliers, hires, retailers, or future investors, people want to know that they are entering into deals with someone who is passionate about their work. Therefore, the happier I am, the happier everyone else will be, too.

Exercising my creativity through products and events is fun, but it also means that I'm constantly innovating. The more products I create, the more organic, healthy, and affordable options there are on the market through Alikay Naturals. The more options available, the more women, men, and children that have access to healthy hair care. The more videos I produce on my YouTube and social media channels, the more knowledge and empowerment is spread about techniques, styles, and treatments for the diverse range of natural hair types. Constantly innovating will not only allow you to flex those creative muscles and keep things interesting, but it will sustain growth in your company's revenue and create compounding value for your customers.

Finally, solving problems for my tribe is my legacy. It is what I hope to be known for when I leave this earth. More importantly, though, it will leave a lasting legacy for women like me at large. For example, one of my proudest accomplishments is creating one of the most widely used methods of natural hair care, the L.O.C. Method™. The acronym stands for "liquid, oil, cream," and is a means of instilling and maintaining hydration within the hair strands for optimal moisture, health, growth, and length retention. One quick search on Google or YouTube and literally thousands upon thousands of results will pop up of other vloggers and everyday women using the L.O.C. Method™ on their curls, coils, and kinks. I consider it one of the biggest parts of my personal legacy, even though by this point I know that many people have no clue where it started or who created it. To be honest, it doesn't even matter. My main goal is to create impact, not receive credit. I am more than satisfied just having contributed to the lexicon of natural haircare and reinforced the arsenal of knowledge surrounding hair education and self-love.

Starting a business will change your life, but it should change the lives of others, too. Before we continue, I want you to take a few minutes and ask yourself all the questions we discussed above. Visualize your business as a strong and mighty tree in full bloom. What are your roots? What are your branches? Remember, your roots are the why behind your company. Your branches are the impact your company will have on the world.

ROCHELLE GRAHAM-CAMPBELL

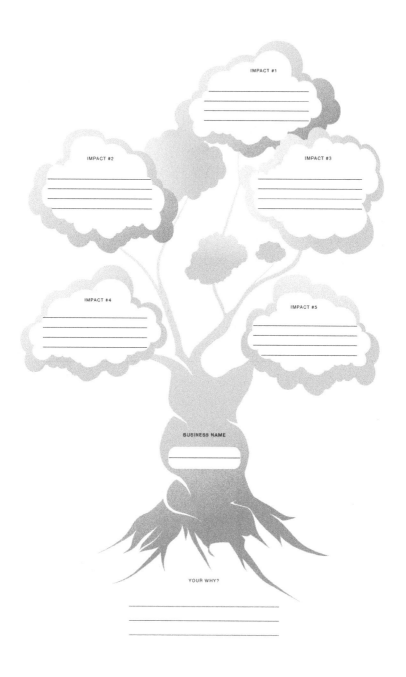

COMMUNITY

Another foundational part of any business is the customer. Your customers are the water that keeps your tree in bloom. They are what will keep your business viable, relevant, and bringing in the cash. It is critical to not only treat them well, but to get inside their heads. As a C.E.O, you must understand your consumer base not as a random collection of individuals, but as a cohesive community with very specific interests, needs, problems, likes, and dislikes. They are not a monolith by any means, but they do share many of the same values, lifestyles, and purchasing habits. Your job as the head of a burgeoning brand is to build a sense of unity between yourself and your customers. They need to feel heard, seen, and represented in all facets. This is how you establish trust from your tribe.

The best thing you can do when starting out is to get to know your customer on paper. Ask yourself the following questions:

Who is my primary consumer?

What is their gender?

What is their age?

What is their race and ethnicity?

Where do they live?

How much do they make in a year?

What are their spending habits?

Where do they shop?

What do they value in the products they purchase?

What do they value in the brands they support?

If you're feeling really creative, you might even give this hypothetical customer a name. The idea here is that imagination sparks innovation. The clearer you define who it is you are selling to, the better you will be able to meet their needs. For Alikay Naturals, the answers might look something like the following:

ALIKAY NATION CUSTOMER PROFILE

Gender	**Age Range**		**Marital Status**	
Female - 97%	14-18 = 1%	36-45 = 30%	Single - 53%	Divorced - 7%
Male - 3%	19-24 = 7%	46-55 = 20%	Married - 40%	Widowed - 1%
	25-35 = 38%	55+ = 4%		

Children	**Household Size (number of residents)**		**Ethnicity**
Yes - 56%	1 person - 22%	4-6 ppl - 27%	African-American - 84% Latino - 7%
No - 41%	1-3 ppl - 50%	6+ ppl - 1%	Caucasian - 5% Other - 4%

Prefer not to say - 3%

Highest Level of Education

High school diploma or equivalent - 11%

Technical training - 5%

Associate's degree - 14%

Bachelor's degree - 32%

Some college, but didn't graduate - 13%

Master's degree - 18%

Doctorate degree - 3%

Other - 4%

Employment Status	Country of Residence	U.S. States (Top 8)	
Below 10k - 4%	USA - 94%	New York - 12%	North Carolina - 6%
10k to 25k - 5%	Canada - 2%	Florida - 11%	Maryland - 5%
25k to 40k - 16%	Other - 4%	Texas - 6%	Illinois - 5%
40k to 60k - 19%	Georgia - 6%	California - 4%	
60k to 80k - 13%			
80k to 100k - 6%			
Over 100k - 14%			
Prefer not to say - 23%			

Shopping Habits

Buys Alikay for themselves or others?	How often do they purchase Alikay products?	
Themselves - 59%	Weekly - 1%	Once every 2-3 months - 48%
Others - 1%	Bi-weekly - 4%	Only during a sale - 30%
Both - 40%	Once a month - 17%	

What prevents them from shopping with Alikay more frequently? (Top 4)

Price point - 52%

Need less due to bigger purchasing sizes - 32%

Not enough knowledge of product - 6%

Most important factors when purchasing hair products

- product price
- natural/organic ingredients
- products free of harmful chemicals
- packaging design
- cruelty-free
- vegan
- positive customer reviews
- social media tutorials
- family/friend recommendations

Most effective advertising methods to persuade to purchase

- customer reviews
- social media tutorials
- sponsored posts on Facebook
- posts from the brand's owner

Top hair concerns/ Pain points

- moisture retention
- growth
- breakage
- dryness
- scalp issues

Knowing this information enables me to create products with my consumer base always in mind. Just like your why, referring back to this illustration of your core customer will keep you on track in the creative process as well as the daily operations of your business.

define your
target audience

Who is my primary consumer?

What is their gender?

What is their age?

What is their race and ethnicity?

Where do they live?

How much do they make in a year?

What are their spending habits?

Where do they shop?

What do they value in the products they purchase?

What do they value in the brands they support?

ALIKAY NATION

The reason I'm so big on vibing with your tribe is because my company would be nothing without the Alikay Nation. They've been with me since day one. I'm talking about the days before my products were sold in major retailers, before I had a staff full of employees, and before my company even had a name. The year was 2008 and I was a college student living with my new husband in a tiny apartment one hour from my campus. Demond and I eloped very young – at 23 and 20-years-old, respectively – and so it was the typical newlywed story: happy, in love, and broke as hell. On top of a full semester's course load of four to six classes, remember that I also worked three jobs as a CNA, a newspaper delivery woman, and an Olive Garden waitress, all just to pay for school and make rent.

Suffice it to say that I was burning the candle at both ends and I needed an outlet. Around that time, my husband and I had dinner with my mother, who had recently cut off all of her hair, a rite of passage that the natural hair community has dubbed, "the big chop." My husband was immediately infatuated. "Oh, my God! Rochelle, is your hair like hers? It's so beautiful! What does your natural hair look like?" The truth was, I had no idea what my hair was like. I had been chemically straightening my hair with a relaxer from childhood, and at the time my hair was tucked away in microbraids. Inspired by my mother's bold new look, I went to the bathroom that night, took a scissor to my microbraids, and cut it all off. By the time Demond woke up later that night, I had about an inch of hair on my head.

Any woman who has ever cut off her hair knows the feeling. There's a wave of euphoria followed almost immediately by a lump of dread in the pit of your stomach. You ask yourself, "what the hell did I just do?" And so, I did what we all do – I went on the internet to figure it out. Keep in mind, at this time there was no huge, mainstream sisterhood of natural hair gurus, but there was Fotki. Fotki was an online message board where lots of women congregated to discuss their natural hair concerns. The platform wasn't created for this purpose, but we made it our own.

Experimenting and trying to grow my hair out, I began posting photos and collages of my journey on the site. I had finally found that creative outlet I needed to blow off steam. For me, it was all just about having fun, experimenting with my new look, and growing my hair; I never once fathomed that anything would come from my posts. Nevertheless, a few of my photos became popular among the community, and as my hair grew longer, women began to message me about sharing videos on YouTube. At the time, YouTube was still in its infancy – just three years old – and I had absolutely no clue what it was. Still, prompted by my Fotki friends, I sat in my tiny apartment bathroom, grabbed an old Canon camera, and balanced it atop a makeshift tripod of toilet paper rolls. Thus, my YouTube channel, Blackonyx77 was born.

Once I made the switch to YouTube, my Fotki family followed. They commented on all my videos, asked for advice, and pumped me up in the comments section. When they saw how rapidly my hair began to grow, they demanded to know my se-crets – and so, I shared. Taking inspiration from my YaYa's love of nature and my Aunty Veda's passion for working with her hands, I created my own oil blend recipe comprised of 17 dif-ferent savior oils. This same recipe would later become the first, and to this day, best-selling product of Alikay Naturals, the Es-sential 17 Hair Growth Oil™ – but at this time, it was nothing more than a kitchen experiment. I recorded a YouTube video sharing my oil blend recipe, but to my surprise, my subscribers weren't having it. They didn't want to make the oil, they wanted to buy it. And so again, I was met with a demand from my in-ternet sisterhood – this time to mix, package, and sell my first ever product.

That's where that extra shift at Olive Garden came in. I couldn't afford to use my regular paycheck to buy materials and ingredients because, as my husband so lovingly remind-ed me, rent was due. Instead, I took the $100 I made in tips and bought some oils, containers, and labels from the Staples down the street. With my new materials, I got to work and whipped up a dozen bottles of the blend. I threw up a photo of the growth oil on my Etsy page, where I also sold handcrafted jewelry from my side-hustle, Nyamani Chic. Before I knew it, all twelve bottles had sold out; I was floored. From there, I con-tinued to make my oil blend, and soon, new recipes followed. I saw a hole in the market for hair products that were actually catered to coarse and kinky textures, and I filled it. The rest was history.

I tell you this story to say this. Trust your tribe. Never take your community for granted because their support will make or break you. Had it not been for my Fotki friends pushing me to make YouTube videos, I might never have made a channel. Had it not been for my YouTube subscribers, I might never have made that first product. These were my first true supporters outside of family and friends. These were the people who spent their hard-earned money on my humble products with the Staples labeling. These are the people who continue to buy, use, share, and review my products online, or walk into stores and make Alikay purchases while beaming with pride. It has been a long journey since preparing recipes in my kitchen, so a win for me is a win for all of Alikay Nation.

BACK TO BASICS

As you get farther along in your journey of entrepreneurship, you will be faced with new and unfamiliar challenges, each one seemingly more difficult than the last. As you advance, it's easy to lose sight of your foundation and get caught up in the rat race of chasing profit. It's hard to see the bigger picture when you're staring at the puzzle piece in front of you. If ever you find yourself feeling lost, overwhelmed, or disconnected from your purpose, take it back to the basics. Remember your roots and why you started. Remember to branch out and consider the impact your business can make. Remember that your customers are the community that you serve. A tree only bears fruit with proper nourishment, so sow your seeds with care. I promise you'll reap more than you can imagine.

Entrepreneur

One who organizes, manages, and assumes the risks of a business or enterprise.

Source: www.merriam-webster.com

Side Hustle

Something that earns an income other than your main job.

Source: Side Hustle: From Idea to Income in 27 Days by Chris Gullibeau

Risk Management

The technique or profession of assessing, minimizing, and preventing accidental loss to a business, as through the use of insurance, safety measures, etc.

Source: www.investopedia.com

Reinvestment

The investing of money or capital in order to gain profitable returns, as interest, income, or appreciation in value.

Source: www.investopedia.com

Ambition

A strong desire to do or to achieve something, typically requiring determination and hard work.

Source: Wikipedia

C.E.O

Short for Chief Executive Officer.

E.O.D

Short for End Of Day.

CHAPTER 2

DEEP CONDITIONING

I n the world of hair care, deep conditioning is the process of treating your hair with a high dose of moisture to nourish strands from the inside out. This treatment helps to boost softness and suppleness and reduces breakage. Can you see growth without deep conditioning? Maybe, but it's the extra level of care and attention that will maximize the long-term health and growth of your hair. The same is true of your business. To sustain a viable company over time, you must condition your mind with the tools for success. Train your brain for maximum growth.

Before we can get into cultivating a business mindset, it's important to know what you're up against. Entrepreneurship is not for the faint of heart and it's extremely difficult, especially for women; even more so for Black women. We're the fastest growing group of entrepreneurs today, and yet only 2% of Black woman-owned businesses ever see the $1 million mark. We receive disgracefully less funding from venture capitalists compared to our white male and female counterparts, if we even receive funding at all. As for my company, our lack of outside funding was actually a choice, but that just makes it all the more incredible that we've been able to have the longevity and success that we've experienced. To put it plainly, in the world of Black female entrepreneurship, Alikay Naturals is a unicorn; there aren't many companies out there that have beaten the odds like we have. We've gone from my kitchen countertop to opening up our own product manufacturing facility; from selling locally to product placement in 16,000 retail locations worldwide. What has made the difference? Of course, it's the product, quality, work ethic, vision, etc. But the biggest factor has been mindset, hands down.

survival of the fittest

The hard truth is that only about 45%-51% of small businesses survive beyond five years. In my experience, most budding entrepreneurs struggle, not because their ideas, products, or services are bad, but because they simply lack the proper foundations and skills necessary to build a business the right way. A lot of companies are failing because they're just doing it wrong – and yes, there is a wrong way, believe it or not. The wrong way encompasses any approach that is too quick, impatient, unfocused, uninformed, entitled; the list goes on. Now, it's okay to go down the wrong path temporarily. Anything you are doing for the first time will have a margin of error. In fact, it's almost inevitable when you're starting out; that's life. The key is to redirect yourself by acquiring the right knowledge and skills along the way. Before we jump into those crucial skills, let's go over some of the main reasons behind early entrepreneurial failures:

1. Lack of Preparation

The first and most obvious reason new business owners stumble is a lack of preparation. These are the folks who have not done the groundwork that we went over in chapter one. They have no direction or larger vision for their company. They haven't established their why or the impact they want to have. Going deeper, they haven't established measurable goals, timelines, or KPIs (key performance indicators). How are you going to track your growth? You just paid a social media influencer $5,000 to advertise your product, but do you know why? What are you getting out of that deal? Are the moves you're making in the best interest of scaling your business? So many people get so excited in the opening phases of launching their idea that they move too quickly. They're not discerning enough in how they allocate funds. They're just making moves, willy nilly; throwing things at the wall and hoping that something sticks. Inadequate preparation will lead you down a path of derailment every time.

2. Lack of Knowledge

Then there are those who do their research but end up with all the wrong information. In the age of social media, we're constantly bombarded with hundreds of coaches looking for a quick come-up. Don't get me wrong. These self-proclaimed business coaches may have pure intentions, but they're missing the qualifications. Where are their credentials? One of my biggest grievances is someone who takes money from a client promising results when they don't have the experience to back up those promises. You wouldn't coach in the NBA without ever holding a basketball. You wouldn't climb Mount Everest without ever going on a hike. Why would you coach people in business if you have no experience starting or managing a successful company? Don't be fooled by a huge social media following. Their coaching business does not count as business management experience if that's the only experience they have. There are so many entrepreneurs hungry for knowledge that simply fall prey to the wrong people with the wrong information. That is why I'm writing this book. I have lived everything that I speak, and all the advice and lessons I'm sharing with you come either from lived experience, or hindsight accrued after ten years of ups and downs. Of course, I want to inspire, but more than anything, I want to educate.

3. Lack of Humility

Entrepreneurs who lack humility fall prey to their own egos. These are the people who swear that they're doing everything right, and yet the sales just aren't coming in. These are the people who feel entitled to success, but too good for the struggle. Newsflash: entitlement is pure poison. No one owes you anything, in business or in life! Hubris tricks business owners into believing that the problem is always with the consumer, their staff, the market, or the universe – never with themselves. They play the victim card when their numbers don't come in as predicted and blame the world for their problems. As a business owner, you must learn to be solution-oriented rather than problem-focused. If you're too proud to reassess your own choices, you'll never see how you may be the one getting in your own way.

4. Lack of Work Ethic

Some people are just plain old lazy. Point, blank, period. They're only doing it for the gram, a.k.a. "Instagram," for those of you who read that and said, what?! They go into their offices or a pretty café, send a few emails, take a photo of the "hustle" for social media, and then leave to go hang out with their friends. Their business is not the number one priority in their lives, either because they are undisciplined, they don't really care enough, or they're overwhelmed and avoid the real work. Other people go into business without considering the kind of worker they are. Not everyone can be their own boss, set their own deadlines, and get things done without a supervisor. If you need constant direction or validation from a source outside of yourself, or if you need to clock out of work at 5pm every day, you're in for a really rough ride. At times, business ownership will feel like a 24/7 job and during those long hours, you'll have to be disciplined in order to produce results. It's the work you execute behind-the-scenes that shows real success in public.

5. *Lack of Resources*

Finally, in my experience, the primary reason that new businesses fail is a lack of resources. I can't tell you how many times I have come across amazing, inspired, driven entrepreneurs – super dedicated people with unmatchable work ethics and instincts – but sadly, they just don't have the resources to sustain their growth. They don't have funding, they don't have the money to hire employees or to increase production, and so their operation grows stagnant, or worse, shuts down altogether. I was fortunate enough to be able to self-fund with the profits from my sales. I also had a husband who was my dedicated business partner, and no kids to feed at the time we started out. This isn't the case for many start-up founders who depend on their profits to feed their children, especially those in single-income households. As for staff, I was blessed with grandparents who supported my vision so much that they were willing to work for me for low starting pay. They gave 120% effort for much less pay than they deserved because they knew it was all I could afford at the time. Don't get me wrong, none of these things made my process easy – employing family comes with its own special set of challenges – however, I would be remiss to ignore the help I received along the way.

For people who don't have resources or a strong support system, the road is even more of an uphill climb. Black women in particular face incredible challenges when seeking funding, no matter how excellent we are. Case in point, between 2007 and 2018, the number of new Black woman-owned businesses increased by 163%. We experienced 10 times the growth of non-minority women-owned companies, and yet still have trouble securing bank loans. Not only are we granted loans less frequently, but we are also likely to receive smaller amounts with higher interest rates. Banks often perceive Black loan applicants as more of a risk due to generally lower credit scores and less available collateral. The story is pretty much the same for those who seek funding from venture capitalists or angel investors instead. These investors are very often older white males who can't – or refuse to -- identify with our lives, stories, and ideas. Thus, they don't invest. Many Black women turn to pitching competitions as an alternative, but the prizes for winning are often modest amounts of $5,000 or $10,000. In other words, not quite enough to grow and scale. There are definitely those who work the system well and walk away with amazing sums, however, these cases are the exception, not the rule. Many of us are turned down, or simply struggle to find investors that are truly aligned with our visions.

So, where does this leave us? It sucks, of course. There's no doubt about it. But as the saying goes, it is what it is. The question then becomes, what are we going to do about it? Even if you can't relate to the specific challenges I face being a quad-minority in business (black, female, young, immigrant), there are still universal glass ceilings you will hit while building your business. If entrepreneurship is your dream and your purpose, you cannot take no for an answer. Don't get bogged down in the limits others place upon you. Instead, search for the nearest solution. Ask yourself, what can I actually control? How can I get around this hurdle? Because the truth is, no one is coming to save you. You have to be your own hero!

No staff? Guess what? You'll just have to play every part on your team until you level up. No funding? Well maybe you can't leave your nine to five just yet. Use your day job to fund your dream and send a portion of your check to savings. No degree? Use the world as your classroom. Even your job can teach you the mechanics of running a successful enterprise. Study the HR department to learn how to handle people. Learn lessons on leadership from your boss, good or bad. Stop viewing work as a burden and pay close attention to the learning opportunities. If you don't know something, Google it, duh! All the information you could ever need is online if you take the time to search. No mentors? Read — voraciously. There are too many articles, blogs, and autobiographies out there to count! Watch interviews, listen to podcasts, study the success stories you aim to achieve. You may not have physical access to these people, but you can still get into their heads and mine their stories for gold. A lack of resources doesn't have to be your demise. Don't get hung up on what you don't have or what you can't get access to. Focus more on what you do have, whether that be creativity, vision, or a number of any other unique assets. Use the strengths that you have and let those be the secret weapons to your success. Besides, for decades, entrepreneurs have always made magic out of thin air. You've got this.

This is why mindset is the most important aspect of business. It's about showing yourself what you're made of and how badly you really want it. Of course, there will be many days when you feel completely underwater, but you can't let yourself drown. Everything in business ebbs and flows. Slow down and tread water until you find the strength to swim again full-speed.

Now that we've covered why so many fail, let's discuss what it takes to win. Condition your mind and spirit to embrace the following ideals and you'll be cooking with gas!

1. Be Patient

You're playing the long game, here. Accept the fact that you will have to do a lot of work – a lot – before you see significant or consistent progress. Most people overestimate their effort and underestimate the time it will take to see results. To put things in perspective, my husband Demond and I were in business for five whole years before we ever even put ourselves on payroll. Five years! In the sixth year, when we finally started taking a salary from our company, we were still the lowest-paid employees at Alikay, aside from our warehouse workers. Now, I'm not saying that this will be the case for everyone, but people tend to think that everything is a rag-to-riches story. In reality, it will be quite some time before you reach the riches. Don't worry about balling out. Keep your head down and do the work. Remember, a watched pot never boils. That is to say, stop obsessing over the future and be present right *now*. Focus on consistency and the results will have no choice but to come.

2. Pivot

"Okay, and…?" This is a question you have to ask yourself a lot. So, your application was denied – okay, and…? Your latest campaign was a bust – okay, and…? That meeting didn't go as well as you anticipated – you catch my drift. Asking yourself this question takes the focus off the hurdle and channels it toward the finish line. It keeps you focused on the end goal and resilient in the face of obstacles. You will hear no and you'll hear it often. Learn how to pivot after roadblocks arise. A no is really just a *not just yet*. The unexpected detour can also be a blessing. Sometimes rejection is protection from things that are not meant for us, people who could be detrimental to our futures, or rooms we are not meant to be in. You may experience feelings of frustration or disappointment, yet still, you have to trust the process. Entrepreneurship is like a maze. There is a goal and there are many wrong turns you can take along the way, but no matter how many pivots you take, you need to stick with it. Eventually, you will find your way out.

3. Take Risks!

Condition yourself to thrive off of challenges and rise to the occasion. Like my mother, jump and build your parachute on the way down. To be an entrepreneur means to live in a state of risk and uncertainty; to seek it out. Sometimes you'll have to do things before you really know how to do them. When I got my first deal with Target, I didn't know if we could produce enough volume of product for the orders. All of our products were still hand-mixed and hand-bottled at that time. My options were: level up or bow out. So, what did I do? I took a risk. Not wanting to entrust our formulas to a manufacturing facility, Demond and I opened up our own. Did we know a damn thing about manufacturing on that scale? Hell no. Did we do it anyway? Yes, and now we can confidently fill massive orders without diluting our formulas and compromising the integrity of Alikay products. Remaining in your comfort zone will only stifle your progress. Growth happens in a place of discomfort, a place that stretches you beyond your current ability or perception. Learn to sit in that discomfort and thrive off of it.

4. Grind Now, Play Later

You have to accept the fact that you will have to give some things up. After your day job, you clock in on your dream. When you're living that 5-to-9 hustle after work, you're going to miss parties, events, and hanging out with friends and even family. You no longer have the luxury of turning work off for the weekend. At least one of those two days should be dedicated to going hard for your business. Club nights will be replaced with meetings, networking events, classes, and conferences. At first, your friends will probably think you're insane – I know mine did, and it was hard (still is) to juggle personal and professional obligations. To help me decide what to prioritize, I play by my "four-to-one" rule. I attend one event for every four I'm invited to. I'm selective and I use discretion. Using this rule-of-thumb still allows you to show effort to your friends and family and let them know you care, but there will be busy periods when you might decline all invitations because you're in a discipline stage. Never be afraid to say no and do so without feeling the need to explain yourself. Looking back now, some of my peers and colleagues say they wish they had the focus I did when I started my company. Sadly, they aren't happy with where they are in life right now, but back then, they didn't see the bigger picture. They didn't understand why I was turning down party invites to mix products in my kitchen. Don't be fazed by the weird looks and judgments. Others will not understand because God did not give them your same vision. Hold fast to your goals and work hard now so you can live the life you want later on.

5. Take Yourself Seriously!

Too many people have business dreams with a hobby mentality. Know the difference between being an entrepreneur and just having a passion project. If your hustle isn't making you consistent revenue, it's not a business. If you want to own and operate a real company, take yourself seriously and *act* like you run a company! That means, stop working for free; stop giving discounts to friends and family. If anything, your circle should be your first customers – a case study for your business. I understand that your family and friends may not actually be your target consumers, but they are a great place to start because they are typically the easiest people to convert. Think about it this way: if you can't convert your loved ones, how do you expect to earn long-term loyalty and business from complete strangers? If you can't effectively reach your neighborhood, how do you expect to reach the nation or the world? Stop being the person that does hair or caters on the side, and start being the businessperson, the mogul, the C.E.O that you are. This means that your side hustle is no longer just about blowing off steam or making a little extra pocket change. A lot of people throw around buzzwords like hustle and fill their time with things that make them busy. What we ought to do is work smart and live productively. What good is a full calendar if you are hustling backwards and running yourself into the ground? My worst fear is being in this same exact position in my business a year from now. A hustling mindset can be good, but will result in temporary wins if you're not careful. A business owner mentality, on the other hand, will give you long-term, ongoing rewards. It's not all about just doing what you love. Even in the things you love, there will be things you absolutely hate, but you have to do them for the advancement of your business.

CORE VALUES AND NON-NEGOTIABLES

A mogul mindset also means clearly establishing your core values and non-negotiables. These are the things that you will never compromise on. What are the words that are synonymous with your brand? For me, they're: organic, quality, premium, affordable, and authentic. The main premise of Alikay Naturals is "beauty without compromise." We have pledged to give our tribe the highest possible quality of product in clean, chemical-free ingredients, effectiveness, and packaging without breaking their bank accounts. Under no circumstances would we ever renege on that promise. Adhering to our pledge is what allows us to maintain and grow the trust between our brand and our customers.

Take a moment to determine your own core values. What are you willing to sacrifice to maintain them? Money? Media placements? What are you willing to put on the line to confidently claim the best product, service, price, packaging, taste, or user-experience? As your company gains momentum, there will likely be many opportunities on the table that will test your character. Offers will be made that may tempt you to stray from your principal beliefs, but that's when you have to hold your ground. Money is a powerful incentive, but remember, it is not your why.

For me, that moment came when I was offered the opportunity to place my products in a certain huge retailer. For two years, I had declined meetings with this particular retailer because it did not align with the vision I have for my brand. Going back to my description of the core Alikay Naturals customer, it was just not a store that she would frequent. I didn't feel that the Alikay Nation woman or girl would find herself shopping in this store, and so I didn't want my products on their shelves. In that third year, however, I wavered.

After confidently saying no for so long, I finally allowed my sales team to talk me into taking the meeting. They informed me that I needed to make this deal because all three of my top competitors were being sold in their stores. Something in my gut told me that this still wasn't quite the right fit for Alikay, but I followed their advice and took the deal. As it turned out, the retailer only put two of my products on the shelf, rather than the amount I recommended. To make matters even worse, they did not include my top-seller, the Lemongrass Leave-In Conditioner™. As a result, of course, our sales were not great, meanwhile in other stores we were selling products so fast that we surpassed sales benchmarks. In the end, I could only kick myself for betraying my intuition and stepping away from my core values.

Ultimately, there are no mistakes without lessons, and so I have no regrets about the situation. If anything, it led me to strengthen my resolve to only do what feels right in my bones. After that ordeal, I implemented policies to better negotiate deals in the future. Now, if a retailer does not take a certain number of products of my choice, I decline the offer. I refuse to put my products in a store if they don't take a minimum number of skus, even if every other hair care brand in the world is sold there. Always remember, *your* brand is yours; stop watching what everyone else is doing and do you. Be a unicorn!

Mindset and intuition go hand in hand. How do you know when something is the wrong fit? Get in tune with your energy, with your own body. When something isn't right, there is almost a dull ache in the pit of your stomach. If you feel uneasy or queasy, abort the plan...run! Still, you have to choose the right moment to abandon ship; you never want to burn a bridge permanently because you never know what you'll want to do in the future. If you're in the middle of a meeting and the vibe isn't right, just take a mental note. It's okay to hold off on saying yes or no. Thank the other party for their time and for giving you so much to consider. Furthermore, tell them you have to review what was discussed with your board members or your team, even when you are the only board member. What they don't know won't hurt them! Don't let big names or faces pressure you into making a premature decision. Trust your gut, sleep on it, journal, pray, or meditate – do whatever it is you like to do to tap into your inner voice. Then, come back with a confident decision in hand after taking time to think clearly. When you stick to your values, things have a way of working themselves out.

Another aspect of a strong business mentality is understanding how to negotiate for yourself. When assessing a potential opportunity for your company, you must be able to determine if it is truly in your best interest. Sometimes people will pay, but the amount may be negligible when compared to the time, effort, or energy expended on your end. For instance, I am constantly pitched to deliver keynote speeches or seminars on business management, which I thoroughly enjoy. While traveling and sharing my expertise with eager audiences fills my cup, these opportunities often require me to take time away from my family to hop on a plane and fly across the country. Even though I may be receiving payment, it doesn't compare to the money I could have made staying home and working at Alikay headquarters – not to mention the money I spend on flights, hotels, food, and transportation during the duration of my stay. On top of that, I have to keep in mind that I'm being taken away from my husband and kids. Sometimes it makes sense to leave an opportunity on the table if its net value isn't high enough. This is why I have a speaking fee that makes all the sacrifices worthwhile.

As a C.E.O, every deal or opportunity you take has to make sense or make cents. This means that if it doesn't get you a nice sum of money, it needs to offer a great deal of value in some other meaningful way. It has to be worth your while. Sometimes smaller organizations cannot meet your rates, and that's fine; we all start from somewhere. If that particular opportunity is close enough to your heart, do it. You may not get a big check, but you'll feel the return in your spirit when you offer your services for things that really matter to you. For me, it's giving back. When I am offered the chance to talk to a group of young girls or give back to my community in any way, I take it as often as possible. These are the things that allow me to become a mentor or a resource to others. I am a firm believer that I have been blessed by God to be a bigger blessing to others.

If, however, someone is offering chump change *and* no other perks, just say no. Don't get in the habit of doing favors for people because you feel bad. Even worse, don't downplay your rates to accommodate what you think other people can afford. The truth is that you really don't know what someone else has in their pockets. If someone seeks out your services or products, it's because they know your worth. That doesn't mean they won't try to cut corners or get a deal where they can. Don't let people get over on you by being too passive. Be firm, hold your ground, and make your rates non-negotiable unless the opportunity speaks to your heart.

GET YOUR HEAD IN THE GAME

The best business owners take their personal development seriously. That means building spiritual endurance, getting mentally tough, and eradicating excuses, especially when you're first starting out. You'll notice throughout this book that I mention God or refer to my faith. That's because it's also a big part of my business strategy. I 100% believe that my success is due to His favour and guided hand on my life. I also respect if you don't believe in a higher power - take from this book what is for you and leave the rest. The foundation that you build in the beginning will support you along your entire journey. Make it a strong one. Don't just read this book and be inspired by my journey - it shouldn't stop there. It's time to take action to create the life, the dream, the business you want. The ball is in your court. Self-belief goes beyond our vision boards. It's what will keep you grounded. Do not doubt yourself. You have to keep a strong hold on the idea that you are destined for greatness and you have the ability to create a powerful legacy. Get your head in the game!

the c.e.o champion checklist

- ✓ LISTEN TO YOUR VOICE
- ✓ AVOID DISTRACTIONS
- ✓ WORK, WORK, WORK
- ✓ WORK HARDER
- ✓ GET YOUR REST
- ✓ GIVE YOURSELF A PEP-TALK
- ✓ PRAY OR MEDITATE
- ✓ GET BACK TO IT
- ✓ SEEK SUPPORT WHERE NEEDED
- ✓ NEVER GIVE UP!

Business Viability

Business measured by its long-term survival and its ability to sustain profits over a period of time.
Source: www.investopedia.com

Capital Funding

Money that lenders and equity holders provide to a business for daily and long-term needs.
Source: www.investopedia.com

Venture Capitalist

Is an investor that provides capital to firms exhibiting high growth potential in exchange for an equity stake.
Source: www.investopedia.com

Equity

Amount of money that would be returned to a company's shareholders if all of the assets were liquidated and all of the company's debt was paid off.
Source: www.investopedia.com

Segmentation

Division into separate parts or sections.
Source: Oxford Dictionary

Aesthetics

A set of principles concerned with the nature and appreciation of beauty, especially in art.

T.T

Short for Turnaround Time.

PART II.

GROW UP TO GLOW UP

"The tiny seed knew that in order to grow, it needed to be dropped in dirt, covered with darkness, and struggle to reach the light."
- Sandra Kring

The middle. This is where you fight. This is where you try and you fall, and you fall again. You grind and you sweat and you punch the wall in frustration. You see the light at the end of the tunnel. Then you watch as it goes out. You cry and you pray and you wonder if you're made for this. This is the part where you fail, over and over and over again – until you reach the other side. This is growth.

CHAPTER 3

THE MESSY MIDDLE

"Be willing to live a few years how most people won't, so that you can live the rest of your life how most people can't."

- Mastin Kipp, *Live How Others Won't So You Can Live As Others Can't*

When the going gets tough, you need to get tougher. Listen, I cannot mask, glamourize, or sugarcoat this part of the journey – nor do I want to. The messy middle is like a rite of passage; a test to see how much you want this. Less than a quarter of small businesses fail in their first year, about a third fail in their second year, and half fail after five years in business. The only thing harder than getting started on your business idea is sustaining it through the difficult middle years. Entrepreneurship is a triathlon – the obstacles and the tasks required of you change along the way, and the path to the finish line is long and winded. You must pass a lot of different terrains to make it to the end.

When you get to this part of your entrepreneurship path, just get focused, keep your eyes on the ground, have all your tools out, and be ready to get your hands dirty and tend to your garden. Cultivate all that you have sown over the years. It's okay to have tunnel vision for a while, and don't let anyone tell you otherwise. Entrepreneurship requires sacrifices and you will have to double down on those when you get to the middle phase. Never forget why you started and use that dream – the end destination – as your motivation to keep going. The sacrifices you make today will allow you to live the life of your dreams for the rest of your years. Wake. Up. Every. Single. Day. With. Your. Dreams.

WHEN YOUR CAR BREAKS DOWN

It was the very first hair expo and show that we had ever signed up for. It was a huge deal for us. My hair expo and show team, at the time, was me, my husband and four of my best friends from college. We decided to go to an expo and trade show in Atlanta, Georgia. My thinking was, *we go big or we go home.* We needed a vehicle for the business, so we saved up our money – self-funded, since we were a cash-based business – and bought one only a couple of weeks before the road trip. It was our first company vehicle ever. I can picture it clearly right now – a white Astro van; we were so excited! Demond and I were so proud to officially own our first company vehicle, and we bought it with cash, at that.

We put everything into this event, and I literally mean every single dollar. We budgeted down to the cent – broke down all of our expenses (calculated how much gas we would need, food for our meals, accommodations) and had just enough to get us there and back. We had no excess, no leeway, nothing. We packed our van, the six of us piled into the seats, and we hit the road for our ten-hour drive to Atlanta. Part way through, in the middle of nowhere in a random town, our van broke down. It was late at night and Demond was making phone calls to different mechanics. No matter what anyone quoted us, I just remember thinking, *this is too much, we can't afford that!* I was on the side of the road in a panic.

We were able to get the van started and drive just long enough to make it to a motel nearby. We got one little room for $50 and all six of us piled in and stayed there that night. There were two beds and a little couch. It was a hot mess and it blew our very carefully planned and allocated budget. Blew our budget like, no-money-to-eat kind of blown. We had packed a few bags of chips and bun and cheese, which became our breakfast, and I just hoped that we would make some money on the first day of the show so that we could buy ourselves some lunch by the afternoon. We were hungry, not just the hungry-for-success kind of hunger, but literally starving for food. Still, Demond and I made sure that at least our friends and staff ate while we toughed it out.

Thinking back to that experience, I realize that I had one of two choices to make – decide that enough was enough and just quit and go back to a normal life, or figure a way out of the situation and keep going forward. I chose the latter, despite how exhausted and scared I felt. The mere fact that we went to this expo with such a huge financial risk was a sign that we were already really driven. Despite how serious the situation was, we just put our heads down and worked to get through it. That was just an extra kick of motivation for us, and it displayed how resourceful we were to not only find solutions to our challenges, but also stick to our original plan and make it happen. We didn't turn around and go back home. Instead, we found a rental and attached a U-Haul trailer to transport all of our products.

In the end, we did the show. We made back our money, plus a little extra. We made just enough to pay our four staff members who came with us, pay for the rental, and still had enough gas money to drive back home. I will never forget that experience. "Messy" really does show up in those middle years of your entrepreneurship journey. It's the transition phase where you are going from a small startup to becoming an official business.

GOING BRICK AND MORTAR

We decided to launch into retail and had to hire more staff to keep up with large orders and increased production. This meant that we had to re-learn how to manage cash flow, even though we had been effectively self-managing it for years. We entered a phase in our business where cash flow was no longer just dependent on us. As a bootstrapped business, money management was always key for us since the beginning. We always knew, for the most part, how much money we were going to make, and we would receive payment upfront from customers online, or businesses we sold wholesale to. We'd then allocate everything and distribute our funds. Once we started selling to big retailers, however, it became a whole other beast.

Big companies place large orders, which is great for business, but they also don't pay all of their invoices on time – not so great for business. The majority don't pay upfront, either. It can take 30-90 days after they receive your goods before they pay. At the start of my entrepreneurship journey, I used to dream about receiving an order for 200,000 units of one of our products. Little did I know about the challenges that come with such a large order.

When we receive a large order from a big retailer, we essentially have to go into debt to fulfill it. I'm not kidding. We don't get paid until we fulfill the order – we buy raw materials upfront, produce the product, package, ship, and deliver it – and then we finally send an invoice for payment. That means we have had to go into the red to buy necessary materials, pay for the labor required, and cover the freight costs. Even then, the payment often gets delayed because of billing issues on the other side. It could be anything from short staffing in the accounts payable department, to someone leaving for vacation, a system issue, or, quite literally, anything else.

As we wait for payment, we will often receive another request for a large order from a different retailer – 300,000 units to be delivered in two weeks! The predicaments and challenges that come with this are very real. Now, we are in the red, we need to make purchases for the new order, and we still some-how have to make payroll by Friday. If we don't take the new order we lose out on business and risk potentially not being able to pay our employees. Basically, you are damned if you do and damned if you don't.

While our products were being sold at large retailers like Target and Sally Beauty Supply, Demond and I were still liv-ing that mac and cheese lifestyle. We thought it was difficult to bootstrap in the early years, but we had no idea what was com-ing our way as we expanded. There were so many payrolls that we just barely made. At the time, our staff payroll once totaled $15,000, and we had $15,300 in our business bank account. This wasn't due to bad money management – this was due to limited cash flow as a self-funded business. At the time, we had a quarter-million dollars in accounts receivable outstanding, meaning retailers owed us all of this money but we were wait-ing to receive it. Unfortunately, when you have employees to pay, none of that matters. You have to have adequate cash on hand to make sure that your employees are paid. Moral of the story – always plan for the worst and prepare for the best. We literally just scraped by and made it. I am not unlucky, nor was the universe out to get me. This is simply the norm during the middle years of growth in your business. It's almost like the shameful secret that nobody talks about, even though it's the reality for most, if not all, entrepreneurs. It's not a question of whether it will happen, but rather, *when* it will happen, and if you will be prepared.

might seem **simple**, but when repeated daily, **positive self-talk** CAN BE VERY **empowering**

— ROCHELLE GRAHAM

CLAIM IT AS YOUR RIGHT OF PASSAGE

As I look back at my entrepreneurship journey thus far, I realize that my messy middle years were actually a blessing. Getting to that point meant that my business was expanding, and getting out of those years meant that I was growing as a person and a leader. That period of time was an essential rite of passage that I needed to go through to be prepared for where I am right now. I want you to claim those crucial years as your right of passage, too. Push through and you'll get to where you are destined to be.

Here are the lessons I learned and implemented along the way to guide me through the messy middle:

Change the Narrative

No matter what your situation is, remember that you are not stuck, and the universe is not out to get you. Take this self-destructive, negative narrative out of your head and change it. Trust me, I know what it's like to be paddling as fast as possible, but feel like the currents of the water are not allowing you to move forward. Even worse, it can feel like you're moving backwards or being pulled out to sea. That's exactly how I felt when we started selling Alikay Naturals products at big retail stores. The negative narrative is completely unproductive; it just becomes one more thing you have to deal with – just another current in the water that is holding you back. Learn to become your greatest cheerleader and focus on the thoughts that are going to help move you forward.

Celebrate your successes, past and current. If you've made it to the messy middle, you've come a long way. Never forget that. Acknowledging yourself isn't just about self-esteem or a confidence boost. It's a reminder of all that you are capable of. Learn to celebrate in large and small ways. Saying positive affirmations to yourself is an impactful way to applaud yourself and change a negative narrative. It's a way to retrain the way you think and focus on thoughts that will help propel you forward.

Reassess What You Are Focusing On

Sometimes it's not that you aren't trying hard enough or putting in enough effort – it's just that you are putting effort into the wrong things. Perhaps you're even exerting energy in areas that will hold you back or slow you down. Misdirected energy is actually a distraction when trying to reach your goals because you think you are moving forward when in fact, you're not. That is why it is important to constantly re-assess what you are focusing on – especially as your company grows.

It's okay to stop and take a breath. Rest, clear your mind, and come back with a blank canvas ready to evaluate all parts of your strategy. Don't be attached to any plan because changing times and needs will require adjustments to your approach. This is your life to live and it is also your life to change paths. Make different decisions and switch things up as you need. Take an audit of where you are and how your needs have changed, and be objective in your evaluation so that you can make consistently smarter and more strategic choices. Also, always be sure to prepare for paradigm shifts. The needs of your business and your customers are going to change over time.

Shifts happen in every industry, and the companies that typically lose or go out of business are the ones that are too stubborn or hesitant to adjust their businesses when those paradigm shifts start happening.

What problems are you currently facing in your business?	What are the possible solutions that you can have in place?

Be Okay with Doing More of the Things You Least Want to Do

Imagine your career, your entrepreneurship journey, as a graph. The horizontal x-axis represents time and the vertical y-axis represents the tasks you have to do as a leader of your organization. The base of the y-axis starts with 100% of tasks that you have to do but don't enjoy doing and, as you move up, that shifts with there being more tasks that you enjoy doing. Generally, this will be an upward curve. Over time you will get to do more of the tasks you enjoy and less of the tasks you don't enjoy – until you get to the middle years. During the middle years, your trajectory will likely drop back down to you, once again, doing more of the things you don't particularly enjoy. This is when you have to double down on grit, resilience, and perseverance.

Remember to stay the course and be disciplined. If it's important, you will make time for it. Build healthy and productive habits early on that will sustain you during your toughest years and most difficult challenges. Nobody is born a master at self-discipline; it's a practice that takes practice. Every day that you exercise your willpower and self-discipline will add to your overall self-mastery.

During your major transition years, your business will require more out of you than ever before. Even if you are experiencing a steady incline in growth and profit, hiring more staff, and expanding into new markets, remember, you are not above or beneath any task that your business needs of you. Be okay with this. I read a book called *Eat that Frog* by Brian Tracy. In his book, Tracy provides great advice on how to stop procrastinating and start tackling undesirable tasks first. During the tough years, it is more important than ever to start your day off with the things that you least want to do. The tasks that you are dreading the most are the ones that require your most energy, effort, and attention. Just go ahead and eat that frog! Get it over with so that you can move on to the things that bring you the most joy.

Entrepreneurship is not easy, but it's worth it. During the messy middle, you may begin to feel like your goals can't be accomplished, or like they are always just out of reach. It can be incredibly de-motivating to get knocked back a few notches, but don't allow the challenges to make you quit. Rather, let every setback be an opportunity to learn; a solution to discover and be better. The messy middle can either make or break you. Either way, you will become wiser and more prepared for whatever life throws your way.

Build Relationships

You are capable of a lot, but you are not capable of doing everything. As your business grows and the needs of your customers and staff change, you will also have to manage your own expectations of how much you can actually do. During the startup phase of your business, you will have had to wear a lot of hats and take on a lot, if not all, of the responsibilities. It is easy to fall into the trap of convincing yourself that you, and only you, are capable of growing, expanding, scaling, or even saving your company. That is just your ego talking. This kind of thinking is a trap because it is simply not possible for one person to do it all, especially not while trying to grow your business. Take the "S" off your chest and recognize that you are not a superhero. This is real life, not a movie. This is why you must build relationships and have people in your corner who you can rely on with confidence.

Learn to ask for help along the way. Receiving support does not mean you are incapable or that you are downloading your responsibilities onto others. Rather, it is a sign that you trust those around you and they, in turn, trust you. Trust is not given but earned. To earn this level of respect from your team, you must build relationships with them.

Having the right team in place is crucial but building a strong relationship with your team is even more important. Treat people like human beings and bring them along your journey with you. Help them understand your why, your mission statement, and your vision. Having strong relationships with your team members will motivate them to help you grow and stay with you through the ups and downs. During the early years when we were tight on cash and unable to make payroll, I had to rely on the relationships I built with my team. Sometimes it was literally like, *who on my team can I talk to about this?* I would have to say, *I'm so sorry but I can't pay you this Friday. Can you give me until Monday, please? I'll pay you then and add an extra $100 on top of your paycheck for the inconvenience.*

Payroll is a major expense and typically one of the highest expenses that a business will face. One of my top C.E.O tips is to hire and grow your team slowly and strategically. Alikay Naturals now has a team of 25 full-time employees, but that didn't happen overnight. Don't take on more than you can handle, and make sure that whatever payroll budget you have is a budget you can afford to pay, even during the slow periods of your business. Small teams can be just as powerful and effective if you have the right people in place. More on building an effective team in chapter ten, "L.O.C. and Key."

When things get difficult, it is not just you as the owner and leader who is impacted. The ripple effect of challenges is felt by those around you as well. One relationship in particular that I have had to work hard to build and maintain is my relationship with my husband and business partner, Demond. We fell in love twelve years ago and eloped at city hall. Our civil ceremony was simple, but our love was grand. As business partners and partners in life, we go through the highs and lows of both journeys together. We have learned to continue to build our relationships as both life and business partners in distinct ways. More on working with your spouse in chapter five, "Self-Care is Good for Business."

Every expert was once an amateur, so don't be afraid to ask for help.

- ROCHELLE GRAHAM-CAMPBELL

— **Rochelle Graham-Campbell**

where

In my business do I need assistance?

when

Is my deadline?

what

Is my ask / do I need?

who

Can help?

A promise to myself to raise my hand when I need something.

Mind the Company You Keep

While it is important to build relationships and lean on others, it's also crucial to remember that not everyone is going to be supportive of your journey. One of the common misconceptions that new business owners have is that they're automatically going to have the support of friends, family members, and colleagues – this is simply not always the case. There will be plenty of people who will doubt you, talk down about you, or cheer you on while secretly rooting for your downfall. Jealousy is real, especially as you gain more success. Many people seem to think that saying the word jealous or identifying envy in other people makes you a bad person – as if you're being narcissistic or petty. If anything, the ability to recognize envy in others and adjust your circle accordingly is a skill that should be honed. Learn to examine the company you keep and allow only the purest, most genuine energy around you and your business.

Unfortunately, I had to learn the realities of jealousy the hard way. One of the most vivid examples that stands out in my mind is also one of the most hurtful. It was the early days of Alikay Naturals when my husband Demond and I were still in college, running the business from our two bedroom apartment. My sister-in-law had come into town and was babysitting the young daughter of one of my friends. The friend lived in the same apartment complex as me, and so I asked my sister-in-law if she wouldn't mind helping me out. I had mixed some of my Alikay Naturals Shea Yogurt Hair Moisturizer™ and asked if she could help me package up some of the product while she babysat. When she agreed, I drove over and lugged my jars, lids, labels, and a plastic tub full of mixed product up the stairs to my friend's apartment. When I arrived, my friend was surprised to see me; my sister-in-law hadn't told her I was stopping by. I told her that I was just dropping off product to be packaged, and she said it was totally fine.

A few moments later, my friend stepped outside and came back in asking where my car was. She must have been confused when she didn't see my beat up old mess of a car, held together by duct tape and a dream. I told her that I had driven my new car, a 2010 Dodge Charger. When she spotted it parked outside of her apartment, she flew into an incredulous rant. "That's your car?" she asked. "You bought it brand new?" When I said yes, I felt her energy immediately shift. She literally told me to pack up all of my stuff and get out of her apartment. She said she didn't want my product making a mess of her place. Ten seconds earlier, she had just said it was okay, and yet now – after seeing my new car – there was suddenly a huge problem. Shocked and confused, I packed my things and hauled them all back down the stairs to my car and drove home. That night, the show went on. I stayed up late to get my product packaged, even if that meant doing it all by myself. Still, I couldn't shake the hurt from what my friend had just done. It wasn't until years later that I finally received an explanation.

Long after the incident and the end of our friendship, she admitted to me that she had been jealous. At the time, she had been in a bad place. She was an ambitious woman, but she had been unemployed for several years and had no car. When she saw my brand new car out front, she was triggered; she was jealous of all the success that I was having with my business. That was when I realized that sometimes, it's not about you. People are going to be mad at you, say hurtful things, and treat you poorly, and it can simply be a reflection of their own poor self-esteem. Her unhappiness made it difficult for her to be genuinely happy for me. It's a lesson that I have kept with me ever since.

Sadly, that wasn't my last experience with jealousy or spiteful behavior. The next instance came from a peer and a woman with whom I thought I had built a genuine business friendship. She and I had started posting as hair bloggers around the same time. Once Alikay began to take off, I stopped vlogging so much so that I could focus on building my company. She, on the other hand, continued on and soon became a top blogger and a go-to favorite of many big brands. By 2011, everyone wanted to work with her and she was at the height of her career. When I came out with some new products for Alikay Naturals, I sent them over to her in a personalized care package with a beautiful card. I wasn't asking for free promotion, but I just asked that she try my products out and let me how how she liked them. If she decided of her own accord to share my products with her followers, that would be great, but at the time all I was looking for was feedback.

Soon afterwards, I received a package in the mail with a huge "return to sender" mark stamped across the top. At first,

I thought that maybe I had sent the package to the wrong address. When I opened the box, however, I realized what had happened. The blogger had returned my products with a note that read, "I did not ask you for this." She simply did not want my products, and what was weird was that she seemed to have been offended by me sending them. I was beyond bewildered. This was a woman with whom I had – until that point – a perfectly amicable relationship. We were both veteran bloggers; both female entrepreneurs doing well for ourselves. To realize her lack of support felt like a slap in the face.

Ever since that day, I had not spoken to her until very recently, when I was at a show promoting one of my products that had gone into retail. To my surprise, she appeared thrilled to see me. She greeted me with warm exclamations of "I'm so proud of you!" It was as if the whole ordeal had never happened. Of course, I remained polite, but in the back of my mind, I remembered what she did and how much it insulted me. Unlike the friend who kicked me out of her apartment, I couldn't blame this woman's behavior on her circumstances. She was very successful and highly sought-after; I was a threat to her in no way. It just goes to show that you can't put a precise face to jealousy. It can pop up anywhere, from people you least expect. That was the spark to another vital business lesson: not everyone who smiles in your face is actually happy for you. As a C.E.O, you have to learn how to stand on your own two feet and thrive off of your own unconditional support. Remember, even when there is no one else in your corner, you always have yourself.

Don't Quit on Yourself

At some point in your journey as an entrepreneur, you will contemplate throwing in the towel. You will want to give up and return to a life of predictability and normalcy. You will remember all the times that you had to forgo vacations or Friday nights out with the girls. You'll likely reminisce and think about how great it feels to sleep in on a Saturday, or not have to think about work at all after 5pm. The second-guessing about your life and career choices will happen – believe me, I've been there more than once. The exhaustion, mental fatigue, stress, and tears are all part of the game; these are the growing pains of running a business. During these moments, none of the hard work, hardships, or successes will feel worth it. But I have to remind you, never quit on yourself. I have literally laid on the floor in my mom's office, cried my eyes out, and had a mini-meltdown. Then, I got up, grabbed my laptop, and got back to work. We are human – it happens!

There are no accidents in life. Whatever your journey is like, just know that it was meant to be that way because you are capable of handling it. You are given all of the tools that you need to get through the challenges you will inevitably face. The fact that you started down the entrepreneurship journey in itself is very telling of who you are. Being your own boss requires a lot of self-motivation, discipline and initiative. Not everyone will take up this path, no matter how enticing the future results may be. It takes a certain kind of person to understand and be okay with the delayed gratification that entrepreneurship comes with. You have what it takes to win. You are more than capable of handling any challenge that comes your way. Don't. Quit. On. Yourself.

Know When to Walk Away

It may sound ironic that I would encourage you to know when to walk away right after encouraging you not to quit on yourself, but there is a big difference between the two. Knowing when to walk away is a decision to move your life and career in a different direction. It is a well-thought out decision based on advice, guidance, and support from the trusted tribe around you. It is an objective decision made by looking at the facts at hand without influence of ego or the emotions wrapped up in it. When you quit on yourself, you are giving up because something is too difficult, or you don't believe you are capable of getting through it. Walking away is about listening to yourself, trusting your gut, and honoring your intentions.

Before Alikay Naturals, I was in the jewelry business. I made handcrafted jewelry and sold it online while in college, and continued to do so after I finished school, as well. As the demand for my product increased and more and more of my focus was being shifted to Alikay, I hired other jewelry makers to meet customers' needs. We grew and became a million-dollar business, but I had to walk away. I was faced with a tough business decision. *Should I continue juggling multiple businesses, or pivot all my attention to one?* Ultimately, I did what needed to be done based on an assessment of scalability and future prospects. I chose Alikay Naturals.

Quality is of utmost importance to me. I did not ship a single product whether it was made by myself or one of the jewelry makers I hired, without thoroughly inspecting it myself. If I found errors, I would have to re-do the pieces myself to get the order out to the customer fast enough or I would have to send it back to the person who made it to have it fixed. It was taking so much of my time that I did not have much of already. I also realized that I could not scale Nyamani Chic any more than where it was and Alikay on the other hand was picking up speed and momentum rapidly. I decided to focus on Alikay Naturals and give it my all. The decision was a difficult one for me to make. Making beautiful handcrafted jewels was a passion of mine and it gave me a creative outlet. I took pride in every piece of jewelry that we shipped to our customers and our increasing success gave me a sense of accomplishment and motivation. However, I knew it was time to walk away.

Walking away takes courage and it comes with its own set of fears. When making this decision, self-reflect on your who and why. It is time to walk away when you no longer feel the same sense of passion and love for your craft. Entrepreneurship is hard and it requires a lot of your time and energy. Do not give up your time and energy for work that no longer feeds your soul. Sometimes your why for starting changes, and the endeavor which once fulfilled your why statement no longer serves that purpose. Other times your life circumstances change, and you have to make decisions according to your new needs. Having children has changed my life. I can no longer make decisions based on my needs alone, the needs of my family have to be considered. Looking back, I know that walking away from my jewelry business was the right decision for me and my family. I have grown all the more as a person and an entrepreneur by creating space in my life and eliminating the responsibilities that came with juggling that business. While I chose to close, remember, you have the option to *sell* your business as well! Whatever you decide, just make sure that it is the right decision for you.

GO WITH THE FLOW

Finally, as a new C.E.O it's important to understand that there is a flow to business. Try as you might to skip the struggles, they are a built in part of the natural progression of things; the sooner you embrace that fact, the better off you will be. Just like your life, your business will have its own unique journey full of ups and downs – the messy middle is just one stop on that ride. Likewise, your products and services themselves will also embark on a journey or a life cycle, and management of that cycle will help you to better plan and support the ongoing success of your business. The chart below is a product life cycle chart, a theoretical model that shows the stages a product goes through on an S curve, with sales in respect to time. These stages can also be applied if you run a service-based business (assume that "product" and "service" are used interchangeably in the breakdown below).

product life cycle

Stage 1: Introduction

As you might have guessed, the introduction stage is when your product or service is first introduced to the market. Your overall growth rate of sales will be low during this phase because your market is small. You are just getting started with promotions and spreading awareness about the existence of your product in order to accrue a larger consumer base. You are also educating your audience on the benefits of your product as well as how it actually works. During the introduction phase, your costs will outweigh your profits.

Stage 2: Growth

A successful introduction leads into a growth stage. This is when people have already discovered your product or service and the sales and profits begins to grow. During a growth phase you can expect to increase production efforts and amounts to keep up with blossoming sales. You may also have to expand operations through additional funds or staff to work quicker and more efficiently on filling larger, more frequent orders. With Alikay Naturals, for instance, the growth phase included product placement in major retailers and opening up our manufacturing facility to keep up with the huge boost in volume.

Stage 3: Maturity

The maturity stage is when your product or service is at its most profitable. Sales will peak as the product reaches market saturation, but your competition will also grow increasingly fierce. Now, the goal is to maintain or boost your established market share. Your marketing efforts are now less focused on educating people on what your product is or how it works, and more focused on differentiating it from other offerings on the market. How do you stand out? What makes you different? You will now face increased competition as others try to duplicate your success or attract your customers with flashy advancements or lower prices. You will have to strategically direct your marketing into showing why your product is still the best out there. This might mean enhancing or making tweaks to your product in order to encourage continued sales or attract new customers.

Stage 4: Decline

Finally, the decline stage comes when a product or service is no longer in high demand. Your profits will decline drastically.

Maybe the market is saturated or the trends have shifted so much that your product is no longer appealing (ie: the decline of physical books and print magazines in the age of digital everything). Of course, a decline will mean diminishing interest and falling sales. Do not be discouraged, decline is a normal part of business. Your best bet may be to increase your efforts in new product development and launch a new offering to create a fresh angle and keep your business relevant. You may also end up dissolving your assets.

Keeping your eye on the life cycle of your products or services will help you predict sales patterns, strategically target your company's marketing efforts, and ultimately endure the messy middle.

Self-Funded

Provide the money for (a project, program, idea or course of action) oneself.
Source: Oxford Dictionary

Personal Assets

Cash and the things you own that have monetary value.
Source: www.investopedia.com

Collateral

Something pledged as security for repayment of a loan, to be forfeited in the event of a default.
Source: Oxford Dictionary

Cash Flow Management

Process of monitoring, analyzing, and optimizing the net amount of cash receipts minus cash expenses.
Source: www.investopedia.com

Cash Flow

The total amount of money being transferred into and out of a business, especially as affecting liquidity.
Source: Oxford Dictionary

S.O.P

Short for Standard Operating Procedures.

Vetting

Make a careful and critical examination of (something).

CHAPTER 4

POPPING THE "BOSS BABE" BALLOON

As a female entrepreneur, nothing makes me happier than seeing another woman walk in her purpose, go for her dreams, and manifest her own reality. It's the reason I wrote this book! In the last few years, I've seen the explosion of this empowering *boss babe* movement, and while I'm all here for the sentiment behind it, something about it doesn't sit quite well with me. I've seen far too many women – women with real potential – cop out on the true work of entrepreneurship; too many women who want to *look* like a success without doing the real work to actually *be* successful.

Being a boss isn't about cute branded mugs, Pinterest quotes, and girl boss decals. I'm dreadfully tired of seeing female entrepreneurship whittled down to frilly pink events and vision board parties. So often I see aspiring business women attending these fufu events where they walk away not having learned anything new. Sure, they may feel inspired or encouraged, but where is the substance? We need actionable steps and concrete advice; mentors, resources, and allies. Before you call yourself a girl boss or a boss babe, let's really get into the nitty-gritty of what it takes to be a boss. It's about being a brand leader and the face of your company, self-accountability, time management, managing a team, goal-mapping, and so much more. Not to worry – your Business Fairy Godmother is here to give you the blueprint.

GOAL-MAPPING

The number one roadblock people face in reaching their goals is that – to put it frankly – their goals suck. This is not to say that their aspirations aren't valid, but that they're ill-defined. When you set a goal that's too general, what you really have is a wish. A rub-on-a-lamp, blow-on-a-dandelion, shooting star wish. Without a plan, there's no way of knowing how to get from point A to point Z of your wildest dreams. Of course, you can never account for everything and any good plan leaves wiggle room for the unexpected, however, approaching your goals with an intentional and detailed plan of action increases your chances of achievement many times over.

BE S.M.A.R.T.

A true boss doesn't just set goals, she sets S.M.A.R.T. goals. S.M.A.R.T. goals are short statements that a person makes to lead them in the direction of what they want to accomplish. The acronym stands for Specific, Measurable, Achievable, Relevant, and Time-Bound. When setting a goal, ask yourself the following questions:

Is it specific?i.e.: what exactly am I trying to accomplish?

Is it measurable?i.e.: how can I quantify my progress?

Is it achievable?i.e: is this realistic for my current abilities and circumstances?

*Is it relevant?*i.e: how exactly does this goal advance my business?

*Is it time-bound?*i.e: have I set a deadline?

The following is a perfect example of a **S.M.A.R.T.** goal:

By October 7th, 2019, my company will improve sales conversion rates by 30% for marketing implementation efforts within the social media department on Instagram and Facebook.

Use the space below to define your own S.M.A.R.T. goals.

Specific
Improve sales conversion rates

Measurable
30%

Achievable
We have the customer base already established

Relevant
Important to the business financially

Time-Bound
October 7th, 2019

With this goal, we know exactly what we're striving for, we have a percentage benchmark by which to measure our success, we know exactly which social platforms we're working to boost, and we've attached a deadline to boost accountability and productivity. Being S.M.A.R.T. about your approach gives you the action plan. That action plan is what I like to call a goal-map, and having a strong goal-mapping strategy is the mark of a true boss. I've created my own Rochelle Graham Campbell Goal-Mapping Method™ to break it down for you.

STEP 1: THANK YOU, NEXT

Before you get down to business, the first thing you need to do is acknowledge and accept the past. Whatever failures, mistakes, or obstacles you encountered before today, accept them for what they were and say "thank you, next" to the past. We can only move onwards and upwards once we relinquish everything else. When we let the burdens of yesterday weigh us down, they only steal our focus and stall the progress of our new goals. Instead, be gentle with yourself, reflect on the past only to extract lessons – never to belittle or shame yourself. Build the habit of pivoting your thoughts toward the here and now.

STEP 2: VISUALIZE THE DESTINATION. REMEMBER YOUR WHY

Once you've let go of the past, it's time to set your sights on what's ahead of you. Picture everything you want in your head as if it's already yours. Use visualization for manifestation! Remember that *why*? Those roots that you established in chapter one for why you started your company in the first place? Well now, work on creating a *why* for each specific goal. With your first goal in mind, complete the sentences below. There should be a targeted purpose and desired feeling attached to every step you take.

I want to feel...

[insert one or more emotions or adjectives]

The purpose of wanting to accomplish this goal is...

[insert whatever comes to mind]

STEP 3: AGREE TO HOLD YOURSELF ACCOUNTABLE

When tackling goals, you are really tackling issues at the core of human nature – predominantly *fear*. Instead of shrinking in the face of that fear, learn to make it your friend. This means staring into the mirror and being completely honest about your shortcomings and weaknesses. It's about asking yourself, where do I need to improve? Where am I slacking? What aspects of my personality or behavior are holding me back? Am I truly going to stick to what I've committed myself to? Holding yourself accountable means being as real as possible, *but* always be sure to self-evaluate from a place of love. Don't waste time self-deprecating. Simply identify your weaknesses and set the right thoughts and actions in motion to correct them.

A simple place to start is taking a look at your environments. Are you maintaining conditions that are conducive to a healthy work-life? A healthy home-life? Physical clutter is often an indication of mental or emotional cloudiness. Hold yourself accountable by clearing out all of the junk in your life. From filing and shredding papers to burning sage and even distancing yourself from outdated, unproductive relationships, take intentional steps to clear out the chaos. Hold yourself accountable to a new standard of peace within your home, office, and life.

STEP 4: THE BRAIN DUMP

If you're unclear on your thoughts, start with a brain dump to get everything out on paper. Get a piece of paper and free-write a list of all the goals that come to your mind. Everything – it doesn't matter how big or small the goal is; the point here is to name it. Consider this a master list of your deepest desires. Don't worry, we'll narrow it down according to priority a little later, but for now, be honest with the things you really want most out of life.

When free-writing, do not hesitate or overthink. Leave judgement out of your process. There is no goal too ridiculous or too big to include. No one is looking at your list except for you! Don't think about your wording, sounding perfect, or even making sense. Simply write and be honest. Welcome each new goal to your list with love and when you're done, accept your list for the hot mess that it is. We'll make sense of everything soon enough.

list your goals

1. _____
2. _____
3. _____
4. _____
5. _____
6. _____
7. _____
8. _____
9. _____
10. _____
11. _____

STEP 5: ORGANIZE YOUR GOALS

Once you have a master list of your goals, you will organize them all into the following four categories: Career, Financial, Spiritual, and Personal. Categorizing your goals into sections helps bring clarity to which aspects in your life appear to be the most important at the moment, and highlights where you are choosing to invest the most time and energy. I've simply chosen the most common categories, but if you think of another that's important for your life, feel free to add it. If by the end you have twenty goals listed under Career and only four under Personal – explore what that means for you. Are you comfortable with that? If not, reevaluate your choices and priorities and shift the weight to better reflect your overall goal plan. The key is to get all of your categories working together in a harmony that works for you.

career

- ☐ _____
- ☐ _____
- ☐ _____
- ☐ _____
- ☐ _____

financial

- ☐ _____
- ☐ _____
- ☐ _____
- ☐ _____
- ☐ _____

spiritual

- ☐ _____
- ☐ _____
- ☐ _____
- ☐ _____
- ☐ _____

personal

- ☐ _____
- ☐ _____
- ☐ _____
- ☐ _____
- ☐ _____

_____

- ☐ _____
- ☐ _____
- ☐ _____
- ☐ _____
- ☐ _____

future goals

- ☐ _____
- ☐ _____
- ☐ _____
- ☐ _____
- ☐ _____

STEP 6: PRIORITIZE YOUR GOALS

Now, let's narrow things down even further by prioritizing your categorized goals from highest to lowest. Take the goals you organized in the previous step and sort them below according to high, medium, or low priority.

high PRIORITY

- urgent and important
- requires your attention and action immediately
- three to six months

medium PRIORITY

- not urgent, but important
- schedule to do later
- three to nine months

low PRIORITY

- tasks that are neither urgent nor important
- six to twelve months

high
PRIORITY

_____
_____
_____

medium
PRIORITY

low
PRIORITY

_____
_____
_____

These are the time guidelines that work well for me, but you may be different. Overlap is perfectly fine – nothing fits perfectly into neat little boxes, but compartmentalizing in this way will help you decide which goals to tackle first and which can wait until later.

STEP 7: MAP OUT HIGH PRIORITY GOALS

Once your goals are identified, categorized, and prioritized, it's time to start mapping! I always recommend starting with your highest priority goals, as these are the most urgent and will make you feel the most accomplished upon completion. To begin, choose a goal and write it on the left-hand side of a piece of paper. Underneath, write your deadline and leave another space for your completion date. Noting your completion date will help you realize how long it actually took you to achieve a certain goal, and help you better choose your deadlines in the future. Now, on the right side of the paper, list all of the steps it will take to reach this goal. For instance, if your main goal is *launch my business website*, your steps might be: research and hire a web developer, decide on website theme, colors, fonts, and layout, send developer my graphic files (images and mood board), type up copy for each webpage, etc. You should then write down a deadline by which to complete all of your steps. Don't worry if you're not yet sure of all the steps you'll need to make – that will be figured out as you begin to work. Simply add in steps as you discover new ones.

goal

_____   _____
Deadline   Completion Date

	_____ Deadline
	_____ Deadline
	_____ Deadline
	_____ Deadline
	_____ Deadline

BLOCKING METHOD

Once you accomplish your first high priority goal, move on to your next one. I call this the blocking method – where you knock each priority section out as a block. Once the high priority block is completed, you can move on to the medium priority block of goals, and then the low.

WEAVING METHOD

Alternatively, you can use the weaving method. With this method, you'll go back and forth between blocks. So, map out one high priority goal and complete, then map out one medium priority goal and complete, and so on and so forth. This will enable you to accomplish two blocks or lists of goals simultaneously and may feel more manageable than the blocking method. Choose whichever method works best for you!

However you choose to map your goals, know that it is not a process of perfection. Try your best to remain flexible and leave room for steps you didn't anticipate, or obstacles that arise. It's okay to push deadlines if you begin and then realize that something will take longer than you thought. Personally, I typically view goals on a one-year timeline; my short-term goals are anywhere within a six month to one year time frame, but you can certainly use the Rochelle Graham-Campbell Goal-Mapping Method™ to map out your three-year, five-year, or even ten-year goal. Just know that the further away the deadline, the less definite of a plan it will be.

STEP 8: LET'S MAKE IT HAPPEN!

Now that you've mapped out your goals, it's time to start executing. If ever you get overwhelmed, simply look back at your why and your map and adjust. Focus only on one mini-step at a time and adjust if necessary, but don't let yourself off the hook. The goal is self-accountability. If you can visualize it and write it down, it can be achieved — it's just a matter of when. Make moves with your deadlines in mind and you should be golden.

When you achieve a goal, celebrate yourself! Taking the time to appreciate your progress only builds momentum for the next task. If a goal was particularly difficult, give yourself time to recover. Treating yourself well during this process will build your confidence and give you the best shot at crossing off everything on your master list.

Finally, once you have some experience mapping and achieving your first few goals, review and reevaluate your plans. If you achieved the goal too easily, make the next one even harder. If the goal took a dispiriting length of time to achieve, make the next goal a little easier. If you learned something that leads you to change other goals, do so. If you noticed a deficit in your skills despite achieving the goal, decide whether to set goals to fix this by acquiring those skills. Everything will be trial and error, but goal-mapping will at least give you a blueprint to follow so that you're not just winging it.

TIME MANAGEMENT

Deadlines are amazing because they are the finish line you're working toward every single day. They make sure that your goals are not some obscure, somewhere-over-the-rainbow vision, but an intentional plan of attack. They also expose your weaknesses. If you have trouble with procrastination or managing your time, you've got to nip that in the bud. Time is your most valuable resource and must be spent wisely.

To make sure I am honoring my own time, I have come up with a list of time management tips.

Rochelle Graham-Campbell's 25 Tips on Time Management™:

1. **Respect your own time.** You wouldn't waste someone else's time, so why waste yours? Don't set deadlines unless you have the full intention of working toward them. By the same token, be vocal about what you are reasonably able or not able to do. Just because someone asked you to do something and you can, doesn't mean you should. Stop squeezing everything into your schedule. Learn to say no sometimes.

2. **Maximize your time.** We all have twenty-four hours in a day. Set certain hours as your productive or "on" hours and make sure to maximize your productivity during that time.

3. **Know your work habits.** You cannot address what you don't know. Take a week or a month to study yourself and your work habits. What keeps you from working

hard? What are you driven by? What kills your creativity? What makes you work harder? Slower? These are all questions you need to know the answers to so that you can be efficient with your time.

4. **Review your schedule in the morning.** Take time in the morning to review your tasks for the day. If something doesn't fit, shift it around. Be in control of the flow of your day.

5. **Write things down so you can revisit later.** When random ideas and thoughts pop up, write them down. At the end of the day, go back to them and determine where you can add them in on your calendar according to your other deadlines. I like to keep a journal with me or simply use the notes app on my phone to record all random ideas in one easily accessible place.

6. **Avoid distractions by being selective of who and what you give your time to.** If you work from home, place a *do not disturb* sign on your door so that family knows not to interrupt your workflow. Do the same at the office if you have employees. You can also put your phone on *do not disturb* mode to avoid the distractions of social media push notifications or social calls and texts. This is particularly important when you're working on a big project. As an entrepreneur, you set your own hours and it is extremely important that your family and friends respect your workday just as they would if you were working for another employer. If you're a

parent, silencing your phone is tougher, but there are ways around it. I typically let my husband know when I'm going ghost, but he knows that if he needs to reach me urgently, calling my phone twice will kick off the DND mode and he will still have access to me.

It's about having boundaries to maximize your productive time.

7. **Focus on opportunities rather than problems.** Be more productive by focusing your energy on finding solutions to problems, rather than dwelling on the problems themselves. Look at the opportunity presented in a particular obstacle. What skill does this hurdle allow you to sharpen? How is it making you better? Not every challenge is designed to break you down. Don't waste time stressing, venting, or being upset. Move forward.

8. **Set alarms daily to remind you about deadlines for tasks.** If I have seven tasks on my list for the day, I'll give myself forty-five minutes to complete each one. I set an alarm on my phone giving myself a fifteen minute reminder that my time is almost up.

9. **Work with urgency!** Always work with swiftness. It's so easy to drag our feet along when we know that our deadline is not fast-approaching, but if you work like every deadline is tomorrow, or even end-of-day today, you will work quicker and with stronger purpose. Lazy thinking is not going to help you. Work like your rent is due tomorrow!

10. **Tackle the hardest thing first**. This was one of the biggest lessons I learned from a book called "Eat That Frog" by Brian Tracy. It's human nature to want to start off our days with the easy things - the ones that don't require much effort. We keep pushing off the biggest and most important things until later, and later becomes *never*. When your mind is fresh and alert in the morning, pull yourself together and force yourself to accomplish the hardest, most uncomfortable, biggest, and most important thing first. Always give yourself a reason to take action. I promise, you will find that you will start to make progress in leaps and bounds.

11. **Track the time you work on each task.** In the past three years, time-tracking has given me visibility on how I spend my time, how much time it takes me to complete certain tasks, and how much time things will take in the future. If I ever have to delegate that task to an employee or family member, I can approximate the time it will take to get it done. If you know this person will work slower or quicker than you, adjust accordingly. Tracking duration is wonderful for delegating and planning future tasks.

12. **Touch it once a.k.a. eliminate procrastination.** Always try to touch on a task ONE time - work on it the very first time you pick it up and try to complete it before you put it back down. Otherwise, you are wasting your time without even knowing it. This is something

that someone very close to me specifically needs to learn from. It is a big pet peeve of mine because this individual will touch on the same task 50 million times before it gets done, and then continue to push it off. By the time it is actually completed, it took three to four times longer than necessary. Do not allow yourself to continuously roll tasks over into the next day. That is a bad habit. When you finally look up at the end of the week, you may have only accomplished two days worth of tasks or agenda items.

13. **Prioritize a task list of six items for the day.** I find that four to six tasks a day is a very manageable amount. If you put too many things on your list, it's easy to become overwhelmed and feel like a failure at the end of each day. Instead, narrow it down, work intentionally, and get things done. I also like to plan my six items the night before. I know that we're often burnt out by the time night comes, but taking a moment to loosely plan for the next day will make things so much easier. It can even be just a quick brain dump of ideas; you can always organize it more in the morning.

14. **Limit the amount of time you allow yourself to be on social media.** No more mindless scrolling. Set an alarm for social media time – thirty minutes to an hour is perfect. Get a weekly screen report. My iPhone started sending me a screen report and I was appalled at the amount of time I was spending on social media and

my phone in general. For Android users, try Google's Digital Wellbeing. Finally, use a scheduling app. If social media is a part of your business operation, schedule your posts ahead of time to reduce screen time. This way they will auto-post and you won't have to log back in.

15. **Set alarms for email time.** I allow myself to answer emails in the morning for thirty minutes to an hour. When that time is up, I close that window and don't reopen it until the next block of time I've allotted for emails at the end of the work day. Back and forth email threads can be a huge time-waster.

16. **Set S.M.A.R.T. goals. Set clear goals.** We've gone over this. Be S.M.A.R.T. so you can tackle goals easily and efficiently.

17. **Control your calendar and meetings, call times, and projects.** Share your calendar with relevant parties like your assistant, partner, or publicist. When people know the flow of your day, they're less likely to interrupt with BS. Also schedule repeat calls with those whom you need consistent check-ins with. This keeps your calls organized and lets you know what to expect each and every week.

18. **Done is better than perfect.** Don't fall subject to paralysis by analysis. Move, work, get things done now. You can always improve and refine later.

19. **Make swift and timely decisions.** When you are a leader or manager in a business or organization, you become a decision maker. Allot yourself a specific set time to think about each decision because delaying the process doesn't make it any easier. Cut down on how many advisers and how much input you need to make every decision. If you ask ten people and each of those conversations take twenty minutes, you have now spent two hundred minutes (or 3.5 hours) asking everybody in the world for advice on what is supposed to be *your* decision. Most times you don't even realize you are seeking this validation from another person or source. Be honest with yourself, and conscious enough to recognize when you do so. You'll find often enough that you still come back to making the same decision that you would've made originally without wasting all that time.

20. **Learn to delegate tasks.** Just because you run the business doesn't mean you are the best person for all the jobs. Delegating is a time-efficient way to move more quickly by making use of your employees' skill sets. Some C.E.Os use the 70% rule. Ask yourself, can this person do it 70% as well as I would? If yes, let it go. Remember, done is better than perfect!

21. **Use project management systems and apps.** Project management tools save time, money, and energy. Instead of an email back and forth, apps allow employees

to just check off a task as completed, and I receive an alert. I can also view the status of projects right from my phone, and quickly assign tasks to myself. Asana and Monday.com are great project management tools.

22. **Multitask.** If something does not require your undivided attention, multitask! For instance, if I'm on hold for thirty minutes on a call, I can use that time to answer emails or plan out my to-do list for the next day. If I'm stuck in traffic, I can use that time to call family and friends to catch up. Maximize your time.

23. **Plan ahead. Work ahead.** This goes back to goal-mapping. Don't work on the fly. Look at your needs and wants months in advance so you can lay the groundwork now.

24. **Remember your WHY.** When I travel for business, I especially maximize my time because I understand the importance of the time that is being taken away from my family and my children. Keeping your *why* in mind will make you much more efficient because you'll remember why you're working so hard.

25. **Tomorrow is another day and another chance to get it right.** Don't be overwhelmed by this list. The point is for it to serve as a guide. Slowly incorporate one or two of these tips into your daily schedule until you find yourself operating like a pro.

And however difficult life may seem, there is **always** something **you can do** and succeed. It matters that you **don't just give up.**

– STEPHEN HAWKING

FROM CREWMEMBER TO CAPTAIN

After goal-mapping and time management, a real boss has also got to learn how to effectively manage her team. Think of your company as a ship. In the beginning, you'll be down on the ground floor, hoisting the sails with the crew. As your business begins to grow and expand, however, you'll have to transition from crewmember to captain. This is a lesson I had to learn the hard way. The very hard way.

The biggest blow-up I've ever had with my staff happened because I didn't understand what leadership truly looked like. For a long time, when my team was getting ready for a hair show, I would be in the trenches alongside my crew: hauling boxes, setting up tables, doing all the heavy lifting and bending. For years, anything that my staff was doing, I was doing, too. It wasn't until one particular hair show that everything changed. I ran into the owner of another natural hair care brand at the show, and she walked over to me as I was sitting on the floor cutting open a box. There I was, sweating in my leggings and t-shirt, and she was dressed to impress. I'm talking high heels, makeup, totally Instagram-ready. I didn't think anything of it at first, but then she asked, "Rochelle, what are you doing? Don't you have staff to do that stuff?" I explained that my staff was there, but I was just helping them set up because blah, blah blah. She smiled at my ramble and replied, "Oh, well, I hire people for that," and walked away.

In that moment, I was so embarrassed. I was so dedicated to killing the hair show and setting everything up perfectly that I failed to consider the optics. The truth is, optics matter in business – a lot. As the C.E.O of a company, you shouldn't be doing the grunt work. You should be dressed to impress. You should be reflecting the premium quality and luxury that your products represent. From that day forward, I vowed never to be in the trenches again. No more hauling boxes and setting up. The next hair show Alikay did, I folded my arms and let my team do the work.

Now, here's where I went wrong. I went 0 to 100, real quick, as Drake would say. While my reasoning was completely sound, I failed to let my team in on the change. I didn't give them a heads-up about this transition, and as a result they felt completely abandoned. For years they had understood me to be one of them; another member of the crew. The team for this particular hair show had also worked for me at Be Fabulous Salon – my salon at the time. I had worn all the hats for so long that they expected me to wear them forever. The sudden change led to anger and resentment that boiled over in the van-ride home.

I vividly remember all of the hurtful things that were said that day. I was accused of being selfish and self-important, of being too good to work now that I was making a little money. My team criticized me for making my sister-in-law – who was pregnant at the time – work the event. The truth was, I had pled with her not to work this particular event because I knew it was very physically demanding. Needing the money, she would not take no for an answer and insisted on working. Still, none of that mattered in the eyes of my team. It was seven against one. They were pissed off, and I had gone from teammate to enemy in a day.

STEER YOUR SHIP

Being a boss teaches you the importance of conflict resolution. After the big blowup, tensions were very high at the salon. Things were extremely awkward because those seven employees had lost respect for me, and I resented them for the nasty things they had said. Still, I knew that I couldn't allow the problem to fester. Ignoring conflict only breeds toxicity in the workplace and so, I took control of my ship.

I called a meeting between myself and those seven irate employees. Truthfully, it was a shitshow. More angry feelings were expressed, tears were shed, and they didn't hold back. The worst part? I couldn't respond the way I wanted to. When you are the leader of a team, you have to learn to suppress your human emotions. You can't yell or cry or throw a tantrum. You have to hear people out and respond in what I like to call the daycare voice. Use a very calm, kind, but firm tone. I gave them the space to voice their feelings, and every time I felt a tear well up I turned my head and wiped my eye. When everyone had gotten everything out on the table, I said my piece.

In that meeting, I finally explained to my team what I should have explained from the beginning. I laid out their responsibilities and my responsibilities and made it clear that we would be playing two different roles moving forward: they are the team, I am the C.E.O. They need not be concerned with my day to day responsibilities, only their own. I explained that Alikay was in a growth phase, and a growing business means that I had to lead from the front, not the back. You cannot successfully lead your business if you are stuck in the day to day operations of running the business. Your efforts as C.E.O must be focused on growing, expanding, and only a small percentage can be reserved for daily operations. That's not to say that I won't get my hands dirty – to this day if you come to a hair show or expo, you will see me playing cashier behind my booth if things are getting hectic. My team knows that if stuff hits the fan, I will not let them drown. However, I am now more discerning when I choose to do those things. I remind myself that if you've hired someone to do a job, you've got to let them do it. You've trained them, now let them fly so you can do what you have to do as leader.

So, what have we learned? We've learned that when making adjustments as a boss and leader, you must expose your team to changes gradually and with transparency. Never do a sudden 180-degree flip. When problems arise – because they will – diffuse the situation in a calm and controlled manner, but be firm on your end point. Don't let your crew steer the ship. *You* steer. *You* are the captain.

FULL-STEAM AHEAD!

After resolution, it's also critical to put procedures in place to prevent the same problems from popping up again. After that meeting, I drafted up processes documents. These documents clearly delineate each and every team member's role and responsibilities moving forward, and they clearly lay out the flow of how I like things done so that I no longer have to be the one doing them! They explain exactly what work is expected for hair show workers so that everyone knows what they are signing up for. Furthermore, processes documents also help to set up an organizational flow within my business which maps out company hierarchy and shows exactly who reports to whom. If ever anything is lost in translation, we can refer back to these documents to double-check.

I've also made it a point to conduct regular check-ins with my staff. I really care about the people that work for me, and I want to make sure that they feel fulfilled and enjoy doing their job. If you don't enjoy your work, you shouldn't be working for me. In our check-ins, I work with my employees to learn their professional goals. What roles do they want to grow into? What skill sets do they want to learn? We discuss classes they can take and steps they can make to advance their careers or just feel more comfortable in their current roles. We of course sit down and have formal performance reviews, but at the end, the focus is always, how can I support you in growing your career? What do you need from me as your boss? I take down their next three goals and we have check-ins every six months or so to measure progress.

Remember, as a boss, your team keeps the ship sailing smoothly. If you want your business to move full-steam ahead, take time to nurture your crew. It will make all the difference.

definitions
every C.E.O should know

Talent Management

Anticipation of required human capital for an organization and the plan to meet those needs.

Source: www.researchgate.net

Human Capital

Skills, knowledge, and experience possessed by an individual or team, viewed in terms of their value or cost to an organization.

Source: Oxford Dictionary

Talent Development

Building the knowledge, skills, and abilities of others and helping them develop and achieve their potential so that the organizations they work for can succeed and grow.

Source: www.td.org

Learning & Development

Strategy is an organizational strategy that articulates the workforce capabilities, skills or competencies required, and how these can be developed, to ensure a sustainable, successful organization.

Source: www.hrzone.com

Business Organizational Chart

An organizational chart (or org chart) is a visual aid used to clarify who reports to whom and who is responsible for what in your organization.

Source: fitsmallbusiness.com

CHAPTER 5

SELF-CARE IS GOOD FOR BUSINESS

Before we continue, let's do a status report check-in. So far, we've tended our roots, nurtured our branches, honored our customers, and managed our employees – but what about us? What about the entrepreneur? Who is tending to *our* needs?

She works hard for the money

So hard for it, honey

She works hard for the money

So you better treat her right!

> \- *Donna Summer, "She Works Hard for the Money"*

Ms. Summer said it best. In the world of entrepreneurship, self-care isn't an option – it's a necessity, and the onus is on *you* to treat yourself right. It's often a lonely lifestyle because you'll find that many of your friends and family members won't be able to relate. Many will deem you obsessive or crazy for pouring so many hours into your fledgling business. Others will call you boring or selfish for passing up on social events and invitations. These kinds of comments can be very isolating. Even if you are blessed to have a strong support system, the sheer instability of your business, bank account, and emotions will have you questioning your own sanity, or at the very least take a toll on your mind and spirit. At times, it's as if you're staring at the world from behind a sheet of soundproof glass and no one can hear your cries.

While researchers are still in the early stages of understanding the correlation between entrepreneurship and mental health, there have been studies that suggest a strong connection. In a 2015 study led by Clinical Professor of Psychiatry at the University of California-San Francisco School of Medicine, Michael Freeman, results found that 49% of surveyed entrepreneurs reported having one or more mental health issues over the course of their lifetime. The study also found entrepreneurs more likely to report depression, ADHD, bipolar disorder, and substance abuse than the control group. The World Health Organization now also identifies burnout as an official medical diagnosis, describing the mental and physical collapse that can happen as a result of being highly stressed or overworked. Entrepreneurs are specifically plagued by the affliction.

Why? Well, think about it. Burnout, depression, anxiety, and other cognitive-behavioural conditions are often triggered by stress. Who leads a very stressful lifestyle? Entrepreneurs. It makes sense, then, that high levels of uncertainty, rejection, and financial insecurity can lead business owners on a downward spiral. The key is recognizing the difference between circumstantial stress and a diagnosable disorder in need of treatment.

SHOULD I SEEK HELP?

First thing's first, let's get something straight. *It's okay to be sad sometimes.* There's nothing wrong with feeling stressed out. In fact, you pretty much sign up for it when you decide to work for yourself. Don't feel guilty for feeling down, overwhelmed, or downright freaked out. It comes with the territory. Entrepreneurs are born risk-takers. We live on the edge, in the grey, and between the rock and the hard place. We are tight-rope walkers straddling the line between failure and flight, and that's naturally a very scary place to live. It's also the same thing that makes us great. Go figure!

In other words, there's nothing wrong with you if you're scared. If, however, that fear has become crippling, interferes with your daily functioning and relationships – personal or professional – or causes you to question your self-worth or reason for living, you must seek help. If you find yourself turning to substances like drugs or alcohol or even excessive sleeping in order to cope, speak to a professional. You may be suffering from situational or clinical depression.

Situational depression is a very normal response to sudden or dramatic lifestyle changes such as divorce, the death of a loved one, or, let's say, a major financial blow to your business. While still very real and potentially dangerous, situational depression often resolves in time. Clinical depression, also known as major depressive disorder, is more severe and may not resolve on its own. Many people require professional intervention or prescription medicine to manage. If you suspect you may be suffering, don't self-diagnose. Take control and make an appointment with your physician.

As these things often go, I didn't take my own advice. A self-proclaimed Superwoman, I tried to handle it all myself: a full college course load, multiple side hustles, a trillion jobs, and a new marriage. Fast forward a few more years and I tacked two kids, a payroll staff, two new businesses, and a self-managed manufacturing facility onto that list. I was doing it all and taking no time for myself – it's in my genes! I come from a family full of "do-it-yourself-ers"; I've always been raised with the example that you power through, figure it out, and solve the problem on your own. It wasn't until I experienced postpartum depression after having my daughter, Serenity, that I finally realized there are some things you just can't fix by yourself. Like so many working mothers out there, I had to learn the hard way to take that "S" off my chest.

MAMA MADNESS

I want to take a moment to talk specifically to the mothers and aspiring mothers out there. Of course, self-care is important for *everyone*, but I strongly believe that working mothers, in particular, need to be reminded to fill their own cups. Mothers live their lives in service to their children, and if you're an entrepreneur, your business is nothing more than another baby. We spend so much time, money, and energy making sure everyone and everything around us is thriving, meanwhile, we're barely surviving. My own journey into motherhood was a deliberate choice and one that I'm so happy that I made, however, it was far from easy on my mind, body, and spirit.

I was married at just twenty-years-old, and by the time Alikay started taking off, babies were the last thing on my mind. Before I knew it, years had passed and my husband and I finally paused long enough to ask ourselves, *shouldn't we have had a child by now?* We had been married for five years and though we weren't trying to conceive, we weren't actively trying *not* to get pregnant, either. It seemed odd that it hadn't happened, and so, forever a problem-solver, I went to a fertility doctor to get checked out. I was informed that I had PCOS and hypothyroidism, common conditions that can increase the difficulty of becoming pregnant or lead to dangerous pregnancy complications or even miscarriage. I was also told that my conditions were likely responsible for my highly irregular periods. Up until that point, I had only been experiencing occasional cycles, but I didn't think much of it. I had chalked it up to stress from life as an entrepreneur and never told my doctors. It wasn't until I was shown the bigger picture that I realized I had been ignoring serious signs from my body, all in the name of the hustle.

Understandably concerned, my husband and I made the choice to seek help conceiving our first child. Too broke at the time to afford in vitro fertilization, we did something called intrauterine insemination (IUI), which only cost around $2,000. It was still a hefty sum for us, but we managed to save everything we had because our desire for a child was that great. Sadly, the treatment failed, and we were beyond devastated, but God saw fit to bless us with our son Landon not too long afterwards – in a miraculous, natural conception, at that! For six years, we continued to grind and build our business until again we looked up and wondered, *shouldn't we have had another child by now?* Not to mention the added pressure of Landon praying every night for a baby brother or sister! Not wasting any time, we opted for IVF right away.

If we thought conceiving Landon was a struggle, it was nothing compared to Serenity. I always say, that little girl was an expensive baby to make! While we could now afford the treatment, additional genetic testing alone was an extra $10,000 on top of the already expensive IVF cycle fee. Keep in mind that Alikay Naturals was (and is) still a bootstrapped business; to say we were tapped out would be an understatement. At the time, Demond and I were still barely taking a real salary from our business, and so we had to use our personal savings to pay for treatment. On top of financial stress, I was still dealing with my health issues, running behind a very active seven-year-old, serving as the public face of a very rapidly growing company, and now, keeping up with a relentless schedule of IVF treatments. When I say it was madness, it was madness! I'm talking, excusing myself out of a business meeting at the Target headquarters to give myself a fertility shot in the bathroom stall. I'm talking, carrying around a cooler of chilled progesterone on the Disney cruise ship when Demond and I took Landon for a family vacation. I was fielding questions from customers in between running to the bathroom at a major beauty trade show full of 25,000 attendees, just to take my shot on time. Mind you, no one knew anything; all of this chaos was happening while keeping my pregnancy private from the world. I did my shots two to three times every day, did acupuncture, and ate any and every food I was told would help the treatment to take: all types of Brazilian nuts, pineapples, herbs, and even McDonald's fries – don't ask. Every single night during my IVF cycle, my husband Demond – who had never given anyone a shot in his life – would have to give me an injection in my lower back/buttocks area. It hurt so bad that my son Landon, who was only five-years-old at the time, would hold my hand tightly and say, "Mommy, it's gonna be okay. Let's be brave together." Not to mention, I was still going just as hard on the business side of things. During that time, I was still traveling and did more hair shows than I can count. I spoke at and attended at least sixteen events that year and launched another business, my photo studio. While the treatments paid off more than I can ever say, this was a period in my life that took immense sacrifice not just from me, but from my family as well.

The last thing on my mind was self-care. To make matters worse, I had to deal with people's public opinions on very private issues. I had gained a lot of weight after having Landon because I had stopped taking my PCOS meds for fear of transferring them through my breastmilk. I was confronted with people's judgement both in person and on social media, and still, no one even knew that I was in the process of trying to have a second baby. It's not that it was a secret – I was simply being protective of a sacred part of my life. God-forbid the treatment failed, I didn't want the world crying with me. I wanted to cry by myself.

By the time my husband and I finally did divulge our plans, even more judgement rolled in. I had other mothers ask me why on earth I would think of having another child. They said I was always traveling, never home; the unspoken implication was that there was no way I could have another child, maintain my business, *and* be a good mother. When I gave birth to Serenity and fell into a deep bout of postpartum depression, I feared my critics were right. For maybe a month after my daughter was born, I experienced a sadness I had never known. On top of the postpartum depression, I had gained another 50 pounds from the fertility treatments and hormones. I didn't look or feel like myself, and no one could pull me out of my darkness, because I couldn't even identify what was wrong. Demond would ask again and again, "What's wrong? What can I do?" I had no answers to give him. Everything made me cry and though I had prayed and prayed for my family, life didn't feel like a blessing. I just felt so sad, like I was failing at everything. I had created a story in my head that wasn't even a reality.

Still, all of that wasn't enough for me to stop and take care of myself. I kept working, thinking I could jump back into the swing of things and be who I was pre-delivery. It wasn't until I nearly fainted while running errands that things changed for me. I had been neglecting my high blood pressure medication and skipping my follow-up doctor appointments. It all caught up to me when, as I was standing in line at the bank, I began to feel spaced out like my body was shutting down. Still doing the most, I didn't call an ambulance. No, Superwoman Rochelle decided to drive herself to the emergency room. When I arrived, I left my phone in my car, so my poor husband and mother couldn't reach me for hours. They drove around making endless calls trying to find out where I was, meanwhile, I was hooked up to machines in a hospital room. As it turned out, my blood pressure was through the roof. I had developed high blood pressure and preeclampsia while pregnant, but I thought they would resolve themselves after having my baby. I had been too busy canceling my follow up appointments for business meetings to know that high blood pressure stays with you. As a result, I was dangerously close to having a stroke. I could have died. That's when it finally hit me: I needed to take better care of myself. Although I neglected my own doctor's appointments, I never ever missed any appointments for my children. It wouldn't be long, however, before I realized that I, too, needed to be a priority.

From that day forward my health became a major priority. No more pushing doctor's appointments or ignoring signs from my body. I finally started checking my blood pressure on a daily basis and actually taking my meds. To this day, I tell my assistant that any health-related appointments in my schedule are untouchable – they can't be moved around for any reason or any opportunity, however huge. I realized that being successful is worth nothing if I'm not alive to see it. I couldn't do that to myself, my husband, or my children. For all of our sakes, I learned that self-care isn't a luxury – it's a non-negotiable. Fast-forward to today, and here I am. I'm taking care of myself and my marriage, all while raising babies *and* businesses! I'm pretty much kicking ass, if I do say so myself!

Get help for yourself, and don't wait until the situation is dire. I never saw a therapist during my postpartum depression, but I sincerely wish I had. I believe talking to a professional would have helped me work through my darkness much easier and quicker. Maybe my husband wouldn't have felt so helpless in his inability to help. Maybe I would have realized sooner that I needed to slow down. I'm actually currently in the process of trying to find a therapist, and I feel like every entrepreneur should do the same. Even if it's only once a month, we need someone to talk to, someone with whom we can take off the boss hat and unload the burdens in our minds to truly be in human mode.

As for the mommy guilt and judgement from onlookers, screw it! They told Cardi B. she was insane for getting pregnant at the start of her career. Look at her now! Motherhood didn't slow Cardi down and it didn't slow me down, either. I was a mom, and that meant I had to keep it moving. I simply strapped my newborn to my chest and brought him to work with me. Toys and pack n' plays would be set up in my office, but the work never stopped. Yes, I was in the middle of my career when I got pregnant. We were just about to move into our first commercial space and had larger orders than ever, but I stayed true to what was important to me, and family was at the top of that list. I remembered that I have *two* sides: the business and the human. Never sacrifice one for the other. I kept my professional and personal lives growing at the same time because they were both fundamental to the vision I had for my life. It was important that I became a mother, and I didn't want to wait or compromise. You *can* have it all, honey. Don't let a Negative Nancy or Petty Patty tell you any differently!

Boy you know you love it

How we're smart enough to make these millions

Strong enough to bear the children

Then get back to business

- Beyoncé, "Run The World (Girls)"

As Queen Bey said, you *can* get back to business. Just make sure that taking care of business also includes taking care of *yourself*. Who runs the world? Girls!

MY WEIGHT LOSS JOURNEY

Being a mother has definitely pushed me to take my health more seriously, but I also did it for myself – I had to make a huge change to save my own life. That change was weight loss.

I had always been pretty slim and in what I thought was pretty good health – that is, until 2012. That was the year I received a series of diagnoses that would change my life forever. My doctors informed me that I had prolactinoma, a benign brain tumor. While the tumor was non-cancerous, it affected my body's thyroid regulation as well as my reproductive system, hence my difficulty getting pregnant. As the tumor was benign, my doctors and I opted against potentially life-threatening brain surgery, and I was simply prescribed monthly medications to prevent the tumor from growing. In addition to my prolactinoma, I was also diagnosed with hypothyroidism and PCOS, or polycystic ovarian syndrome, all of which led to a swift and significant weight gain. At the time of my diagnosis, I was around 165 pounds; by the time I got pregnant with my son, I was sitting at 175. After I gave birth, however, I made the decision to stop taking my medications for fear that they would be transferred to my son through my breastmilk. Choosing Landon's health over my own, I came off the meds that were regulating my body and quickly gained a whopping thirty pounds.

I hovered around that new weight – 205 pounds – for years. It wasn't for a lack of trying, though. I tried everything to lose weight, but my PCOS and hypothyroidism made it nearly impossible. I maintained that weight until 2017 when I started IVF treatments to conceive my daughter. Between my preexisting health conditions and being pumped full of hormones from the fertility treatments, I had gained another 50 pounds just trying to have Serenity. Before I knew it, I was standing in the mirror at 240-something pounds, barely recognizing myself and wondering how on earth I had gotten there. Determined not to spiral into depression, I tried my very best to boost my self-esteem by dressing up in cute clothes. I tried to embrace my body and work with what I had, but I just wasn't happy. On top of everything, I was in real physical pain. I remember how badly my feet would ache when I would step out of bed every morning. I could no longer run or play soccer with Landon, or ride bicycles in the evenings, which had been our family ritual for years. I was fatigued all of the time and the worst part of it all was knowing how little control I had over the situation. Still, I carried on doing my best to live life despite the physical and emotional toll of my health struggles.

One day, I accompanied a family member to a doctor's appointment. She had opted to have VSG, or vertical sleeve gastrectomy, and I was there purely for moral support. Like the commonly known gastric bypass, VSG is also a bariatric surgery. The main difference is that gastric bypass surgery shortens the digestive track and reroutes the path of foods and beverages after consumption. Since the larger part of the stomach and intestines are bypassed, the procedure limits the nutrients and calories that the body actually absorbs from food. VSG, on the other hand, is the surgical removal of a part of your stomach. About 80% of the stomach is removed, leaving behind the smaller 20% portion. This results in a quicker and longer-lasting feeling of satiety or fullness without altering the body's process for absorption of nutrients and calories. During her own consultation, my family member suggested to her doctor that he should try to convince me to have the VSG surgery as well. Shocked and mortified, I immediately went on the defense. I didn't care what she said, what the doctor said, or what my previous weight loss struggles had indicated – I just *knew* I could do it on my own. I didn't want any help.

Knowing there was nothing he could say to change my mind, the doctor presented me with a deal. I would set a weight loss goal and try my very best to reach it on my own. If in three months I proved unsuccessful, I would come back and set an appointment to talk about VSG. Albeit reluctant, I couldn't argue with that logic, and I ultimately agreed that I would come back if I couldn't reach my goal of 20 pounds down in the next three months. From there, I was on a mission; I became a woman, obsessed! I tried every diet there is under the sun from Atkins, to Weight Watchers, to the Ketogenic diet. I even did an entire week of a green smoothie cleanse – no food, just smoothies full of fruits and vegetables. I ran myself so ragged that my body began to rebel. I vividly recall being on the road with my husband on the way to make an appearance at an event. Demond had to keep pulling over just so I could throw up the green smoothie contents of my stomach again and again. After three months of trying, I returned to the doctor. To my dismay, not only had I not lost any weight, but I had actually *gained* five pounds! After all of that effort, I weighed in at 247 pounds. That night, I went home and cried my eyes out.

I am a born-entrepreneur – that means I am a go-getter. I set goals and I don't stop until I reach them. All of a sudden, I was being confronted with a problem I couldn't solve on my own. I had to humbly accept the fact that I needed help – medical help – not just to lose weight, but to save my life. I scheduled my VSG surgery for July 2018, seven months after the birth of my second child. While I would have been covered under my insurance, I chose to pay out of pocket. If I had gone through my insurance I would have had to wait through an extra six months of further evaluation before my surgery, and to be frank, I simply did not want to see where I would be in another six months. I couldn't stand to gain any more weight than I already had, and I was ready to make the jump. I got my surgery and I have never once regretted the decision. On the anniversary of my surgery, I weighed in at 146 pounds, a full 100 pounds down from my starting weight. Do I have loose skin? Of course. Do I still deal with body image issues? Yes, just like everyone else.

Contrary to what many people may think, weight loss surgery is not a quick fix to your physical or emotional struggles. My surgery was merely a tool used to help me gain control over a problem that was quickly snowballing and threatening my wellbeing, my future with my children, and my very life. While it obviously helped me shed the weight, there are very real side-effects to surgery. Recovery was brutal as I dealt with post-op dehydration and even lost my hair – by month four or five, it was all falling out in clumps. Some people experience complications from surgery that lead to overly severe weight loss and hospitalization. I had to readjust to the limitations of my new, smaller stomach and hold myself accountable. Like many entrepreneurs – busy with work or constantly on the road – I hadn't developed the best eating habits over the years. I would skip breakfast, scarf down a snack or a quick lunch, and eat dinner late at night after my children had gone to sleep. After my surgery, all of this had to change. Now, I have to make sure that I eat the right portions of the right foods, frequently enough throughout the day. I've joined Facebook groups to find VSG communities full of other people on the same journey. I make sure to hit my protein goals and workout to increase my strength and muscle mass. I take my meds and go to all my doctor's appointments. The point is that even on the other side of successful weight loss, it still takes effort to maintain strong physical and mental health.

Currently, my weight generally fluctuates between 150 and 155 pounds, but it's not about the number. I am happy and I am healthy – I am happy *because* I am healthy. Still, I would be lying if I said I had fully recovered mentally from my surgery. I haven't even fully recovered from IVF. The truth is that both of these journeys have been brutal. They've been mentally, emotionally, financially, and spiritually-taxing, but worth it, nonetheless. When you get your health back, you get peace of mind, joy, and the freedom to imagine a future where you're around to reap the fruits of your labors, watch your children grow, and grow old with your partner and loved ones.

As entrepreneurs, we are extremely prone to high-stress lifestyles, and stress releases cortisol (the primary stress hormone). A little here and there is normal, but when your body experiences an excess of cortisol due to a constant state of stress and worry, there can be damaging long-term effects. Like me, you could experience high blood pressure or weight gain, but chronic stress also puts you at risk for anxiety, depression, sleep issues, heart problems, headaches, and more. Learn from my story and take care of yourself sooner rather than later. Self-care isn't just a good idea – it's imperative.

SO, WHAT IS SELF-CARE, EXACTLY?

This might seem like an obvious question, but you'd be surprised how many people have no definition. I know I sure didn't. Back when I first started Alikay while in college, I was so busy between all of my jobs, classes, and online businesses that I hadn't stopped to consider what it meant to take care of myself. Perhaps I didn't find it necessary. If you had asked me, I might have said self-care looked like a day of pampering: massages, manicures, pedicures. Either way, I had no time or money for any of that.

As a grown woman, I've come to understand that self-care looks different to different people. It's whatever you need to do to feel better taken care of, and to find peace and calm. For me, it's knowing when to stop and retreat from the world. Shutting the world down and going into my own little hole to build myself back up. It's sitting down and bingeing a television series – my current obsession: *The Marvelous Mrs. Maisel*. When I'm very busy, self-care often looks like a stay-cation. I go to a hotel maybe thirty minutes away from home and stay there for a night or two all by myself – no husband, no kids. It's as simple as having that alone-time just to have a bath, drink some tea, and get some good sleep. Maybe I'll get a massage or meditate on the beach, maybe not. The key is the solitude. I find that being alone with my thoughts, away from meetings, people, and obligations, helps to renew me. Furthermore, it boosts my creativity when I can get in tune with my own emotions, independent of anyone else's input. Whether it's a solution to a tricky problem, a new ad campaign, or an upcoming product launch, I always find my best ideas after some time on my own.

When I really want to indulge, self-care is a real vacation. I try to take a trip to somebody's country, island, or resort at least once every three months or so. My husband may think it's a little extra, but it's so important. Traveling has become integral to my spirit; it sparks joy in my life. To be clear, I'm talking about an adult vacation, not a family trip. Even family vacations can be hectic and stressful when you're a mom running after energetic kids. We take family vacays once every year so our kids can experience new countries with us, but self-care vacations are separate. I mean, a poolside and drinks, *How Stella Got Her Groove Back* vacation – well, minus the steamy shenanigans with the hot local islander. My quarterly trips remind me that I'm human – not just a mom, wife, or entrepreneur.

When I'm not taking a staycation or vacation, self-care looks like sleep. Yes, sleep. I'm not one of those *team no sleep* people. Hell no. I need my rest, thank you. Demond knows the drill: after the kids go to sleep around 8:30, he's got about two more hours alone with me before it's lights out. Don't worry, folks. We do spend a lot of time together during the day and weekends as well, but my bedtime is sacred! I go to bed by 10:30 most nights because I'm an early-riser. Funnily enough, I don't even set an alarm unless I'm waking up to travel or take a meeting. My body wakes me up naturally anywhere between 5:30 and 7 am, depending on the day. I propel out of bed because that's how much I love what I do. I know it sounds cheesy, but it's true. To live this entrepreneur life, you've got to fall in love with the process, with the struggle. I get my sleep in so that I can function at full capacity. That whole sleep when you're dead thing just isn't for me.

Don't get me wrong. There will definitely be times when you have to lose sleep – lots of times, actually. Any time I'm in the middle of a product launch or a huge campaign, sleep is the first thing I sacrifice. I go from my typical seven or eight hours to maybe four or five. I call these times my unhealthy grind modes. I'll be working sixteen hour days or more, staying up late, waking up early, and eating cheap, convenient, processed foods when I'm on the go. Is it ideal? No, but it's sometimes necessary to get things done. The key is to keep these grind modes in moderation. I make sure not to let them become a lifestyle. Once that project or launch is over, I often block out a week of recuperation time just to get back into my normal lifestyle.

Finally, another part of my personal self-care is prayer and meditation. I like to say that prayer is asking God questions, and meditation is being still enough to hear His answers. Unlike lots of self-help gurus out there, I don't believe you have to meditate every single day – although I did while I was pregnant. Forcing it defeats the whole purpose. Instead, I just take fifteen to twenty minutes a couple of times a week to still my mind. Years ago, I read a book by Russell Simmons and Chris Morrow called *Success Through Stillness* that really taught me how important meditation is for entrepreneurs. For those who have struggled with meditation, don't overcomplicate it. Sit in a quiet place, – for me it's a little poolside swing in my backyard – shut off your phone and devices, and clear your head. For the first five minutes or so, my mind usually gets more hectic. Thoughts start buzzing around about my checklists and schedules, but after some effort, I'm able to zone out. I remind myself that this is my time to commune with God. I take that very seriously.

Whatever your preferred method of self-care turns out to be, prioritize it. Make the time and schedule it into your calendar. If I've learned anything over the course of my life, it is that you have to protect the asset that is yourself. *You* are your most important asset. Without taking care of you, everything else falls to pieces.

PICK THE RIGHT PARTNER

While your happiness is in your own hands, I can't stress enough how important it is to align with the right people. From family members to friends and employees, the people you surround yourself with will bring either positive or toxic energy to your journey. That influence is magnified tenfold when it comes to your spouse. Think of your significant other as your partner in progress, productivity, and in my case, profit. My husband Demond and I have been blessed enough to maintain a happy marriage and successful business partnership for the last twelve years and counting. Here are a few tips I've learned along the way for working with your spouse and maintaining both of your sanity:

MARRY SOMEONE DRIVEN

Firstly, make sure you're choosing a mate whose goals or visions for life align with your own. To be honest, some people are just not very driven. They may be okay with living a life of simplicity that doesn't require much ambition beyond making ends meet. Some people want a lowkey life of low pressure and high comfort and that's okay – that's their choice! However, if you were born to be an entrepreneur, that's exactly the kind of energy you want to avoid. Choose a partner who is hungry for the hustle, who always wants more and better for themselves and their life. Even if they themselves don't want to be an entrepreneur, it's okay. You just need someone who is driven and who will support you and cheer you on during your entrepreneurship journey. Pick someone who will never let you off the hook with the goals you set for yourself because they hold themselves to the same standard of accountability. This is not to say that you and your spouse need to be identical. Demond and I are different in many ways, however, we are both extremely ambitious at our cores. That kindred energy has set a solid foundation for our relationship in love and business.

Another critical consideration to make when you marry as an entrepreneur – particularly for my female entrepreneurs – is whether or not you want to legally change your last name. My husband and I got married on June 21, 2007. I did not legally change my last name until June 20, 2019. That's right – it took me *twelve years*! In practice, I was Rochelle Campbell, for all intents and purposes; that's how I made everyone address me. However, when it came to legal documents from my social security card to my driver's license and my business documents, everything remained under Rochelle Graham. At first, I didn't change my name simply because the process seemed too time-consuming. I was young and in college, working a million jobs, and running a brand new business – I didn't have the time. As the years passed, it became a branding issue. Everything from my media placements to my websites had me listed as Rochelle Graham. I was worried that I wouldn't be recognizable or that my social assets would vanish if I changed my name so late in the game.

Ultimately, I ended up making the decision to hyphenate my name. I am now legally, Rochelle Alikay Graham-Campbell. While my business is important, my family is my everything.

My love for my husband has always been 100% undeniable, but we are both happy that I can now proudly and publicly declare my new last name to the world. It feels like an extra way to honor my marriage and feel even further connected to my children. The best part is that I didn't have to compromise and give up the name that has carried so much personal importance within my heart and professional significance within my brand. I simply issued a rebranding campaign within my company to incorporate my new legal name. Yes, it was an extra step, but it was worth it. If your name is central to your business branding, be sure to consider your options carefully when you get married. I'm sharing with you what I did, but remember, you must ultimately do what's best for you.

IDENTIFY ROLES AT WORK AND HOME

By establishing your individual roles both at home and within your company, you and your spouse will avoid many fights. Demond and I discovered that we have different strengths. While we appreciate each other's input, we allow one another to work in our own individual areas of genius and what we each enjoy doing within the company. This keeps us from stepping on each other's toes or having too many cooks in the kitchen.

I am the C.E.O of Alikay Naturals while Demond is our C.O.O. Just by virtue of our titles, sometimes my decision has to trump his. When we're home, however, I respect my husband as the leader of our household. I'm the captain at work and he's the captain at home. Neither of us makes big decisions without talking with the other, but we also trust and respect each other enough to relinquish control and let the other person take the reins.

KNOW WHEN TO TURN OFF WORK MODE

I am an early bird and Demond is a night owl. I want to talk about everything in the morning and he wants to talk about them at night when I am mentally exhausted. It didn't take long to realize that that wasn't going to work, so we came up with a very important boundary. As soon as we leave the office, we are no longer the C.E.O and C.O.O, we're Rochelle and Demond. Once we leave those doors, we have to ask each other permission to talk about anything work-related. *Hey, I have something I want to run by you, but it's work-related. Are you good?*

Since we're both workaholics, we don't always stick to our rules perfectly, but I'd say we follow it about 80% of the time. If ever we get to rambling about company talk and one person isn't feeling up to it, they have the power to shut it down. *Hey, I really don't want to talk about business right now. I need to be in human mode. Can we table this until tomorrow?* Simple language like this helps us to distinguish between our work and human personas.

HAVE SEPARATE IDENTITIES

This is a big one. Demond and I literally create two alter egos in our heads. So, I have my husband, Demond, and then I have my business partner, Demond. If I'm angry at something my business partner did, I don't carry that over to how I treat Demond, my husband. The same goes for how he treats me. It sounds really weird, but we've become really good at being able to separate the two.

SCHEDULE YOUR DATES

If it's not in my calendar, it's not happening. Like business meetings and conference calls, Demond and I make sure to schedule our date nights in ahead of time. This reminds us that our marriage is just as much a priority as our business, if not more, and also allows us to replenish our human sides. Our bond existed way before our business came to be, so prioritizing our relationship keeps that foundation at the heart of everything we do, from pursuing goals to raising our two amazing children. We agree never to sacrifice our household for our careers. Be sure that you and your spouse are on the same page about that.

SCHEDULE YOUR MEETINGS

On the other side of the same coin, we also schedule our one-on-one meetings together. I know, it seems odd to have to schedule an appointment to talk to your husband, but I have to remember – I'm not meeting with my husband, I'm meeting with my business partner, my C.O.O. We are two legitimate, independent professionals with hectic schedules, and we have to respect each other's time the same way we would for a meeting with a retailer. These meetings are typically when we review the higher up issues in our company and strategize the future of Alikay.

DON'T DISRESPECT EACH OTHER IN PUBLIC

Like I said earlier, entrepreneurs are human, too. Our emotions can get the best of us and sometimes we get the urge to let the other person know exactly how we're feeling without mincing words. However, it's critical that you learn how to disagree in a respectful manner, especially when it's in front of other people. Our team has witnessed us disagree, and we are both very, very passionate people, but we never go about it in a nasty way. We know when to pull the other person to the side and say, *let's finish this later.* There's a difference between disagreeing and arguing. Arguing is never productive, especially in front of your team. When addressing our staff, Demond and I make sure to maintain a united front. I'm not saying that we're perfect – it took years of trial and error to get this part right. For the sake of the business, we actively try to remember that we are always on the same team.

ASK FOR SUPPORT WHEN IT'S NEEDED

There's a quote from Iyanla Vanzant that I love:

"When you give to others to the degree that you sacrifice yourself, you make the other person a thief."

Basically, when you get stuck in the habit of giving, giving, giving, without asking for anything in return, you breed resentment for others. In the early stages of our business, I would be so resentful of the fact that Demond had the freedom to go out and do certain things. I was tired and felt like he had it better than I did, but at the same time, I had never spoke up and asked for help. I hadn't said to him, *hey, I feel like I'm carrying way more weight in this business. I need you to do more.* It took me some time to learn that my husband should not be expected to read my mind; a closed mouth doesn't get fed. Communicate so that the other person knows where you need their support. Harboring resentment will be poison for your business relationship and your marriage.

REMEMBER THAT YOU ARE A TEAM

Lastly, if you choose to go into business with your spouse, remember the two of you are a team – you are *the* most important team within your company. If you guys are not aligned or in sync, it will throw off everything else. Remember that this person is not out to get you. If they're tough on you, it's only because they want to push you to reach the greatest version of yourself. Always be 100% honest and transparent and communicate at all times and you can absolutely make it work.

Demond and I eloped when we were in our early twenties. Our families thought we were crazy to tie our lives together so young, but everything we have today we owe to that decision. Twelve years later and we are planning to renew our vows, this time with a small, intimate ceremony – white dress and all. They say you shouldn't mix business with pleasure, but I believe that Demond and I have dispelled that myth 100 times over. Not only is he my greatest love and most trusted business ally, he and the support he provides are an integral part of how I manage this crazy life of mine. There is no one else that I would rather take this journey of building a family and growing a business with. Entrepreneurship is extremely stressful and it can take a toll on you as a person and on your marriage if you aren't careful. Focus on the love that you and your partner share and hold on tight to each other during the tough times.

SETTING BOUNDARIES

Another major part of my self-care is maintaining healthy boundaries. When I say no, no one is exempt! Not hubby, not babies, not employees. Boundaries help me maintain control over my time and energy so that I can focus on what I need to get done without giving myself away to a million other people at once. Nothing and no one is worth me sacrificing my inner peace and mental health.

NO MEANS NO

> "*The difference between successful people and really successful people is that really successful people say no to almost everything.*"
>
> – *Warren Buffett*

It might seem extreme, but this is a quote I live by. There was a time in my career where every business opportunity seemed like gold. If I was asked to speak on a panel, I did it. If I was asked to teach a business master class, I did it. If I was asked to fly across the country to make an appearance, I did it. All I could see was exposure for my brand. Eventually I had to consider what I was losing by saying *yes* all the time: bonding with my children, date nights with my husband, presence with my staff, and time for myself to rest and recoup from my demanding C.E.O schedule. I realized that declining on an opportunity didn't make me mean or ungrateful, it made me a smart businesswoman. Time is a huge resource and it shouldn't be wasted.

Saying *no* more often also taught me to operate from a place of abundance. Oftentimes when we're afraid to say no, it's because we think we're passing up an opportunity that will never come again. We think we're blocking a blessing. The truth is, however, that you have got to move as though your opportunities are limitless. What is meant for you will never pass you by, so don't live your life from a place of lack and scarcity. Say no with confidence because when you're great at what you do, there will always be something bigger and better down the line.

DO NOT DISTURB

Another tactic I use to establish boundaries is hanging a do not disturb sign from my door. I do this for both my home and work offices, and it works wonders. When you are the captain at the helm of the ship, it's only natural that your crew will come to you with questions. While I keep the lines of communication open, it's also crucial that I don't leave myself available to others on-demand. If I did, I would never get any work done.

In reality, I only actually go into my work office two days out of the week. The rest of the time I'm at home or working from a café if I need a change of pace. When I do go into the office and my do not disturb sign is hanging, my team knows not to interrupt me. Unless it's an urgent situation with one of my children, they know to figure it out on their own. If it's something they can't address among themselves, they know to table it until my sign comes off the door or save it for a team meeting on another day. When I'm working on something especially important and I absolutely cannot risk being disturbed, I go as far as to go to my downtown studio, apart from my staff. There, I have complete focus. Of course, I still remain available through email and text, but I refuse to give the world 24/7 access to my physical presence.

I'm also a huge fan of the do not disturb function on my smartphone. This keeps me from scrolling social media when I should be working, and blocks any unnecessary social texts and calls from interrupting my work flow. Even my husband is subject to my DND modes, but he knows that should anything pressing pop up, he can simply call me twice and that will deactivate the setting so that he can reach me.

SCHEDULE BLOCKING

Schedule blocking is one of the greatest weapons in my entrepreneurial arsenal. This is when I lump all of my conference calls, emails, and meetings into a specific block of time every week. For me, it's Tuesdays and Wednesdays. Every Tuesday and Wednesday, I conduct back to back meetings with my staff. I may only get fifteen minutes in between each appointment, but I make sure that every single department gets my undivided attention. These meetings are when my employees get the opportunity to ask all those questions they couldn't ask during the week. I even schedule my check-in calls with friends! That's right – I map out calendar time, outside of work hours, specifically for girlfriend catch-ups.

Thursdays are my execution days – pure action steps. This is the day I allocate to executing on all problems or concerns raised during Tuesday and Wednesday meetings. Not only does this make it super easy for me to keep track of my weekly commitments, but it also ensures that each meeting's agenda items are actually prioritized, addressed, and tackled.

By contrast, Fridays are my off-limits days. On Friday, no one calls me – my phone simply does not ring. My team knows better by this point. That is my one day a week to really work on planning projects for the future and so it is sacred. Keeping that day strictly for C.E.O planning also sets the tone for my weekends.

Finally, even my emails and travel are schedule blocked. Too many people waste time answering emails back and forth, all day long. I choose to set aside a specific block of time, even if it's only for thirty minutes or one hour at the start and/or end of each workday. This is the only time I tackle my inbox, leaving the rest of my day free for running my company. As for travel, my assistants know that I'm very particular about how they schedule my trips. For example, I hate early morning flights – not because I'm not a morning person, but because they interfere with my routine. As an entrepreneur and mom, my time with my children gets interrupted enough. If I can take a later flight and leave my morning open so I can still drop my kids off to school, I prioritize that. It's so important for me to maintain a sense of normalcy in their lives, and having their daily car rides with mommy is a big part of that. By the same token, I don't take any calls after 4pm so that I can pick my daughter up from daycare. These moments are sacred and schedule blocking keeps them untouched.

BALANCE IS BS!

For a long time, I thought these boundaries would help me find balance in my life. While they're extremely important for my sanity, the truth is that balance is a bunch of bull. It doesn't exist! Not in my world, at least. Balance implies that all the aspects of your life get equal time, equal effort, equal attention. No. I find that life is more of an organized juggle. There are several moving parts, and while you have your hands grasped firmly on a few, the others will be up in the air. You can't touch everything at once, but you never drop any of the balls.

That's life as an entrepreneur. One ball is your business, another is your children. A third ball is your marriage or relationship and a fourth is your health. You can also throw in your relaxation or down-time, friend commitments, and whatever else is dictated by the circumstances of your life. It's *your* juggling act; you decide best how to keep everything afloat. Don't kill yourself aspiring to some unrealistic standard of balance. Everything won't always be equal, but everything should be stable. Stability – that's the goal!

One week I might be focusing on Alikay and my kids. I might ask myself, okay, when was my last mommy-Landon or mommy-Serenity day? What play date can we have this week? The following week, maybe I'm prioritizing my marriage. Okay, let me schedule in a date night with Demond or make time to cook his favorite meal. The next week might be about catching up with family and friends I haven't checked in with in a while. The truth is, if I don't schedule these things, they won't happen, and I don't allow myself to feel guilty about that. I do what I have to do to keep everything working, it's just that one or two things might take priority at a given time depending on my most pressing needs.

SELF-CARE SOLIDARITY

While you're taking care of yourself, try to remember that your circle needs support, too. Especially if you know other entrepreneurs, check in with them, ask them what they need and how you can help, remind them that they matter. Not long ago, I was ill with the flu. On top of feeling and looking like a hot mess, I was stressed about not being at my best for work. One of my fellow female entrepreneurs, Kendra actually took the time to send me an Amazon get-well care package! It had everything from teas to chicken noodle soup, and when I received it, I just felt so incredibly loved. More than that, I felt *seen* as a businesswoman and a human. She didn't have to do that, but she reached out a hand in sisterhood because she knew how I was feeling.

Ever since that experience, I try to make sure that I'm standing in solidarity with my fellow businesswomen. I'm the friend who will send over a bottle of wine because I know you're in the middle of a hectic product launch. I'll have a bouquet of your favorite flowers sent over to your office on a day I know you're in, just to brighten up your day. Like I said, this can be a pretty isolating lifestyle, so showing your peers that you understand goes a long way. Not to mention, they'll be likely to remember your kindness and return the favor when you're in need of some compassion.

YOU DESERVE IT!

So many entrepreneurs neglect self-care because they simply don't think they deserve to feel good. They think rest is synonymous with laziness and that they haven't earned enough success to slow down. Furthermore, because we identify so strongly with our brands, we take any blows to our businesses as personal defeats. If an idea fails, we think that we are failures. If you relate to any of these feelings, I want you to know that you're not alone.

I still struggle with these thoughts every day. Because my desire for greatness is so strong, I tend to be overly harsh on myself. I take care of everyone else before stopping to consider my own needs, and sometimes making time for myself feels selfish or even frivolous. I ask myself, *isn't there something more productive you could be doing right now?* While it's an ongoing struggle, I remind myself of what I know to be true: I deserve good things. I deserve to feel good, and so do you. Let's dispel the myth that we are indestructible. Take better care of yourself so that you can operate at 100%. It's what you, your staff, and your customers deserve!

Self Management

Management of or by oneself; the taking of responsibility for one's own behavior and well-being.
Source: Oxford Dictionary

Body Positivity

Self-acceptance of one's body and the changes it goes through in a lifetime, and belief that all human beings should have a positive body image.
Source: www.psychologytoday.com

Faith

Complete trust or confidence in someone or something.
Source: Oxford Dictionary

Executive Assistant

A person employed to assist a high-level manager or professional with correspondence, appointments, and administrative tasks.
Source: Oxford Dictionary

Generational Wealth

An abundance of valuable possessions or money passed down through generations.
Source: Wikipedia

Accounts Payable

Money owed by a company to its creditors.
Source: Oxford Dictionary

Accounts Receivable

Money owed to a company by its debtors.
Source: Oxford Dictionary

CHAPTER 6

TOP NOTS

Entrepreneurship is not a one-size-fits-all path. Hopefully by now you've realized that each and every person's journey is unique, and we all have to learn our own lessons. Still, in my ten years of experience I've picked up on some ideas that I consider to be universal truths – things I've had to learn the hard way that I can help you look out for. After all, what kind of Business Fairy Godmother would I be if I didn't show you the pitfalls? So, buckle up. I'm about to school you! The top knot is one of the most popular and trendy hairstyles out there. In this chapter, I'll be giving you my top *nots*, or what *not* to do when running a business.

WITH YOUR STAFF...

DON'T OVEREXPLAIN YOURSELF

As the C.E.O of your business, you want to keep the peace in your workplace. Sometimes this leads to you killing yourself trying to make everyone happy with every decision you make. Cut it out. The plain truth is, you don't have to justify all of your choices and actions with your team. You don't owe them an explanation for every move you make – you owe it to *yourself* to do whatever's in the best interest of your company. Sometimes, you're going to piss people off; decisions will be made that rub people the wrong way or cause them to talk behind your back. Let it happen. As long as no one's safety or well-being is being threatened, don't feel bad for doing what you feel is best. It's your business and you have to follow your own intuition. Make sure you're not lighting yourself on fire to keep everyone else warm.

As cliché as it sounds, it sometimes really is my way or the highway when it comes to my business. That's not a matter of ego, it's a matter of establishing a culture of leadership. If I make a decision that turns out to be wrong, so be it. I'd rather learn a lesson having stuck to my guns than drive myself crazy answering to everyone on my payroll. Part of effective leadership is making swift decisions. By swift, I do not mean hasty or poorly-thought-out. I mean that you must learn to be firm and decisive, and take action quickly and confidently. If you get into the habit of clearing every decision with your staff just to be liked, you'll end up paralyzed.

DON'T BE OVERLY NICE

Every email or conversation with your employees doesn't need to begin with a small talk session. *Hello, Susan! Good morning! I hope your weekend was fantastic. How are the kids? How is that cut on your toe? How are you feeling? Is your tummy okay?* Cut the fluff! I am a friendly person, but work mode is work mode. I cannot waste time on unnecessary pleasantries – I like to dive right in. *Hello, I need an update on this. How are we doing on this project? I am available today between 2 and 3pm, call if you need me.* I don't want to flood anyone's inbox with anything other than pertinent, problem-solving information and I appreciate the same courtesy in return. It's not about being cold, it's just about picking your moments. In our downtime or slow time, that's when I check in with my employees. *How is your nephew doing? Did he make the team? I know you said your goddaughter was just born. Can I see a picture?* There's a time to catch up, for sure, but I am careful not to build these moments into my everyday interactions. Don't worry about being perceived a certain way. If you've established a good rapport with your team, they know your character and who you truly are. You shouldn't feel the need to win them over with every single conversation.

By the same token, pleasantries do have their place, particularly in interactions outside of your internal team. When you're networking, meeting new contacts, and potential partners, clients, or retailers, that's the time for niceness. Checking in with people helps build relationships. Just be sure to pick your moments and know when to rein it in.

DON'T GET TOO CLOSE

When it comes to your employees, you can be friendly without being friends. Never lose sight of the fact that your staff works *for* you, not with you. This means that certain behaviors are just not appropriate. For example, I don't skip out to every Friday happy hour my employees invite me to. I don't gossip about people on my staff. If we're at a company event, I show up, I take pictures, I engage with people, but I don't drink too much. I realized that my staff does not need to see the fun, "turn up" Rochelle. I like to remain composed at all times and I try not to put myself in situations that will compromise my boss-employee dynamic. This is a policy that I implemented over time. When I was a younger, newer C.E.O, I allowed myself to have a lot more flexibility and fun around my employees. As I grew and my roles and responsibilities expanded, I made the necessary adjustments.

Traveling is a perfect example. If ever I have to fly somewhere with my staff for an Alikay event, I try not to sit with my employees on the flight if there is another available seat. This is actually a suggestion that my husband gave me. Sitting next to your staff on long flights is a perfect storm for getting too comfortable. Before you know it, you'll be chatting all about your employee's fresh divorce or ex-boyfriend drama. When you're overly personal, you may learn information that makes it hard for you to effectively do your job. For instance, it's much harder to fire someone you need to let go if you know all about their struggles as a single mother of three. As a rule of thumb, I do like to know a little about the people I employ because I only want good energy on my team. However, I don't like to know too much. I maintain a warm and respectful distance and that works best for all involved.

DON'T PANIC

Many entrepreneurs have what is called chicken little syndrome, or perpetuating and crippling belief that the sky is falling. Don't allow that toxic energy to infect your team. If you struggle with anxiety, seek help and find coping mechanisms to manage your symptoms. What you absolutely must *not* do, however, is spread that panic to your staff. How is your team supposed to stay calm if you're running around like a chicken with its head cut off? Don't inform your team of every little piece of bad news. Vent to your journal or your business partner, maybe even your spouse or your therapist, but never sound off your worries to your employees.

DON'T UNDERVALUE YOUR EMPLOYEES

While it's critical to maintain separate roles for yourself and your staff, don't underestimate the value that your employees can contribute. Sometimes, because they are the ones on the ground floor of company operations, your staff will see things you can't see. They'll catch details that can streamline your processes or even save you money. They can offer up creative ideas that you hadn't thought of. For instance, while only myself, my husband, and my brother-in-law have the actual formulas to Alikay Naturals products, my staff frequently participates in the product naming process. They come up with tons of cute, original ideas and I like to keep the air of creativity flowing. I'll even bring in some fragrance samples after narrowing them down to my favorites and have my staff vote on their top picks, as well. This makes them feel like they are a part of the process and also shows them that I value their opinions. By letting them know that they have a voice, I've established an atmosphere of community and collaboration. If your employees feel undervalued or unappreciated, they won't have a safe space to share and you will potentially miss out on some great ideas. When you treat people with respect, they'll want to see you win and they'll work hard to make that happen.

WITH YOUR COMPETITORS...

DON'T UNDERESTIMATE THE UNDERDOGS

Many times, when entrepreneurs are evaluating their competition, they tend to only look left and right at their top rivals. Don't forget to look behind you, as well. The brands in your industry that you consider small or irrelevant are the same brands coming for your spot. Underdog companies are often run by some of the hardest-working people because they're still hungry; their drive is unparalleled because they haven't yet made it to the top. I wouldn't say Alikay has yet made it to the top either, however, we've had significant enough success and growth to earn a spot as one of the leading natural hair and beauty brands on the market. Still, I fight to maintain the same fire with which we started. Don't let your hustle spirit die and don't take your eye off the smaller brands. They just might eat the food right off of your plate.

DON'T STALK YOUR COMPETITION

Market research is a part of business; you have to do it. It's important to study the habits and strategies of your competition so you can see what works and doesn't work. My team sits down for competitor analysis usually every quarter just to see what's happening in the industry: who is on top right now?

What brands are most talked about on the blogs? When people talk about their favorite hair brands, who is being mentioned? Are we on that list? If not, what are we missing or doing wrong?

It's important, however, not to become so obsessed that you are checking these brands' pages every single day. My competitor analysis is very strategic. We don't look at what our competition is doing on an everyday basis because that's how you run the risk of copying what someone else is doing. There are several ways to copy someone else's work or ideas, the most infamous being plagiarism. Plagiarism is when someone blatantly and intentionally copies the work of another person, brand, or business and tries to pass it off as original work. This is — without exception — a major no. Not only is it unethical, but plagiarism can also land you in legal hot water if you are found to have copied a trademarked name, slogan, or entity.

Then, there are two other types of copying that many people may not even be aware of. The chameleon effect, for example, is a social psychology term referring to imitation stemming from casual, frequent observation. More specifically in the world of marketing, we are constantly exposed to so many ads, emails, and social media pages that different brands begin to adopt each other's marketing styles. From diction to aesthetics, marketing campaigns and strategies begin to look strikingly similar within an industry simply because everyone is adapting, like a chameleon, to the larger, industry-wide marketing climate. The assumption is, *if it ain't broke, don't fix it*, and brands are all adopting the same rules and regulations in an effort to get in the game. Alternatively, there is cryptomnesia -- the concept that you can incorrectly remember an idea or thought as original, when in fact, it came from an outside source. Your brain essentially creates false memories, leading you to believe you conceived an idea you actually picked up somewhere else. Cryptomnesia is tricky because it leads to unintentional plagiarism — if you release a campaign that's the same as another brand's, no one is going to care whether you *thought* it was your idea. Plagiarism is plagiarism regardless of intent, which cannot be proven.

Cryptomnesia, the chameleon effect, and plagiarism all present similar problems. The main issue is unoriginality, which leads to boring, monotonous, and uncreative content. In other words, no one stands out when everyone is blending in, and the strategies you adopt — even subconsciously —may not necessarily be the best fit or approach for your specific company and your specific consumer base. Even if you do have integrity, your team – the people who create your ads and run your marketing – might subliminally integrate ideas that they've seen elsewhere. While there may be no malintent, it's still something you want to look out for! Don't over-consume your competitors' content, or else your pages will seem unoriginal and uncreative before you know it because you'll be doing the same thing as everyone else — and customers will notice!

Case in point, I recently had a very uncomfortable experience where I had to confront the owner of a competing brand. I was receiving tons of direct messages from Alikay Nation, my Alikay Naturals community, informing me that this brand seemed to be recreating my ads and images almost word for word. My supporters were sending me screenshots and everything. Noticing a clear similarity, my team and I decided to release a decoy ad. Surely enough, the brand replicated our experiment image just two days later, confirming our worst suspicions: they were copying us! When I confronted the brand's owner, she was very defensive. Even worse, she told me that it didn't really matter who did something first because there was – in her words – enough money and food for all of us to win. Even if that's true, copying your competition is never a good move. I made sure to address it directly and shut that behavior down because as the C.E.O of my company, it is my job to protect my business. This behavior of copying only demonstrates a sad lack of creativity, integrity, and ultimately, a lack of sustainability for your business.

It's possible that the intent wasn't malicious. Maybe her team was simply over-watching our pages. They might have actually thought the ideas were their own by the time they pitched them to her. I understand that inspiration can turn to imitation all too easily. That's why I make it a hard rule not to stalk the competition and keep my eyes focused on my own paper. The Alikay Naturals goal is to be an industry leader, not a copy-and-paste follower.

DON'T LIVE OUTSIDE YOUR MEANS

Comparison is the thief of joy, and it can be the thief in your pockets, too. As the owner of a bootstrapped business, I've had to learn that I simply cannot afford to live and operate the same way as other entrepreneurs. Companies that receive outside investments – be they from banks, venture capitalists, or angel investors – can be a bit flashier. They can afford the fancy company vehicles, huge, luxurious events, and extensive influencer campaigns. The owners of these brands can even pocket some of their earnings for spending cash. For years, Demond and I could not, and even once it became a possibility, we strategically made the decision not to.

Almost every dollar that Alikay Naturals makes goes back into the company. It's set aside either for purchasing ingredients, manufacturing products, marketing, or making payroll for our employees. Can we afford a higher quality of life than before? Of course, but we make sure to remember that Alikay is always our bottom line. I refuse to go broke trying to keep up with the Joneses because I know that if we mismanage our funds, no one is coming with their checkbook to bail us out. This means that when we upgrade, we do so modestly and gradually, and it has to have a greater purpose that makes sense for our family. It's a marathon not a sprint; we are always thinking of the long term effects of our current decisions. For example, we're currently in the process of building our dream home after ten years of work. Could we have bought a home earlier? Sure, but we made the choice to live below our means so that we can ball out in the future. Now, with two kids, we feel it's time to level up and so that's what we're doing.

Sometimes, I worry that I'm a bit *too* good at living modestly. Every month I put aside some fun money, which is just money in my personal finances I can spend on myself. No matter how much fun money I save up, though, I always seem to have trouble actually spending it. For years I wanted a Chanel bag. I'm not obsessed with labels, but it was the one thing I wanted to treat myself to because it represented luxury and class. Last year for my thirty-second birthday, I finally got my fun money to where I could buy this bag without blinking. I went to the store with my mom, tried it on, fell even deeper in love, but still, I just couldn't allow myself to buy it. I left the store empty-handed.

Eventually, after many pep talks from my mom and myself, I finally bought myself the bag for Christmas. It is now eleven months later and the bag is still sitting untouched in the box it came in. I never opened it, and truly, it's a little ridiculous. The moral of this story is this: don't live outside your means trying to flex like your competition, but do allow yourself to live a little! You've earned it, you deserve it. With that being said, I'm giving myself eight weeks to force myself to open the package and rock my Chanel purse proudly because I earned it! This is something I know a lot of entrepreneurs struggle with once reaching success, especially those of us who have built ourselves up from having nothing to having more than we ever dreamed of.

WITH YOUR FINANCES...

DON'T UNDERESTIMATE YOUR COSTS

I cannot stress this enough: as a business owner, you have to become very comfortable with understanding, discussing, and handling your money. So many people come from a scarcity mindset where money is something to be feared. That fear will only inhibit your growth. If you own a business, you must prioritize financial literacy so that you can not only profit, but scale your business as you continue to expand.

Rule number one: always have an emergency fund. Unexpected costs are a normal facet of entrepreneurship. There will be registration and licensing fees, overdue invoices, and potential legal fees. I know firsthand how impossible it can feel to accrue a decent amount of savings as a new business owner, especially if you're self-funded. However, every little thing counts. Even if it's only 5%, take a percentage of each and every payment you receive and put it into a rainy-day fund. Your company should *always* have extra spending money, even if you don't. Three to six months of business operational costs in savings is the goal.

Rule number two: keep track of where all of your money goes. At this point in my career, I am blessed to have an excellent money team. Between my husband, my CPA, and my CFO, my entire life is budgeted, and my bookkeeping is impeccable. Before we had the means to hire an accountant or a bookkeeper, Demond was the one-man-machine behind our finances.

While he was and is excellent with the books, we knew we needed to upgrade our tracking. "Mo' money, mo' problems," as the saying goes. You don't want to run into any problems with the government — once you're on the IRS list, you're on it forever. Outsourcing our bookkeeping to trusted professionals has increased our stability and comfort tenfold.

Before you freak out about the expense, you don't have to keep a bookkeeper or accountant on a monthly retainer. When Demond and I hired our first accountant we only paid her four times a year to file our quarterly taxes. Then, we paid her to file our annual business and personal taxes as well. You don't have to break the bank. If you still feel that you'd rather do your own bookkeeping, just make sure your financial literacy is up to par. Take a class and do some research; really learn the ins and outs. Something that helped Demond and I was keeping multiple bank accounts. To this day we have a merchant account which holds all of our total incoming revenue, no matter the source. Then, we have an operating account where all of our money goes out for shipping, packaging costs, etc. Next, we have our savings or rainy-day account, and then an account for tax savings where we transfer money on a weekly basis to prepare for the following year's taxes. Finally, we have a payroll account completely separate from everything else. It might seem excessive but trust me. Separate bank accounts help immensely with being able to see where all of your money is coming and going. Also, having your own understanding will prevent you from being robbed or taken advantage of by any outside hires.

Rule number three: shop around. It may take you two or three tries to find the right team for you, and that's okay. Don't be alarmed or embarrassed. The first accountant Demond and I hired got us on the right track, but they weren't really the right fit. We hired them because they were cheap, and cheap doesn't often buy you the best. They didn't spend the time to find all the areas where we could be saving money. As a result, we moved on to a larger CPA firm, thinking that they would have a higher attention to detail and yield us better results. As it turned out, we ended up being overlooked and lost in the shuffle because the firm prioritized their bigger clients over small businesses. Years later and we've finally found the right team to meet all of our needs. It's all about trial and error.

Rule number four: take a financial literacy class. The *you* you are today is responsible for the financial future of your older self. If you don't learn to save, invest, and spend your money with wisdom and discernment, you'll find yourself out of luck in your old age. If you don't set up a retirement fund — guess what? — you won't have one. When you really start making money, make sure that you take your financial education and money management skills into your own hands. This is not a suggestion, this is a *must*. Either enroll in a finance course or find yourself a reputable financial advisor to sit down and explain your personal finances (in addition to your business).

Allow me to share a little gem from one of my favorite books, *Profit First* by Mike Michalowicz:

"Here's the deal. There is only one way to fix your financials: by facing your financials. You can't ignore them. You can't let someone else take care of them. You need to take charge of your numbers."

- Mike Michalowicz, Profit First: A Simple System to Transform Your Business from a Cash-Eating Monster to a Money-Making Machine

DON'T FORGET TO READ THE FINE PRINT

When signing contracts, the fine print will make or break you every time. I've seen excellent entrepreneurs come close to losing everything simply because they didn't fully understand the terms of their agreements. Sometimes, when you're offered a deal you might be so excited by the dollar amount that you overlook the details. That's a huge mistake. If you don't have the patience or understanding to pour over a contract with a fine-tooth comb, find someone who will. For me, it's Demond. My husband absolutely loves reading the fine print. When it comes to contracts, he is detail-oriented in a way that I am just not. He can read a contract and tell me exactly what we're signing up for, exactly what makes sense and what doesn't. Then, I step in and take over the negotiations role. If you don't like something, negotiate. Speak up and ask for better terms.

If anything at all doesn't sit well with you, *do not sign*. You'll often find yourself in situations where you'll be pressured to make a decision. Take your time anyway. Before I even had a board of directors, I would conclude retailer meetings by saying, "Thank you for your time. I need to go over everything in detail with my board. We'll get back to you once we've had time to review." Not only does it reassert your authority as an active participant in the deal, but it gives you time to figure out what the heck your contract actually says. If you need to, hire an attorney – again, you don't have to keep one on retainer. You can pay an attorney to review contracts with you as needed and explain in layman's terms all of the legal jargon. Pro tip: never accept an attorney referral from the people with whom you're making a deal. You never want to run the risk of being cheated out of ownership in your own company. Trust me, I've seen it happen. Go the extra mile, get the extra help.

I vividly remember a conversation I had with my mother years ago. We were standing in her kitchen, and I was reviewing one of my very first multi-million dollar retail contracts. I was nervous and wasn't sure how to negotiate for myself without running the risk of blowing the whole deal. My mother stopped me and gave me a piece of advice I will never forget: your business is your baby. Protect it like you would protect your child. She told me to imagine that Alikay was my son, Landon. I would go to war before signing anything that would harm him or work against his best interests. Following my mom's advice, I marked up that contract with all my alterations. To this day I always tell others, protect your business like you would protect your child. Fiercely!

WITH YOUR CUSTOMERS…

DON'T NEGLECT YOUR EXISTING TRIBE

A huge mistake many entrepreneurs make is throwing all their attention, efforts, and money into bringing in new customers. We think that the more followers or customers we have, the more money we make. Not necessarily. There are actually three ways that a business makes money. Firstly, yes, acquiring new customers. Secondly, getting your current customers to buy more frequently. Thirdly, getting your current customers to buy at a higher volume. What many people fail to realize is that the cost of acquiring a new customer is actually far greater than the cost of getting a previous customer to repurchase. Why? Well, your previous customer is already aware of your product or service and they already have a user experience. The cost of reaching them is lower because you already have access to them via your ecommerce platform, social media, and email listserve, as well as through their direct mail address and/or phone number. You already understand who that customer is and what their needs and pain points are. With a new customer, you're starting from scratch. You have to get onto their radar, find what they like, market to them, and convert them. Familiarize yourself with something called the Pareto Principle, or the 80/20 rule. In the world of entrepreneurship and marketing, the rule is that 80% of your sales come from 20% of your customers. That 20% is the loyal customer base that you should always be catering to. While you should never stop seeking new business, don't neglect the business you already have from your 20%.

I would say about 70% of Alikay Naturals' marketing activities are focused on how we can appeal to customers we already have. This is because I know the power of word of mouth, especially within the beauty industry. I don't take my tribe's purchasing power for granted because I know that they don't *have* to repurchase. People have choices; it's my job to figure out how to make Alikay that choice. Maybe it's by sending a thank you note, maybe it's by checking in with them or sending them a special customized message from the C.E.O on their birthday. Whatever you choose, make sure that you are consistently investing and engaging in your community.

DON'T BE AFRAID TO BE A CREEP

Okay, hear me out. The same way you conduct competitor analysis, you should be analyzing your customer – and don't be afraid to go deep! Figure out where your customers or potential customers hang out and go there so you can study them. Don't be weird! One day I actually sat in the corner at a retail store for almost three hours with my phone and just watched the way people operate. I don't care how big I get – I will still go to the store and hang out in the middle of the aisle. I'll act like I'm buying band-aids or something – it doesn't matter. I'm really there studying my audience, especially the multicultural consumers. Did they stop and pick up a hair product? What did they say to each other? What product did they grab first? Was it mine or was it a competitor's? I analyze my products on the shelf just like a traditional merchandiser would. What's my brand presence? Do we stand out? How does my packaging look? Are there any improvements we can make? Is there a problem with products in stock that I can bring to the attention of my retailer partners? This is the ground floor of market research. Get out there, get your hands dirty, and just learn as much valuable information as you can.

Figure out what events happen in your industry, go to consumer shows, trade shows. You have to meet people and ask questions. I always suggest signing up for all the industry publications that you can, both online and at least some in print. I study the beauty industry from both a multicultural and non-multicultural lens. If there's something I need from my community, I open my mouth and ask for it. Need a review? Ask for it. Need referrals? Ask for them. Always be sure to engage with your consumer without harassing them. How else will you get to know their needs?

WITH YOURSELF…

DON'T WASTE TIME ON LOW-LEVEL ACTIVITIES

Do yourself a favor and fire yourself from every job other than the C.E.O. Become a delegating machine and hand off any responsibilities that aren't absolutely necessary for you to do yourself. This will free up your time to focus on those unique and high-level tasks that only you can accomplish. If someone on your team can do a job 70% as well as you would, let them do it. Remember, you are the captain, not the crew.

DON'T RELY ON PEN AND PAPER

Oftentimes we'll be struck with an epiphany or a moment of genius, and we'll break out a notebook or journal to write down the idea. Fast-forward a ridiculous amount of time, and the idea is still sitting on that page, collecting cobwebs. Take your brilliance from simple ideas and convert it into a plan with concrete goals. Don't allow your ideas to become stagnant. Put action behind them by focusing on creating automated processing and systems of operation within your company. For example, it took me some time to realize that I needed to create physical employee manuals for every role in my business. For too long, the job requirements only existed in my own brain, and so whenever there was employee turnover, I ended up being the one to have to train the new hires. A waste of time. Now, because I've created and distributed operations manuals, the onboarding process can happen with little direct oversight from me. Systems like this will make your life so much easier.

In addition to systems of automation, make use of technology. I don't know what I would do without Asana – like, literally. Asana is an online project management tool that allows me to assign responsibilities and tasks to different employees – and myself – without an email thread full of a million unnecessary exchanges. I simply assign a task and a due date, and the designated employee and I receive an alert when it is completed or when my input is needed. Then, he or she can simply check off a task when completed, and I'll be alerted that it's done. Boom. I also rely a lot on voice notes for quick and easy communication. If I think of something on the fly or don't want to spend the night typing away in an email, I'll simply send my managers a voice note. I find that audio also eliminates many miscommunications due to misinterpretations of tone in written text.

DON'T BE A FAKE C.E.O

Growing up, so many of us had the same idea of what an entrepreneur looked like: typically white, male, and middle-aged or older. Now, entrepreneurs wear t-shirts and blue jeans. Think of Mark Zuckerberg or Steve Jobs. They didn't try to be anyone other than themselves, and neither should you. Don't feel like you have to look or dress a certain way to be in business. Yes, you should always look professional and well put-together, but that doesn't have to mean pant suits and blazers – though I love a good blazer, myself! We're living in an age that is increasingly accepting of different personal styles and aesthetics. Find a way to let yours shine through. I had a friend who would consistently wear these horrible oversized suit jackets. He was trying to look the part and shoving himself into an outdated mold of what he thought a businessman looked like. You don't have to look like anyone other than you.

Something I like to do is create a quick and easy professional uniform. A professional uniform is a simple outfit variation you can go to on the days where you don't want to have to think about what to wear. My go-to is a company logo shirt, or an all-black outfit. This way, I can hop out of bed and dive right into my C.E.O tasks while still properly and professionally representing my brand in appropriate workplace attire.

Don't be a fake C.E.O also applies to behavior. Never adopt behaviors or management styles just because you *think* that's how a boss is supposed to act. Case in point, one day I was talking to my son Landon about what mommy does for work. He asked, "Mommy, why do you have to go to work and why do you need to work so hard?" I explained to him that I have to work hard to set an example for my staff and show them that it's important to do a great job. He replied, "But bosses don't work! Bosses sit at their desks, put their feet up, and boss people around while drinking smoothies all day!" Stunned and amused, I asked who on earth had told him that to which he replied, "Nobody! That's just what bosses do on TV."

My son had seen a certain portrayal of bosses on television shows and cartoons and assumed that was how mommy should behave — in my experience, many new C.E.Os are no different! Whether it's being the cool, fun boss that makes friends with everyone, or the evil, hard-ass a la *The Devil Wears Prada*, new business owners often fall into the trap of imitating an idea of a boss instead of actually becoming a leader. If you want to be a real C.E.O, focus less on playing a part or controlling other people's perceptions, and more on sharpening your people skills, honing your leadership style, and setting a clear direction for your company.

DON'T TAKE REJECTION PERSONALLY

Do you know how I first learned to deal with rejection? My father. He rejected me and to this day we still don't have a real relationship. As sad as it sounds, once a parent rejects you, you kind of learn quickly how to brush things off. If anything, I'd say it made me resilient. I now understand that other people saying no doesn't necessarily have anything to do with me. I don't take rejection personally because I understand that business is business. A no is not the end of the discussion. When I first started Alikay, I would go around to all the local beauty supply stores carrying my humble little bottles and ask them to sell my products in their stores. I worked on my pitch, I had my presentation folder, my price lists, my samples, everything. How many times do you think I was told no? More than I can count. I eventually got a yes, but it took countless rejections to get there. Somehow, I was never deterred. I remember one store owner would even hide in the back of her shop when she spotted me coming. I was that relentless.

When you get a no, always ask for the why. Never take rejection at face value; you should always get something from it. Why did they say no? What can you do differently? What would make them say yes? Get your feelings hurt and then get on with it.

DON'T BURY YOUR FAILURES

For that one business that someone was able to grow into a six-figure or million-dollar company, there are usually a handful of failures behind it – it's just that no one talks about them.

I think that's a huge missed opportunity for us all. I myself had quite a few failures. My first company was D and R Customer Solutions. While in college, Demond and I had the bright idea to do customer service for other companies from home, but we were not able to scale or keep up with the demands. We soon called it quits.

My next failure was my handcrafted jewelry business, Nyamani Chic. This one stung a bit more because it was my first official, real high dollar-generating business. I made multiple six figures from that company, but ultimately decided to close down when Alikay started to see major growth. I saw that Alikay was something I could scale, whereas my jewelry was not. I definitely tried, though! I went as far as to hire other local artists and jewelry makers to come in and learn how to make my earrings. They would bring me the earrings and then I would inspect and fill the orders myself. I soon realized, however, that the quality was too inconsistent, and I no longer had the time to sit and make everything on my own. Thus, another company bit the dust.

Not one to give up, my next business failure was my salon. I owned an establishment called Be Fabulous Salon for three years. Oh, how I loved my salon. It was amazing with girly, glammy chandeliers, mimosas for clients, Alikay Naturals products on the shelves – all the works. I wanted to create a space where people could not only purchase my hair products, but they could come in and have qualified stylists use Alikay products to style their natural hair. We were financially successful, but I did not have a strong enough management team in place to run the business and keep the vision going. I realized that I didn't have the bandwidth with time to be at my salon daily to monitor and ensure things were being run up to my high standards of excellence. I also came to the realization that I preferred product-based businesses over service-based. With product-based, I could create amazing quality products and I knew that, no matter what retail shelves they were on around the world, every person that purchased would receive that same amazing quality. With a service-based business like my salon, I couldn't control that level of quality because I had to depend on other people to carry that out in my absence. Lastly, we could not fulfill the needs of the customers we had coming in. We were consistently booked out months in advance and people could not get appointments in a timely manner. While I had four full-time stylists, I had a hard time finding two more for my last two stations that matched my expertise expectations. I couldn't focus on Alikay, my manufacturing facility, *and* the salon all at once, so I made the executive decision to close up shop.

Many times, business owners try to bury their failures in the sand and forget about them. Others try to spin them: *it wasn't a failure. It just wasn't the right time or circumstances.* Not me. I own my stuff. Those businesses were failures because they *failed* to last, they *failed* to scale. Even if they could have panned out, I decided to quit on them. That was my decision and I stand by it because it was the right choice for my business and my future. I didn't care who judged me or who whispered and snickered behind my back because I had failed. I took each failure as a lesson to help me better myself as a C.E.O. It's time to take the stigma out of these words. When done strategically, failing and quitting can be some of the wisest things an entrepreneur can do! I am not defined by those failures, but they sure as hell taught me what not to do and what I didn't want with Alikay. I'm a better businesswoman for having gone through those experiences. If your hang-ups about past failures are weighing you down, shake it off! Focus your energy on your next million-dollar idea.

DON'T MAKE DECISIONS ON YOUR WORST DAYS

There will be many days when you're tired, stressed out, out of answers, or downright pissed off. Don't make decisions on those days. Bumps in the road are nothing to be alarmed by, but if you're consistently hitting a wall on the same problem, you need to sit down and evaluate: Should I rest, pivot, or quit?

Maybe you're just stressed, and you need to take a break and come back to the problem with fresh eyes. Or maybe you need sleep because your mind and body are exhausted. If that's the case take a break! Get some rest. If that doesn't help, perhaps the situation in question simply isn't working and you need to adjust. Maybe you're targeting the wrong audience or investing in the wrong type of advertisements. How can you pivot to turn things around? Lastly, if all else fails, maybe you simply need to quit like I did. There's no shame in figuring out something isn't right for you. You are the C.E.O of your life.

Whatever you choose, make your decision from a place of calmness. Never make rash decisions in the middle of a hectic work day or after a bad call or meeting. Always be measured, reasonable, and logical. If you need to, use someone you trust as a sounding board before making a final move.

DON'T WAIT TO SMELL THE ROSES

Finally, don't put off your happiness until you've attained a certain level of success. I can tell you right now, you will never – never – be successful enough. It's in your DNA as an entrepreneur. You will always want more. If you never let yourself enjoy what you have where you are right now, you'll never feel the sense of fulfillment you seek. Take that vacation, buy that car (if it's within your means to purchase). Live your life! You are already living a bigger life than many around you will ever fathom. You're being brave, taking risks, and your efforts are paying off. Relish in that a little and clap for yourself!

Bootstrapping

Building a company from the ground up with nothing but personal savings and the cash coming in from sale.
Source: www.investopedia.com

Partnership

An association of two or more people as partners.
Source: Oxford Dictionary

Revenue Model

A revenue model is a framework for generating revenues. It identifies which revenue source to pursue, what value to offer, how to price the value, and who pays for the value. It is a key component of a company's business model.
Source: Wikipedia

Outsourcing

Obtain (goods or a service) from an outside or foreign supplier, especially in place of an internal source.
Source: Oxford Dictionary

Liability

A thing for which someone is responsible, especially a debt or financial obligation.
Source: Oxford Dictionary

End User

The person who actually uses a particular product.
Source: Oxford Dictionary

Asset

A useful or valuable thing, person, or quality.
Source: Oxford Dictionary

PART III.

PASSION TO PURPOSE

"If you can't figure out your purpose, figure out your passion. For your passion will lead you right into your purpose."
- Bishop T.D. Jakes

W hat will be the stamp you leave on this world? How will you make a difference as a C.E.O? How will you impact the lives of your customers? Your staff? Your family? Yourself? Harness the power of your passions to create not only profit, but immeasurable purpose and peace in your life.

CHAPTER 7

OWN YOUR THRONE

While entrepreneurship is extremely challenging, it also comes with an extraordinary bonus: you're in charge! From company vision to marketing and promotions, from brand identity to scheduling and establishing workplace culture, it's all up to you. Like Mufasa said to Simba, "Everything the light touches is our kingdom." Your business is your domain. Sure, running a company comes with a ton of responsibility, but it also grants you the freedom to explore, lead, and create as you see fit. It's your kingdom – act like it!

You would be surprised to see how many entrepreneurs take off because of their big ideas, only to shrink themselves as they see more and more success. Oftentimes, we think we are prepared to be the orchestrator of our lives, but when finally put in a position to do so, we feel unqualified, unprepared, and unsure – we dream big and then make ourselves small. This phenomenon is called imposter syndrome.

SHAKING IMPOSTER SYNDROME

Basically, imposter syndrome is when you convince yourself that you are undeserving of the successes and opportunities that come your way. Those that suffer typically attribute their wins to luck, chance, or some mysterious oversight. By the same token, they typically amplify any losses or rejections as confirmation of their self-perceived inadequacy – *See? I knew it was too good to be true!* No matter how confident we think we are, imposter syndrome can get the best of all of us, especially during times of great growth or change.

For me, the self-doubt began to set in once I started to grow my company and hire people who were smarter than me. As a rule, I believe it's vital to work with people who know more than I do. After all, if you're the smartest person in the room, you're in the wrong room. I've made it a point to hire professionals with more experience than me, whether that be on the educational front, training, or on-the-job experience. The upside? I have a stellar team of top-notch talent that challenges and pushes me to my greatest potential. The downside? All that excellence played tricks on my confidence. I began to wonder how I could possibly lead a team of people with more years in the game than I had.

Imposter syndrome also popped up as I began walking into bigger rooms and meeting high-level executives outside of my own company. As Alikay took off and started getting attention from retailers, I would have lots of pitches and deal meetings with the top players in the industry. To further my nerves, these meetings were often with boardrooms full of people who looked nothing like me. Contrary to what many may think, the heavy hitters of the beauty industry are often men – rich white men – and here I was, a young black woman, walking in to sell them on a brand for a niche demographic to which they didn't belong or relate. Those meetings were intimidating, to say the least, and the perfect fuel for imposter syndrome to thrive.

So, how did I shake it? I had to remember who I was! I had to remind myself that Alikay was *my* kingdom. When it comes to leading a team, remember that no matter how much knowledge or experience is on the table, no one knows your brand better than you. No one is as invested as you and no one sees the vision as clearly as you do. Starting a company is like being a first-time parent. You'll get tons of advice from experienced parents who have seen and done it all, but at the end of the day, no one is more suited to raise your child than you. Your company is *your* baby. Be confident that if you created it, you are more than capable of leading it.

As for boardroom blues, convince yourself that if you were invited to the room, you deserve to be there – you just need to act like it and carry yourself accordingly. Don't let a lack of confidence make you cower or miss out on opportunities that you've earned. I think the reason so many new entrepreneurs struggle to accept their wins is because they never stop to appreciate just how far they've already come. We convince ourselves that we're not experienced enough, not ready enough, not deserving enough for the big leagues. We want to shine, but in the future, not right now – now is too scary. Even when we're receiving praise and monetary gains, it doesn't fully set in because we haven't truly given ourselves credit for all the things we've accomplished. This makes all the accolades and huge deals feel premature or misplaced.

They're not. Trust that all of your wins are right on time. Abiding by thoughts and emotions that keep you playing small is nothing more than self-sabotage. It's okay to be surprised by a big win but take it in stride. Step up to the plate and own your throne.

CLAIMING YOUR SPACE

Easier said than done, right? I know. Owning your rightful place as top dog of your business can be hard, especially if it feels contrary to your DNA. I know that many business owners struggle with confidence and leadership for a variety of reasons. Maybe they didn't grow up with examples of strong leaders to model themselves after. Perhaps they live with anxiety, or maybe they're extremely introverted and have a hard time commanding attention. If entrepreneurship is your dream, however, you've got to set systems in place to help yourself power through and claim your space.

THE POWER OF INTROVERTS

So many introverts count themselves out before they even step into the ring. They think *I'm not strong enough to be a leader. I'm too quiet to be a boss.* Think again. You don't have to be loud or bossy to be a leader. As a matter of fact, sometimes those qualities are a recipe for disaster. Just because someone has a huge personality doesn't mean he or she is a good leader, especially if that personality leaves no room for the wants and needs of the team as a whole. I see plenty of entrepreneurs all the time who are loud and proud, strong and wrong, and it's reflected in their workplace culture. If you identify as an introvert or an ambivert like me, be the best leader you can be by being *yourself*.

Introverts are often keen observers. They have amazing people-watching skills and are usually very smart and perceptive. This is something I admire about my husband, Demond. A lot of people think that he's shy or mean because he is quiet, but that couldn't be farther from the truth. He actually has a very big personality; he just chooses to be quiet and observe. He has a way of reading people's personalities and intentions, not by listening to their words, but more so by watching their actions. These are crucial qualities for a successful C.E.O because they help you navigate the multiple personalities of your staff. Being quiet teaches you how and when to listen and helps you learn how to cater to different team members effectively. Instead of trying to be some caricatured version of what you think a boss should be, try playing up your own strengths. It'll get you farther every time.

LEAP OUT OF YOUR COMFORT ZONE

While playing to your strengths is important, it's no excuse to remain stagnant. You must still be constantly challenging yourself to try new things. You don't have to be someone else, but you do have to evolve. For a successful business owner, evolution means stepping – no, leaping – out of your comfort zone. My leap came after the birth of my second child.

Prior to having my children, I had no problem being the face of my brand. My photo was on every product, label, and webpage, and doing those photoshoots was actually one of my favorite parts of the job. After giving birth to my son Landon, however, I was extremely uncomfortable. I had gained a significant amount of weight and it started to mess with my head. I have loved myself and looked chic and stylish at every size, however, forever thinking about the business first, I began to feel as though maybe I no longer had the right look to represent my own brand. For the first time, I casted an influencer as the model and face of a huge campaign launch. We even flew out to meet her in another country for the photoshoot; it was basically my dream shoot and I gave it away to someone else. The shoot itself worked out fine, but as you'll find in business, there was no extended loyalty there. After the terms of the agreement were up, I realized that the deal wasn't worth the investment we had made. I had to remember that I was the heart and soul of my company, and no one else would care or authentically connect with my audience the way I would. I knew I had to get over myself and put myself back out in front.

Oprah was actually a huge inspiration and example to me at that time. I remember thinking to myself, this is a woman who lives her life under a microscope. We've seen her lose weight and gain weight countless times. We've seen the media scrutinize and praise her, all depending on her looks, but you know what? Her face has remained plastered in the center of every O Magazine for as long as I can remember. She doesn't push herself to the back or run to the shadows. Why? – because it's *her* magazine. It's *her* brand and *her* empire. There's no other celebrity or model she could hire to do it justice. Taking a cue out of Oprah's book, I leapt out of my comfort zone. Two months after I gave birth to my daughter Serenity, I had another face of the brand photoshoot – only this time, I was the model. I claimed my space and it felt damn good.

The most **alluring** thing a woman can have is **confidence.**

– BEYONCÉ

ROLE MODELS

This brings me to my next point: the importance of having role models. So much of entrepreneurship is winging it out there on your own. It's important to have people you can look to for inspiration to know that your dreams are possible. Even if they work in a completely different industry, you can always mine the stories of others for gems to apply to your own journey. As a female entrepreneur, it has been crucial for me to have fellow female business owners to learn from and look up to.

OPRAH WINFREY

Like almost everyone under the sun, Oprah has been one of my biggest inspirations. Not only because of what she has taught me about owning my brand in every phase of life, but also because of her ability to adapt and transform. From news anchor to talk show host, to media executive, television producer and actress, Oprah has reinvented herself more times than anyone can count. Furthermore, she's maintained a standard of excellence in every title she holds. Because of her example, I know that I can do so much more than make hair products. I've already expanded to skin and baby care products and launched other companies and projects which I hope to grow to the heights of Alikay Naturals and beyond. Oprah is also a wonderful example of what it looks like to align the success of your career with intentional and ongoing spiritual exploration.

AYESHA CURRY

Despite the hate she receives in the media, Ayesha Curry is another woman whose journey I personally admire. She is a perfect example of building your own empire and maintaining independence within your relationship. Even though she's married to Stephen Curry, a millionaire NBA player, she has still maintained her own interests and built them into thriving business endeavors of her own. Since marrying Curry and putting her acting aspirations on hold, the now mother of three has launched her own cooking show on the Food Network, penned a cookbook, and created her own home and kitchen collection. I think Ayesha Curry is a lesson to all female entrepreneurs on maintaining your own sense of self and building a name separate from that of your partner.

SARA BLAKELY

Sara Blakely took a hosiery idea and approximately zero business experience and turned it into the billion-dollar business we know as Spanx. I am blown away by just how quickly her company grew, and the fact that she is still the sole owner all these years later. At just forty-one-years-old, she became the youngest self-made female billionaire, a far cry from the college student who failed the LSAT and wound up working at Disney World. Blakely's humble beginnings remind me of where I started at Olive Garden, and her amazing success shows me where I'm headed.

Other femme fatale founders I love include Jessica Alba (Honest Company), Jamie Kern Lima (IT Cosmetics), Maureen Kelly (Tarte Cosmetics), and of course, Beyoncé Giselle Knowles-Carter, who pretty much owns the world at this point.

Take a moment to consider who inspires you. What can you learn specifically from each of their journeys about how to own your throne?

CREATE YOUR ALTER EGO

Even with all the role models and inspiration in the world, your success still boils down to *you*. You have to grow into a version of yourself that is equipped for all aspects of entrepreneurship. Something that has been a game-changing factor in my own growth as a businesswoman is developing a strong alter ego. My alter ego is basically just the business side of my personality – the default mode I activate when everyday Rochelle just won't do.

When I first started my business, I was extremely nice – too nice. The problem was that I was operating my company the same way that I maneuvered through life as a human being. It got to the point where I would onboard new employees and they would expect me to be soft and sweet like the person they had seen making videos on YouTube. It took me some time to realize that I needed a clear distinction between YouTube Rochelle, or BlackOnyx77, and C.E.O Rochelle. To start, I realized that niceness has little place in business. You can be courteous and respectful, even compassionate, but you have to leave the fluff for your personal life.

Rochelle the human is very bubbly, very silly, and giggly. I'm loud and sweet and I speak in a squeaky voice that may be annoying to some. That's just who I am. Rochelle the businesswoman, on the other hand, she's an entirely different story. My professional voice drops down several octaves and carries a certain authority that commands attention. I also speak much slower and enunciate much stronger in professional environments, whereas human Rochelle talks a million miles a minute. Human Rochelle worries about being too mean or rubbing her employees the wrong way; C.E.O Rochelle tells it like it is with no apologies. Again, it's not about pretending or being someone else – it's about cultivating a different side of your personality. I've learned that having an alter ego with her own voice and mannerisms has made people take me more seriously. Furthermore, it's given me more confidence in myself as a leader.

Whenever you come across responsibilities or parts of the job that make you uncomfortable, default them to your alter ego. Whether it be firing someone or reprimanding an employee, turning down a deal or negotiating for more money, access your bolder side to get the job done. By thinking of this other side as its own persona, you get to run your show without losing yourself or compromising your human side in the process.

BE YOUR OWN CHEERLEADER

Creating your business persona will take some time. Don't worry if it doesn't feel natural at first. If ever you feel like a fraud or you sense that imposter syndrome swooping in to steal your shine, shut it down. You literally have to be your own cheerleader, your own hypeman or hypewoman! It is especially important to hype yourself up around big meetings or potential deals. I have a very specific method of preparation for these moments, and it's all about blocking out the negativity and getting in tune with myself.

First, protect your energy at all costs. When I have a big meeting or call coming up, I put myself into a positivity bubble. In the week or so leading up to a big day, my family and team know to keep all bad news away from me. Unless the world is ending, I don't want to hear about it. This goes double for friends who need to vent. I'm sorry, but when I'm working on something huge, I can't be a shoulder to cry on. That week is my cherished time of solitude and selfishness to get my head in the game for my company.

Of course, I also use that time to consider WCGW – or what could go wrong. I don't dwell on the negative or project bad energy, but I do come up with contingency plans just in case an unexpected question is asked, or the meeting doesn't go as planned. After that, it's back to positivity. I visualize myself as the rockstar of the meeting. For those ten or fifteen minutes of my presentation, all eyes are on me. Only I have the power to answer any questions or ease any doubts that arise. I give myself permission to shine because that gives Alikay permission to shine. Rock on, Rochelle!

It may sound silly, but you literally have to be your own number one fan! Especially if you are someone who deals with stage fright or anxiety with public-speaking, find a way to cheer yourself on. For some, that might mean power-posing in the bathroom before the meeting. My mother taught me a trick of picturing everyone in the audience in their underwear. For a long time, it helped to diffuse the tension and ease my nerves. As I've gotten older, the tip that has worked best for me is simply to talk to people as if you've known them forever. Before I enter the room, I inhale confidence and exhale all fear and anxiety. When I walk in, I imagine that everyone in the boardroom or on a stage is an old friend, and it really helps to kill any lingering nerves.

A WOMAN IN A MAN'S WORLD

Like I mentioned before, the beauty industry is surprisingly dominated by men. While women may design and create the products, it's the men who are often the decision makers and gatekeepers. It's hard enough being an entrepreneur, but when coupled with the weight of being a woman it can be downright paralyzing. It's important to me to speak directly to my fellow female business owners, because I've experienced firsthand some of the hurdles that you are bound to run into. To this day, I still have to deal with phone calls where I'm asked, "Hello, ma'am. May I speak to the person in charge?" I have people come into my company headquarters only to assume that I am the receptionist or secretary. Not to mention that what earns a man the title of boss or leader often gets a woman called a – well, you know the word – simply because she is confident, commands power and respect, and makes her expectations and boundaries known. My years in the industry have taught me that while sexism is sadly to be expected, it is *never* to be accepted. Here are some ways I've learned to navigate as a female entrepreneur in a male-dominated world.

LAY DOWN THE GROUND RULES

When it comes to establishing my role within my team, I am very direct. Because Demond and I work together, I find that unless I am assertive, it's easy for people to defer to his judgement, assuming he is the big boss while disregarding my role or importance. Remember, this is my kingdom – I have to set the tone. I do this by laying down some ground rules as soon as anyone new is introduced to the team. *Hello, this is who I am, this is how I speak, this is how I prefer to be addressed. Here are my expectations, here are some do's and don'ts of working with me.* Boom. Quick, clear, and to the point.

Leading with these ground rules lets people know right away what to expect when they interact with me. It may come off blunt to some, but I don't like my time wasted. Laying out your boundaries minimizes the chance that lines will be crossed, and eliminates the time spent on damage-control or cleaning up awkward messes. It's better that employees know how I am upfront.

FLIP THE SCRIPT

As for dealing with executives outside of my team, it can be a bit trickier to navigate. While I try to only do business with people I respect, sometimes you run into a few bad apples that only reveal their true colors once the ink on a deal has dried. If I ever find myself having to deal with sexist comments, rude remarks, or inappropriate names like honey or sweetie within the context of a business meeting, I flip the script to take back my power. Most of the time, men use these names and make these comments because they can; it's a way for them to flex their power. I like to take that power away by refusing to answer. If I'm in a meeting and I am called out of my name, I will simply ignore the person and address my next remark or question to someone else. *Oh, were you talking to me? I'm sorry. I did not hear my name.* A simple response like that does nothing to impede the business discussion, but also clearly redirects the conversation in a way that says you are not to be played with.

If the inappropriate behavior persists, I will simply pivot and let it be known that I refuse to work with that particular rep for that company. *Our business may continue as planned, but I will be requiring a new company rep moving forward.* Never feel backed into a corner. If someone makes you feel uncomfortable, do not deal with them and definitely don't take meetings with them one-on-one. People will only continue behaviors that you allow. Flip the script and take your power back!

TWICE AS GOOD

If you are a female entrepreneur of color, the hurdles are only further magnified. As the saying goes, Black people have to work twice as hard or be twice as good to get half as much, and I've found that proven true time and time again. The sad truth is that Black entrepreneurs are playing a different game. We are often locked out of certain rooms and deals because vendors and retailers assume we cannot scale. We've already addressed how much harder it is for us to secure loans from banks and investors. To add insult to injury, we're also often put in a box that we didn't ask for.

For some reason beyond my understanding, there's this unwritten expectation that Black entrepreneurs only make products and services for Black customers. I can't explain how many times I've had white customers message me asking whether they can use my skin or baby care products. They see what I look like and they assume my products aren't for them. I even have a friend in the linen business dealing with the same issue. She makes luxury sheets and comforters, and yet she still fields questions from shoppers asking, *are your products only for Black people?* It truly is ridiculous.

As if that weren't enough, we get the same pressures from our own communities. Whenever Black business owners begin to scale and try to expand their marketing to be more inclusive, they risk a backlash from the Black community. We're so used to being locked out of upward mobility for so long that we fear being abandoned by our own. While I understand the concern and personally strive to keep my demographic at the core of my vision, I also feel for the entrepreneurs crippled by these limitations. Not only do they affect our bottom line by keeping us cut off from potential new avenues of income, but they place a burden on our backs that makes us afraid to move too far in any one direction.

I myself have had to confront the realities of being a Black businesswoman very recently. I've had meetings with retailers who wanted to sell my baby care products – great! However, they wanted to place them, not in the section along with all the other baby care products, but in the multicultural or ethnic aisles. Why? Why the separation? It's this kind of subtle marketing that screams, *you don't belong here. You're too different.*

The worst part is that it can be tempting to overlook the discrimination when there are dollar signs attached. I've seen many business owners be so blinded by a check that they compromise on their non-negotiables, and I refuse to let that happen to my company. As a double-minority entrepreneur, I come to the table already knowing that I have to break down barriers. I have to change more minds and open more eyes than my White male counterparts. It may be unfair, but it's the truth. The key is not to let that make you bitter or resentful; don't become a victim. If anything, use it as fuel. Always be twice as good and if they won't make room for you at the table, build your own.

WHAT'S YOUR SUPERPOWER?

How do you get twice as good? You have to identify your *it* factors. Ask yourself, *what is my superpower?* Once a year, I recommend you do what's called a S.W.O.T analysis, both for your business and for yourself as a C.E.O. A S.W.O.T analysis is a strategic planning technique to determine one's strengths, weaknesses, opportunities for growth, and threats to success. Why is this important? When you're the C.E.O, you are the highest on the totem pole. There is no one there to check you or hold you accountable but yourself, and that can easily work to your detriment. Conducting a S.W.O.T analysis will help you see not only your superpowers, but your blind spots as well.

PERSONAL S.W.O.T

Strengths
What are my winning points? Where do I excel as a leader? What do I have that no one else can copy?

Weaknesses
What complaints or concerns are consistently expressed by my staff? What areas of leading my team make me feel the most uncomfortable? Where am I making myself small or clinging to my comfort zone?

Opportunities
What classes can I take to sharpen my skills? What resources do I have to improve my leadership? Who do I know that I can call for advice?

Threats
What is distracting me from operating at my highest level? What urgent matters have I been avoiding?

BUSINESS S.W.O.T

Strengths
What makes my company stand out? What do we have that our competitors don't? What is that special sauce that keep my customers coming back?

Weaknesses
What complaints or concerns are consistently expressed by my customers? What K.P.I.s are we failing to hit? What areas of our operations are least efficient?

Opportunities

What events are coming up that we can affiliate ourselves with? What new trends can we participate in to expand our reach and clicks? What have we not tapped into yet?

Threats

Who are our top competitors? What is preventing us from scaling? Which aspects of our operations are not working? What needs the most immediate attention?

When conducting a S.W.O.T analysis, you've got to completely remove your ego from the process. Hold a mirror up to yourself and your company and really be truthful about what works and what doesn't work. By being honest about where you're lacking, you can plug in the gaps and take yourself and your business to new heights.

OWN YOUR PAIN

Let's talk about those weaknesses for a moment. Those can be pretty difficult to examine, especially for those of us who have been through a lot in our lives. It can be hard to stare our weaknesses in the eye because oftentimes they are scars from a past that has damaged us. It is so easy to tuck them away and pretend they never happened, but I am here to tell you that the best thing you can do to fully thrive as a businessperson and a human being is to own your pain. Use the negative experiences you've lived to become a victor. Use them to become a superhero. Use them to rewrite your story and reconstruct the narrative you've been telling yourself about who you are. So many people – including myself – have been through so many traumas and trials in their lives. I was abused by the very people who should have loved and cared for me most, but guess what? I am still standing, and so are you.

When you leave old struggles behind, new ones will come to take their place. As an entrepreneur there are going to be days that are absolute garbage. There will be times when you're trying to fix one problem, and five more pop up. It's called the snowball effect and it's inevitable. On those days when you just feel so tired, beaten down, and defeated, I want you to remember my words. Close your eyes and tell yourself, *this, too, shall pass*. It's something my mother used to say to me, and it's continued to provide me with so much comfort throughout the years. *This, too, shall pass.* Never give up, never quit. Rest, of course, but never stop. You have to get up and fight. Find that grit and determination to carry you through all the frustrations, all the obstacles, and all the doubts that pop up to test your commitment to your dream. I triumphed, and you can do the same. It's all about deciding that you want a better life. Know that you hold the pen and you control the story. Who you've been doesn't have to be who you are today. Own your pain to own your power.

FIND YOUR JOY

On the other side of pain is joy. Never forget that you should enjoy what you do! Yes, you have your why and the impact you want to leave on the world, but you also became an entrepreneur because you wanted freedom. You wanted to work for yourself and live your life doing something you're passionate about. Of course, doing what you love doesn't mean that you'll love everything you do. As an entrepreneur you will always have things on your agenda that you detest, especially at the beginning when you're wearing all the hats. However, as your company begins to grow and pick up steam, prioritize those things that bring you joy.

For me, mixing and making my own products has always been one of my soul's greatest pleasures. It's how I started Alikay, just playing around with ingredients and seeing what I could come up with. When the company took off, however, I was blindsided by the workload, and shifted all of my focus to operations. I was busy opening a facility and managing a team, pitching to retailers and making deals with vendors – I stopped mixing altogether. Before I knew it, seven years had passed with no new products or collections. I had allowed myself to stray so far away from why I started and the things I initially loved about my business. The self-proclaimed mixtress wasn't mixing, wasn't concocting, and I wasn't creating content for my initial base of supporters on YouTube. One day I looked up and realized, I was seeing success, but I wasn't happy.

Owning your throne is more than just handling your business. It means feeling like the queen or king that you are. I had to pivot and return to my roots. I went back to experimenting with ingredients and playing with scents and mixtures because that's what I needed to be happy. Furthermore, the happier I got, the more Alikay benefited through new collections and product launches. When you win, your company wins.

You've also got to think about what brings you peace. When you look at an opportunity that you are presented with, consider not only what it's costing you in time and money, but also what it's costing your spirit. Money isn't everything, and while you may need the revenue for your business, not every deal is worth making. Ask yourself, *is this money worth my peace? Is this money worth my happiness? Is this money worth me compromising my values or my loyalty to my customers?* If the answer does not sit well in your spirit, just say no.

HUMBLE WITH A HINT OF KANYE

Finally, don't be afraid to feel yourself, just a little bit! One of the main concerns as you begin to see success is remaining humble. People see you making money and a name for yourself, and they put all this pressure on you not to change.

> *Everybody look at you strange, say you changed*
>
> *Like you worked that hard to stay the same*
>
> *- Jay Z, "Most Kingz"*

As famously stated by rapper and business mogul Jay Z, you didn't work that hard just to stay the same! Give yourself permission to feel good. I spent so long trying not to have an inflated ego that I think I wound up with the opposite. Don't get me wrong ⊠ I'm confident in who I am, what I do, and how I do it, but I think I can stand to let it shine a bit more. When I leave events, I am floating on cloud nine! I meet my longtime customers, they give me handwritten letters of love and support, and I am able to see firsthand the impact I have made through my products. I take those compliments and I bottle them up in my heart. It sounds cliché, but on my hard days and tough times, those are the things that boost me up and keep me going.

So, my motto for the upcoming year is, "Humble with a hint of Kanye." I will always strive to remain grounded but moving forward, I give myself permission to shine and feel the weight of the work I've done. One of the lessons that my stepdad, Richard, always taught me was, *you are a light in this world.* He said it to me all the time as a kid, and even still, to this day! He has never let me forget it and I take that lesson to heart. Richard taught me that, by being brave and confident, myself -- even and especially when I just want to run and hide in the corner -- I then give other people the freedom to be brave and confident, too. And so I will leave you with an excerpt from one of my all-time favorite quotes:

> *"We ask ourselves, Who am I to be brilliant, gorgeous, talented, fabulous? Actually, who are you not to be? You are a child of God. Your playing small does not serve the world. There is nothing enlightened about shrinking so that other people won't feel insecure around you. You were born to make manifest the glory of God within us. It's not just in some of us, it's in everyone. And as we let our own light shine, we unconsciously give other people permission to do the same. As we are liberated from our own fear, our presence automatically liberates others."*
>
> *- Marianne Williamson, Return To Love*

Acknowledge how great you are. You deserve your success. Own it.

definitions
every C.E.O should know

Trademark

A symbol, word, or words legally registered or established by use as representing a company or product.
Source: Oxford Dictionary

Scalable

Able to be changed in size.
Source: Oxford Dictionary

Counter Offer

An offer you make in response to an offer made by another party.
Source: Wikipedia

Research & Development

Work directed towards the innovation, introduction, and improvement of products and processes.
Source: Oxford Dictionary

Status Report

A report describing the current situation with regard to a business, project, matter, etc., especially one in a series of such reports summarizing a changing state of affairs.
Source: Oxford Dictionary

Mock Up

A model or replica of a machine or structure, used for instructional or experimental purposes.
Source: Oxford Dictionary

K.P.I

Short for Key Performance Indicator.

CHAPTER 8

PAY IT FORWARD

If you feel insignificant, you better think again

Better wake up because you're part of something way bigger

You're part of something way bigger

Not just a speck in the universe

Not just some words in a bible verse

You are the living word

Ah, you're part of something way bigger

Bigger than you, bigger than we

Bigger than the picture they framed us to see

But now we see it

And it ain't no secret, no

- Beyoncé, "Bigger"

In the wise words of Queen Bey, you are part of something way bigger – we all are – and that something is your purpose. As we discussed in chapter one, a true entrepreneur's vision extends beyond him or herself. The reach of your impact can be as small or as grand as you imagine it to be. For me, it's important that my impact on the world ripples beyond my personal pool of influence. I have a purpose beyond profit, and that purpose is serving others. When I'm not managing my company or spending quality time with my family, I'm trying to figure out how I can reach a hand back in solidarity to pull the next person up behind me. It's part of the reason I'm writing this book. I'm here, first and foremost, to liberate myself, and then to help others do the same. If you haven't already, consider how you will use your name, brand, money, and influence to pay it forward.

GIVE BACK

I know from experience – philanthropy isn't even a realistic thought on the radar for many new entrepreneurs. We're too broke and too stressed trying to keep ourselves and our families afloat, let alone trying to help anyone else. I know the financial strain that building a business can take, especially if you have loans to repay. However, if you can't afford to give money in the beginning stages of your business, you should consider at least giving your time.

I make it a rule for myself: I must give back to my community in some way at least once every quarter. Whether that's speaking on a panel, giving a workshop, or whatever other volunteer opportunity I'm asked to participate in for a greater good, I'll do it as long as my schedule permits. I understand that many non-profits and budding organizations simply cannot afford my fees for speaking engagements or media appearances, and I don't hold that against them. If I decide to offer my time for free, it's because the cause, mission, or organization has spoken to me in some way. I'm especially partial to interacting with children – I'm a sucker for babies! Sometimes it may be a toy drive, sometimes it may be going to a school and talking to young girls about female entrepreneurship. Giving back has always been in my nature because It presents me with the opportunity to blend my business and human sides. I can't take that for granted.

One opportunity in particular that stands out in my mind was a complimentary speaking engagement I did with a local non-profit organization for young girls. The girls in the program came from low-income households and many were exposed to unthinkable terrors such as drug abuse and domestic violence. Always searching for new organizations to support through my Alikay Cares Foundation, I arranged a meeting to take a tour of the program facility. Not only did the girls receive access to amazing teachers and private counselors, but they also participated in a merit-based incentive program where they would earn credits to shop the facility's toiletry and beauty closet. Many of the girls' parents simply could not afford beauty products, and so I donated over $1,000 worth of Alikay Naturals products to restock their supplies.

Later, my mother and I got the chance to sit down and talk with the girls. We shared our stories and listened to theirs. I bonded with the girls over my somewhat-tumultuous childhood, and encouraged them to keep walking along the right path. For many of the students, attending college was a far-fetched dream, and financial freedom, an even greater fantasy. I shared my personal testimony to show the girls that they, too, could grow up, work hard, and become successful. If I could do it, they could do it. After exchanging tons of hugs, I remember sitting in my car and getting emotional. I saw myself in almost each and every one of those girls. Hearing their stories reminded me that my success paves the way for the next person. My story just might light that spark that convinces a young girl to go to college, or become a C.E.O herself. These are the types of engagements I like giving my time to - the ones that touch my heart and reignite my spirit.

As for financial donations, I don't pressure myself to hit a certain monetary goal. While I've seen amazing success in the past ten years, my business is still self-funded. Most of our profit goes right back into the business, and soon we'll be seeking fiscal support from investors so that we can scale. I do, however, like to do campaigns around the holiday season. Alikay Naturals will typically have holiday sales, and I'll instruct my staff to donate a percentage of proceeds to different causes and organizations. Whether we make our donations public or not, campaigns are just a way we like to give back as a team. Another way we give back is through the Alikay Cares Foundation. I started the foundation in 2016 as an initiative to provide resources to underserved communities. Sometimes I'll pack up the family and my staff and we'll all volunteer together. It's important to me to share that philanthropic energy with my children and my employees.

give
back

How often can I commit to giving back/philanthropy?

What are some local and global causes
or charities that speak to me?

How can I offer my services?

BE GENEROUS, BUT WITHIN REASON!

However you choose to give back, be it through your time, presence, or money, make sure that you are only giving within your means. Oftentimes, entrepreneurs fall into the trap of feeling like we have to save the world. We want to serve our families, serve our customers, serve our teams, and serve our communities so badly to the point where we might bite off more than we can chew. Be careful of overextending yourself for two reasons. First, you never want to agree to give your time to a cause only to back out at the last minute. It not only reflects poorly upon your brand, but it also makes you seem disingenuous as a person. Second, you may end up harboring resentment towards giving back because you've depleted yourself of time, energy, and funds. Giving should be done with a free spirit and come from the heart – never obligation. Moral of the story? Make sure you have boundaries set firmly in place – yes, even for charity. Don't tap yourself dry. Again, take that "S" off your chest. You don't have to save the world, especially not at the expense of yourself.

ANNIE MALONE

For a lesson in the importance of mindful giving, I turn to nineteenth century entrepreneur extraordinaire and one of my personal business sheros, Annie Minerva Turnbo Malone. While Madame CJ Walker is often credited as the mother of black hair care, she was actually mentored by Annie Malone, the forgotten beauty entrepreneur and the true first black female millionaire. I don't want to take anything away from Madame CJ Walker's amazing legacy, however, her success would not have come if not for the tutelage and business model provided by Annie Malone. Even though she was two years younger than Walker, Malone actually launched her wildly successful hair care enterprise of Poro beauty products four years before Walker started her own business. In fact, Madame CJ Walker even worked for Malone as a Poro agent, selling Poro products door-to-door in the sales agent system later popularized by Mary Kay.

In addition to being a great businesswoman, Annie Malone was also a magnificent philanthropist. She did amazing things for the African-American community, such as donating huge amounts to charities and historically black colleges and universities like Howard University. She also founded Poro College, the first American educational institution devoted specifically to black cosmetology. Through her college, Annie Malone employed hundreds of people and trained and graduated tens of thousands of students. She also incentivized her employees with cash rewards for attendance, workplace anniversaries, and investing in real estate, and also purchased homes for her family members. Annie Malone is a true example of leaving a legacy that was bigger than herself and her individual success.

So, why is it that Madame CJ Walker has become a household name while Annie Malone has all but fallen to the shadows? As it turned out, Annie Malone's generosity and philanthropic efforts were ultimately a large part of the downfall of her business. Focused on giving back, she entrusted the daily operations of her business to her husband and a number of managers who mismanaged her money and ultimately drove her business into the ground. Coupled with a divorce settlement, lawsuits, and the Great Depression, Malone's business could not survive. While her generosity was noble, it came at a time before her business had fully stabilized, causing it to be unsustainable. On top of that, former employee and mentee Madame CJ Walker actually went on to mimic Malone's business model with her own Walker agents and created similar products – one of Malone's Poro hair preparations was known as the Special Hair Grower while Walker went on to sell her Wonderful Hair Grower. While Madame CJ Walker also made philanthropic contributions, she did so more moderately and did a much better job of maintaining her success and reinvesting her money back into her business.

Many may not know of Annie Malone's legacy as a hair care pioneer; I myself didn't hear about her until after I became an entrepreneur. Still, she remains my very favorite entrepreneur in history because of the valuable lessons I have learned from her story. Annie Malone has taught me that philanthropy is crucial, but should not be done frivolously. Without having proper company and money management systems in place, your success will be short-lived. She has also taught me to be careful who you mentor. Sharing your expertise is wonderful, but you never want to give away so much that you end up mentoring your next big competitor. Be mindful of the company you keep and protect your business at all costs. It's not about being selfish, it's about being a smart business owner.

PROVIDE OPPORTUNITY

If and when you begin to experience success in your business, you will likely experience at least one time when people begin to identify your wins as their own. Many times, it's family and friends who feel obligated to a piece of your success, but it's not always for the reasons you'd suspect. The issue may not be greed or entitlement. Sometimes, people who have genuinely supported or helped you out in some way simply feel proud of you. When you make it, they feel like they've made it, and they may see you doing well from the outside and assume that you're doing well enough to help them out financially.

Success does provide an awesome opportunity to give back to friends and loved ones, however, just like anything else, it must be done with discernment. Be wary of feeling indebted to everyone who ever smiled in your direction. Also, consider that you can repay old favors in ways other than money or gifts. For example, I may not be able to buy a new house for every loved one or friend who has ever helped me out, but I have been able to hire several family members onto my full-time or part-time staff.

Of course, hiring family and friends comes with its own set of concerns and might not be a smart move for everyone. If you can make it work, however, onboarding family is a great way to provide opportunity for others to empower themselves without breaking your pockets. I've been able to employ family members from my brother-in-law and father-in-law, to my grandfather and even my Yaya! For Yaya, not only does the job provide income – it also provides purpose. She fell into a deep depression after attempting to retire and finding herself lonely and stagnant at home by herself. Having a job gave her a place to come to work alongside her husband, a place to contribute and feel helpful. I've seen how much working has reenergized her entire spirit, and at this point, she can come in as frequently or infrequently as she wants. My point is giving doesn't always mean loans or gifts. Give *opportunities*. Don't allow yourself to be used as a crutch, but help others as you see fit.

INSPIRE OTHERS

ON A SMALL SCALE

Another way to give back is simply through leading by example. You never know who might be watching your journey in admiration, learning from your trials and tribulations, and wanting to follow in your footsteps. For example, I have a good friend named Marilyn. She and I go way back; she was actually studying for an exam while I was mixing up the first bottles of Essential 17 Hair Growth Oil™ on my kitchen stove. Even though she had a full-time job, she would always help Demond and I out with Alikay whenever she could. She has been at every hair show I have ever done, she was a part of my hair show team when I couldn't even afford to pay her and little did I know, she was watching my entrepreneurial journey the whole time. Years later, and now, Marilyn is a publicist for a major Florida university and runs her own PR and event planning firm. She is also my event planner for my Natural Hair Expo that grew from 100 to 1,500 attendees!

It wasn't until Marilyn sat me down and thanked me that I even knew how closely she had been paying attention. When she ultimately had to close her first company, I talked her through those hurdles and encouraged her to pivot and keep going. When she started doing events, I hired her as the event planner for my FABU Expo and reassured her that she could absolutely pull it off. Now, she has events with 1,000 plus people under her belt, and more and more offers are coming in all the time. I absolutely knew that she could do everything she wanted, but in my head, I was just encouraging a friend; putting in my two cents. I never stopped to consider the fact that watching me go for my dreams pushed her to pursue her own.

Even my own mother tells me all the time that I've inspired her. Seeing me start my own company and figure everything out along the way prompted her to open her own medical practice after a lifetime of working for others. The thought that I – as the child – had a hand in inspiring my own mother is so incredibly humbling and eye-opening for me. Sometimes when you're so busy keeping your head down and doing your work, you fail to appreciate the effect you're having on those around you. You don't realize how many people you're inspiring in real life, not just on social media.

When you do catch wind of the effect you're having on others, relish that. That's God's way of letting you know that you're walking in your purpose! It's not about bragging or taking credit for other people's success, but it's about being grateful that you could play a part – however small or brief – in someone else's story. So, pay it forward by being authentic and sharing as much of your story as you can. You never know who's watching.

"To whom much has been given, much will be required" – Luke 12:48

ON A LARGER SCALE

While it's easiest to see your influence on those closest to you, don't be afraid to dream big. Remember, *branch out!* The larger and more successful my company has become, the greater urge and responsibility I feel to help more people. Your reach will only go as far as you extend your arms! To make sure I touch as many people as possible, I started the Rochelle Graham Business University™(RGBU).

Rochelle Graham Business University™ is a business education enterprise that I launched in 2019 to reveal everything that business school won't teach you. Oftentimes, I'll get emails, direct messages, and in-person requests from aspiring entrepreneurs who just need a little help. They've laid the groundwork and have done their research, but are just seeking the personal touch of a mentor to help them navigate the unsteady waters of entrepreneurship. As much as I would love to help, I have to be realistic. I know that I cannot possibly commit the time and energy necessary to truly mentor someone. I strongly believe that being a mentor is an honor and a responsibility; you have to invest yourself, and I simply don't have the bandwidth to bring on an apprentice at this time. Rochelle Graham Business

University™ is my solution. It's basically my opportunity to mentor the masses!

Much of business is actual, factual information like licensing, meeting codes and regulations and more. We'll get into those things more in depth in the next chapter, "Open Up Shop." What many people don't consider, however, is that some of the information you can only glean from experience. A textbook can never teach you about grit, resilience, and coping with failure. Your professors can't teach you about vision, creativity, or trusting your gut. That's where RGU comes in. I designed my university to share the real life, practical applications of lessons I learned the hard way. The content is about 20-30% textbook need-to-know information, and 70-80% real life. The first course I'm launching is about how to create a product that sells. Next, we'll be covering how to vend and sell your products successfully at small events or large trade shows, and the next will be about the fundamentals in launching your own business successfully. Moving forward, I'll share tips on how to enter and survive in the retail world. Basically, I want to help people build strong, solid, and scalable business foundations and add to the wealth of knowledge available out there for novice entrepreneurs. I'm also creating a Facebook community for my students to be able to share testimonials and support each other on their entrepreneurial journeys, guided by my advice along the way.

Ultimately, it's more than inspiring people to become C.E.Os or make lots of money. It's about inspiring people to love themselves, to bet on themselves, and bank on their abilities. That's the mission at the core of Alikay Naturals. Of course, I wanted to create products that would sell. Yes, I wanted to make products that would actually work and make people look good. Even deeper than products, though, I wanted to inspire other women to find the beauty in their hair and the beauty in themselves. I wanted mothers to feel safe and educated enough to do their children's hair with full confidence in the integrity of the ingredients. I wanted to expand the lexicon of beauty and natural hair care so that the next generations would never question the beauty and versatility of their tresses. *That* is how I feel like I'm paying it forward, more than anything else.

SHARE EXPERTISE

While I don't have any one-on-one mentees, I never mind giving advice or answering questions. As an entrepreneur, sharing your expertise will always be easier when people ask the right questions in the right manner. Personally, I prefer in-person interactions over emails or messages. In person, I can be more mindful and present in the moment. When I am asked questions via email, I have to type it out and worry about things like tone or formatting. I'd rather just keep it as real and raw as possible.

Another thing that helps is when I'm approached with a concise, well-thought out question. If you're seeking advice, don't lead with fifty million things about your backstory. Most entrepreneurs are pressed for time; they may want to answer your questions but need you to help them help you. When seeking advice, be prepared, efficient, and brief. When giving advice, be engaged, detailed, and transparent.

Finally, I will answer almost any question I'm asked, so long as it is in good taste. As an entrepreneur, know when to share, and when to keep things to yourself. For instance, I don't appreciate when people ask me proprietary questions – it's rude. People will walk up to my booth at a hair show, grab a product, read the ingredient list right in front of me and ask me specific questions about my formulas. When giving advice, never give away your product secrets.

GO FORTH AND PROSPER!

"When I stand before God at the end of my life, I would hope that I would have not a single bit of talent left but could say, I've used everything you gave me."

– *Erma Bombeck*

The biggest and best way you can help others is by being a badass! Shine! Go for it with all you've got, endure all the bumps and bruises that may come, and leave nothing on the table. What better way to repay all the support you've received than by absolutely killing it?

As a self-funded business one-decade-deep in the game and a company that I started in the middle of the recession, Alikay Naturals is a unicorn. There are not many other businesses out there in our niche that have had the longevity that we've had or scaled the way we've been able to scale thus far. As a result, the advice we've received from peers is few and far between; many of them are looking to us as pioneers. For those rare gems who have actually reached out and offered me some sort of advice or support – maybe they whispered something in my ear or mentioned a name that I needed to know to get my foot in the door somewhere – I am eternally grateful. The best thing that I have been able to do in my career is to show them that gratitude by knocking every single opportunity that comes my way out of the park. I have to make sure that I'm returning on their investment.

Underperformance is not an option. In every area of your life, walk in and not only do the job, but show them why you were *built* for it. Some people will be blessed to have many doors opened for them and many opportunities thrown their way. They might not value each and every one of those opportunities because they came relatively easily. Your goal, as you grow more and more successful, should be to maintain that gratitude and that mindset of humility, and yet also keep that hunger and insatiability for progress and evolution so that every single person who helped you knows that their efforts were not in vain. Show them that betting on you was the right bet!

Bylaw

A rule made by a company or society to control the
actions of its members.
Source: Oxford Dictionary

Scalable

Able to be changed in size.
Source: Oxford Dictionary

Philanthropy

The desire to promote the welfare of others, expressed
especially by the generous donation of money to good causes.
Source: Oxford Dictionary

Business Model

A design for the successful operation of a business,
identifying revenue sources, customer base, products,
and details of financing.
Source: Oxford Dictionary

Grant

Agree to give or allow (something requested) to.
Source: Oxford Dictionary

Fiscal Year

A year as reckoned for taxing or accounting purposes.
Source: Oxford Dictionary

R.O.I

Short for Return On Investment.

PART IV.

ROCHELLE'S RULES

"While they were saying it couldn't be done, it was done."
- Hellen Keller

Y ou've made it through my trials, tribulations, and heard my C.E.O testimony in full. Now, it's your turn. I know you've been paying close attention and doing your homework as we've gone along. You've jotted down notes and if my suspicions are correct, by now, these pages are filled with underlines, highlights, and asterisks galore! A strong entrepreneur's thirst for knowledge is never quenched, however, so prepare yourself. The work is far from over. In these next two chapters, I will provide you with my comprehensive syllabus for Small Business Management 101. I'm giving you all my secrets, hacks, and practical advice for opening and operating your new business. I will also be providing you with three C.E.O checklists to monitor your progress along your journey. Use my thirty, sixty, and ninety-day checklists to remember your priorities and mark your growth during each phase of your business from conception, to launch, and operation. These check-ins will push you to hold yourself accountable, set a solid foundation for a viable company, and create real forward momentum toward your dreams of entrepreneurship! Your progress is in your hands. The time for dreams and hypotheticals is over, people. Stuff is about. to get. REAL. Welcome to Rochelle's Rules of Business, a jam-packed guide to walk you through your first ninety days to C.E.O.

CHAPTER 9

OPENING UP SHOP

If you've made it this far in the book, congratulations! So far, you've established your why and laid down your roots and branches. You've conditioned your mind for the messy middle, popped the boss babe balloon, and brushed up on the importance of self-care as an entrepreneur. You've learned the ins and outs of my journey, and it is my sincerest hope that my story can serve as an example to you along your own path. However, I know firsthand that you need more than just an example.

As a fledgling business owner, you need more than success stories and inspiration. You need practical, actual advice – actionable steps and tips to get your business out of your head and into reality. I meet so many aspiring business owners who have the vision and the dedication down, but they just need more directed guidance. They wish someone would just sit them down and tell them what it *really* takes to finally open up shop. Well, your Business Fairy Godmother is here, and your wish is my command.

In these next two chapters, we'll be going over the exact steps you need to take to get your business up and running.

We'll cover everything from naming your company to securing the right legal licenses and titles; and securing vendors to building a solid team of employees. Of course, all of this information comes from my husband's and my own professional experience. We cannot guarantee that your steps will be exactly the same as ours, because every company and every entrepreneur is different. Even the regulations for opening and running a company will vary depending on your state of operation. Still, we've learned lots of pertinent information as well as some pretty useful business hacks along the way, and it is my pleasure to share them with you. So, without further ado, break out your pen and paper and let's get down to business!

DETERMINING VIABILITY

I know this is your dream and you're eager to get started but hold your horses. Before we can even think about selling a product or service, we need to determine whether your idea is viable. Determining viability is a crucial first step to starting a business that many people overlook because of enthusiasm and spontaneity. Yes, you should be passionate, but when it comes to business, passion without a plan is pure chaos.

CREATE A BUSINESS MODEL

Distill all the ideas in your head into a clear and concise business model. A business model is a conceptual blueprint for how your company will generate profit and should clearly outline what products or services your business will offer, your target customers or market, and any and all predicted expenses. A business model is vital to keeping you organized, focused, and most importantly, viable.

The first step is deciding whether you want to start a service-based or product-based business. If it's the former, what service are you going to offer? Are you going to be the sole person offering this service, or will you have employees and contractors? If you are bringing other workers on-board to help expand your service, how will you train them? Do *you* already have the professional training, skillset, or experience needed to offer this service effectively and with integrity? Asking yourself these questions will determine your next steps. For instance, maybe your dream is to open a mobile salon service because you've always had a passion for hair and makeup. While interest is great, there are steps you'll need to take to go from mere passion to a profitable and legitimate service-based business – like getting your cosmetology license, for instance. Even if you are confident that you can go out and get clients tomorrow, obtaining further education and expertise within your field is a great way to boost your legitimacy and ultimately attract even more customers. For instance, someone might hire you for your personal training services because you're in shape, but they're more likely to *remain* a loyal and recurring client or refer your services to a friend if they know that you have certifications in personal training and nutrition.

If you want to start a product-based business, the same rules apply. Is this product something you have already created, or are you starting it from scratch? Can it be handmade or will you require specific machinery for assembly? Where will you source the components or ingredients for your final product? Deciding on a product-based or service-based business model is the first major decision that will dictate everything else you do moving-forward. Be sure to head over to rgbusinessuniversity.com and check out my "How To Create A Product That Sells"™ course for more information.

VALUE PROPOSITION

A hugely important component of your business model will be your company's value proposition. A value proposition is a description of the products or services your company will offer, as well as the ways in which those products or services will provide value to consumers in a unique and sustainable way. Think of it like an elevator pitch, but for your business. Your value proposition should be specific and speak to your company's allure. Clearly define what it is that makes your business stand out from the crowd. What makes you different than everyone else and why should customers want to purchase your product or service over the next brand's?

In the space below, take a moment to brainstorm a possible value proposition for your business:

Value Proposition template

Example:

For freelance writers who have trouble getting their clients to pay on time, our software package tracks past-due payments and sends automated reminders so you can spend your time earning money, not tracking it down.

https://www.smartsheet.com/value-proposition-positioning-templates

REVENUE MAP

Once you've established a strong value proposition, it's time to determine the profitability of your product or service. In other words, can you actually make money off of your idea? And if so, how? There are two main steps to determining the profit-making power of your business idea. First, figure out all of your potential expenses. Second, determine your potential revenue.

Expenses will include each and everything needed to get your business off the ground floor and to keep it operating. Things to consider include: the cost of ingredients, the cost of manufacturing, the cost of renting an office or workspace, the cost of hiring a staff, the cost of transporting goods, and the list can go on. As a side note, this is why I highly recommend starting off small. The more hats you can wear when you start out, the less money you have to pay to employees or contractors. Remember, I started out hand-mixing products in my apartment kitchen/lab. My husband did all of our bookkeeping and I printed all my own product labels with labels I purchased from the local Staples. By being a jack of all trades, I not only learned a ton, but I also kept my expenses low by eliminating manufacturers, employees, and expensive commercial offices. I'm telling you, work with what you've got until you can't work it anymore! It'll save you a ton.

As for your potential profit, I recommend that new business owners do what's called a **revenue map**. A revenue map is a diagram which lays out all of your company's potential streams of income. For instance, if your goal is to start a catering business, your primary income will come from the events that you cater. Perhaps, however, you can also make money by offering prepackaged meal-prepped lunches and dinners, hosting beginner level cooking classes in your community, and selling branded merchandise through a website. All of these avenues are high-value goods that you can market to attract new customers or increase your volume of sales from existing customers.

Before you actually make your map, I want you to sit down with a pen and paper and brainstorm all the ways you can possibly see your business making money. Don't be shy! Every idea counts as long as you believe it can generate revenue. Once you have your brain-dump list, it's time to organize and prioritize these items with a revenue map.

How to make a revenue map:

Step 1: Put your potential company name in the middle of a piece of paper.

Step 2: Draw a web with multiple lines extending out from the center and draw little bubbles at the end of each line. In each of these bubbles you will write down one of the potential money-making services or products from your brain-dump list. Things to consider: main product or service, brand merchandise, consulting or coaching services, public speaking services, etc.

Step 3: Decide which of these products or services will be your core elements, or your new business' first offerings. These should be the offerings that you are most confident will generate high-revenue and allow you to hit the ground running. Draw a star or a number 1 next to these items to indicate phase one. Every bubble left unstarred or unnumbered will be phase two or three items, or your business' secondary product or service offerings. You will save these items for a later time while you continue to grow and scale your company around your phase one selections.

Use the space below to start your first revenue map:

Voila! There you have it, an organized map of exactly how your new business will bring in money. When you're brainstorming additional products and services, it's okay to get creative, but make sure everything you plan to offer makes sense for your niche and your industry. For example, no one wants to buy makeup services from their local flower shop. Make it make sense, but also, don't offer everything at one time. The reason that we release new products and services in phases is so that we can effectively manage our time, resources, and efforts. Master your two or three phase one offerings first. Then, listen to the feedback from your consumer base and see what else they are asking you for. What did they like about your phase one products? What didn't they like? From there, you can then build out and decide which one of your other idea offerings is an appropriate next fit. Some businesses may never get around to their secondary or phase two offerings. To be honest, it's completely okay to work with just a couple of core items. When you're in the brainstorming phase, however, it's a good idea to note all of the possible options for generating revenue to leave yourself and your business somewhere to go.

If phase one proves successful and you do eventually proceed with your phase two ideas, make sure that they are semi-automated, or that they won't demand too much extra bandwidth from you or your staff. As you launch other products and services, you never want to abandon your phase one offerings. You really want to make sure that your core functions, services, and products are always being served first, even when you're adding new things to the table. Remember, phase one is the foundation of your business and these offerings generate the highest and most consistent revenue for your company. As you're adding on new offerings, be mindful of whether they will demand too much extra time, money, or staff power. If so, you're going to need to expand your team and your operations to carry the weight of that extra burden. There's no rush to expand – slow and steady wins the race.

Lastly, you also want to think about whether your phase two or three ideas actually fit within your current business model. If not, it is possible that you may want to open a separate business down the line specifically for those other offerings. For example, my official company name is Black Onyx World LLC, and this umbrella company houses all of my beauty-related businesses, including Alikay Naturals. My new businesses, however, – Rochelle Graham Business University ™ and Rochelle Graham Business Consulting™ – are not beauty-related, and therefore they do not fall under Black Onyx World LLC (because they don't fit the business model). To house my non-beauty related businesses, I opened a separate company, RG Legacy Enterprises, to act as the parent company to all of my education and business-related services. It's okay if you don't have all the answers when you're first starting out, but taking the time to brainstorm for the future will help you bigtime in the structuring and launching of your first business. Always think long-term.

Once you begin actually selling your products or services and building an idea of your predicted monthly expenses and income, you will begin to understand how your company needs to function in order to be viable or profitable. For instance, if you determine that you need to make $20,000 a month in revenue to surpass your startup and operation costs and your company offers services at a $2,000 per month retainer, that means that you need to have at least 10 clients minimum every month to hit your revenue goals. If we're talking products, it's the same thing. Figure out how many products you need to sell on average per week or month and track your progress diligently. If you're underperforming, that's an indication that something needs to change. Perhaps it's your product, your marketing, your customer service, or some other variable. You will only build a viable business by diving in, tracking your growth, and seeing what works and what does not.

CONSIDER YOUR INDUSTRY

Your value proposition and revenue map are all about how you will be good to your prospective consumer base, but when determining viability, it is also crucial to consider how your consumer base will be good to you. In other words, you need to consider the current climate of your particular industry and whether it works in your favor. Are people buying what you're selling? Is there a high demand? Is the industry healthy or is it in decline? No one in their right mind would start a DVD rental business in today's age of streaming, right? That's because the demand for how the public consumes content has shifted drastically, and entrepreneurs have followed suit. We have moved away from physical movies and CDs to streaming and subscription services; we've shifted from tangible books to podcasts and audiobooks. These shifts are entirely dictated by the wants, needs, and behaviors of the consumers. When starting a business, always consider the industry that you're entering, the people you're selling to, and whether they align with your particular idea.

Another important consideration is the competition within your industry. It might sound great to be the lone wolf in the market but guess again. The truth is that while competing companies present a threat, they are also a great indication of possible success for your new business. Competition actually confirms that you are entering a viable industry, because at least you know that other businesses similar to your own have launched, sustained, and thrived or scaled in that space. You can also study your competitors to learn from their successes and mistakes. Remember, never imitate someone else, but market analysis is critical to the successful operation of any company.

WRITE A BUSINESS PLAN

Now that you have your business model it's time to write a business plan. Yes, there is a difference! Your business model is mainly conceptual – you may write things down like your value proposition and your revenue map, but at the end of the day the model is for you to understand the structure and direction of your new company. A business plan, on the other hand, takes that concept and puts it into tangible, written, and easily digestible form for others – mainly for investors.

As a bootstrapped business (more on that later on in this chapter), Demond and I never created a concrete business plan for Alikay Naturals. As the sole financial contributors, we didn't have to present a written plan to anyone else. Even so, I still recommend writing a business plan because you never know when you'll need it. Ten years down the line and Demond and I are finally at a point of growth where we will soon need to seek outside funding so that we can scale our business. When that day comes, you better believe that a business plan is the very first step. If you are seeking outside funding from the start, however, a business plan is not just a good idea, it's a requirement. Investors and banks look to your business plan as an indication of whether or not to financially back your company. The more solid your plan, the more viable your business, and the more confident funders can be in your success. Ultimately, that adds up to potentially more generous investments for you!

The length can vary anywhere from five to ten pages for a mini plan to ten, fifteen, twenty, or even thirty pages for a comprehensive business plan. Regardless, the first component of a strong business plan should always be your **executive summary**. This is where you give a brief explanation of all the information to come in the remaining sections. Your executive summary should include the idea for your company, long and short-term goals, as well as strategies for execution, industry and market research, analysis of competitors, information on your team or internal structure, and of course, financial requirements to fund and execute on your plan. Think of the opening summary as the bait for your investors. This will determine whether or not they are even interested in hearing anything further.

After the executive summary, here are some of the most important components of a business plan:

Customer profile and analysis – Who is your target customer? What are their primary wants, needs, purchasing habits, and demographics? (Refer back to the core customer profile you created back in chapter one.) The most important thing is detailing your customer's main problem or pain point.

Product or service analysis – You've identified your customer's problem. Now, explain how your product or service will solve it! What is your company going to offer and how does it work? Why will it stand out in a meaningful and profitable way? You also want to identify your company's USP or unique selling proposition. This is basically the special factor that separates your product or service from everyone else. Your USP should be concrete – it can't just be your work ethic or faith that sets you apart. Examples of strong USPs include: unique design, original formula or ingredients, affordable price point, superior quality, etc.

Market analysis – This is where you prove that you know your stuff. Pack this section with facts and statistics that demonstrate your detailed knowledge and understanding of your market. What are the current trends? What are the big success stories and failures? Why is this a good market to enter?

Business model and revenue map – Good news here! You've already got this covered! You'll want to include your business model and revenue map within your business plan to prove to investors just how your company will function and how it will generate profit.

Competitive analysis – Here is where you demonstrate your understanding of your competitors, as well as how your company will compete. What are your competitors offering? What are their USPs? Where do you fit in in a way that makes you a real contender?

Marketing plan – What is your strategy for marketing all of these selling points? How will you attract new customers or encourage existing customers to buy more or more frequently? What marketing materials and strategies will you implement?

Team introduction – Of course, your potential investors will want to know who they're doing business with. Show them you've assembled a qualified and driven team by listing all names and titles, and detailing the experience and credentials of everyone on board.

Financial projections – Finally, you've got to be clear and straightforward about all things money-related. What will be your startup costs and expenses? How much do you need right now and how much will you need in the future in order to effectively execute on your business plan and secure their investment as a viable and profitable company? These things may be hard to know exactly when you first start out, but it is important to provide your best guesstimates. Make sure to have a budget laid out and let potential investors know that you have an organized plan for how you will allocate their funds.

Whether you self-fund or seek financial help, the most important thing to remember is that your business plan is not a static document. This is a document that you will revisit time and time again and update as the years go by, and the picture of your business becomes clearer and clearer. Even if you only update your plan once a year, that's perfectly fine. Just make sure that you leave room for future adjustments to accommodate the evolution of your company.

CREATING A PRODUCT THAT SELLS

Now that you've determined viability and brainstormed potential sales funnels, it's time to actually develop your product or service. Maybe you've been working on this for years – if so, great! Even so, there are always ways to tweak and enhance things and go from good to great. After all, you don't just want a product, you want a product that *sells*, big-time.

In my most recent brand, Rochelle Graham Business University™I have gone in-depth for new and aspiring C.E.Os on how to build a strong foundation for a strong business. If this book is a comprehensive overview, RGBU gives a true play-by-play and I'm there as the coach, walking you through each and every step. In our very first course, for instance, I go over what it takes to create a profitable, quality product. This information can be applied for creating quality services, as well. As a sneak peak, I will share with you my method for determining the value of potential goods. This method is tried, true, and pretty S.I.M.P.L.E.

_S_IMPLE:

Your product or service should take the guesswork out of how it will solve a customer's problems. Could someone look at your product or read a description and understand it imme-diately?

INTERESTING:

How do you stand out from the crowd? What makes your product different from your competitors' products? What is unique about the service you provide or the manner in which you provide it? What makes you interesting?

MEANINGFUL:

If you create a product or service that solves a problem people care about, it will likely sell itself. How are you making a mean-ingful difference?

PRODUCTIVE:

Your product or service needs to offer a means to do something faster, better, easier, or in a more cost-effective manner. How will you increase the productivity, convenience, and quality of your customer's life?

LONG-LASTING:

A successful product or service has longevity. It will provide a meaningful solution to a customer's problem that's more than just a fad. Does your product have the power to withstand mul-tiple generations? Will it be referred and passed along for years to come, or is it a one-off type of deal?

ENTERTAINING:

Lots of people love movies and video games, but not because they're productive. If you can provide excitement or enjoyment through an entertaining product or service experience, you've got a winner on your hands.

If you can confidently check off all or most of the above, congratulations — your product or service is high-value and likely to sell, but evaluation is only step one. From there, we'll also cover how to differentiate your goods from the competition, design your product packaging and test a prototype, identify your production plan, source materials, qualify manufacturers, measure costs and price accordingly, and create an extensive launch plan with a stellar marketing strategy. For all of this exclusive information and more, be sure to sign up for the Rochelle Graham Business University™ at rgbusinessuniversity.com.

NAMING YOUR BUSINESS

So, your company idea is viable, and you have an amazing product or service. Awesome. Now, let's talk names. I named my company Alikay Naturals because it speaks to who I am and what my brand is about. Alikay is my middle name and *Naturals* points to the ingredients in all of our products. It's a name that points undeniably to my niche (organic) within my industry (natural hair and skin care), and is also unique enough not to be confused with any other brand. These are all things that are important to consider when coming up with a name for your company.

TIMELESS vs. TRENDY

If you want your business to stick around for the long-haul, I strongly recommend choosing a name that is timeless. This means that your name will transition well through the years and will age gracefully along with your target demographic. You don't want to risk your brand sounding dated or aged in the future. Stay away from trendy names – this includes slang terms or names derived from fleeting hashtags or pop culture moments. People are fickle, and what's popular right now might not be so popular later on. You don't want to look up in five years or even one and cringe at a company name you've outgrown. Imagine seeing a brand today called YOLO Inc. Did you cringe? My point exactly.

CONSIDER YOUR LEGACY

Your best bet is to go with something simple. Simplicity means that you most likely won't regret it, and your customers won't forget it! What's simpler than your name? Naming your company after yourself is a great route because it's easy, effective, and aligns you with your brand right off the bat. Think of Robyn Rihanna Fenty's Fenty Beauty, or Oprah's Harpo Productions. When we hear those company names, we know exactly who the founders are ("Harpo" is "Oprah" spelled backwards). Naming a company after yourself establishes you as its face and helps you to build your legacy as an entrepreneur. Remember, it's about owning your throne!

Another important thing to consider is the legacy of your company itself. For some people, the goal may not be longevity. Some business owners can benefit from trendy names if their company is only meant to be short-term. Sometimes trendy companies arise where there is amazing growth and revenue over, let's say, a two-year period, and then it disappears. Maybe those entrepreneurs go in with the full intention of selling their company or phasing out of leadership after a certain period of time. That's totally okay. However, if your goal is longevity, do yourself a favor and stick with a name that's clean and timeless.

Finally, ask yourself, *what is the goal for my branding down the line?* Do you plan on starting other businesses? Maybe this first one will be the parent company to several branch businesses down the line. If that is the case, consider choosing an umbrella name under which everything else can fall. For example, Black Onyx World is my LLC or parent company. Alikay Naturals and all of my other brands fall under the Black Onyx World umbrella, but more on that in a bit!

Now that we know a bit more about what makes a great name, let's take some time to brainstorm a few ideas. Grab a sheet of paper and follow the steps below:

business name brainstorm

Step 1   Write down all of your prospective business names.

Step 2   Write a short description explaning why you like each name.

Step 3   Do an online search for each name.
Is it available or has it already been taken?

Step 4   If the name is not yet taken, ask 5 friends/family members for feedback. Have them rank each name on a scale from 1-10.

Keep in mind that naming your business in your head is only one aspect. To become a legal entity and protect yourself from copycat brands, you'll need to secure your name by registering with your state and local governments and trademarking with the United States Patent and Trademark Office. More on that a little later.

REGISTERING YOUR BUSINESS

Before you can truly begin conducting business, you have to officially register your company. In order to register, you first have to decide on a legal structure. Your business' structure is what makes your company a legal entity and will have subsequent effects on your daily operations and what taxes you will be required to file.

COMMON BUSINESS STRUCTURES

Some of the most common business structures are listed down below. These are general synopses, but keep in mind that rules, responsibilities, liabilities, and taxes for each structure will vary depending on your state of operation.

Sole Proprietorship – Sole proprietorship is open to entrepreneurs planning to go into business alone and is probably the simplest of all the legal structures out there. In fact, most new small businesses in the U.S. operate under this structure because of its relatively easy and straightforward process.

Pros: Owner has full control over all business decisions and operations. Zero corporate tax payments, fewer legal fees, requirements, and less paperwork than other entities.

Cons: As the sole proprietor, you alone will be held personally responsible for any debts or liabilities incurred by your business or employees. Investors are also sometimes reluctant to invest in one-man or one-woman operations. Sole proprietors often have to rely on their own savings or family loans to assist in funding.

Partnership – The simplest structure for a business with two or more owners. You can choose to open as a limited partnership, in which there will usually be one general partner with unlimited liability and control, and then limited partners with limited liability and limited control over operations. Alternatively, there is also the option of a limited liability partnership (LLP), where all partners enjoy limited liability so that no one owner is legally responsible for the actions of another (beneficial for professional practices ie: physicians or attorneys).

Pros: Zero corporate taxes, shared financial burden and decision-making support.

Cons: Shared profits, possible disagreements, shared liability (unless opened as an LLP).

Corporation or C corp – A C corp structure is considered a completely separate legal entity from its owners. This means that any debts or obligations incurred by the company are not considered personal debts of the owners, offering more protection and less risk to the shareholders' personal assets. Because a corporation is an independent entity, it will continue to exist even if a shareholder dies or sells his or her shares.

Pros: Offers the most protection from personal liability, can continue with little disturbance if a partner leaves, dies, or sells his/her shares, can raise more capital through the sale of company stocks.

Cons: Double taxation (taxed on company profit as well as dividends paid out to each shareholder), more expensive to form and operate.

S Corporation or S corp – An S corp is similar to a C corp except for the fact that it avoids the double taxation of a C corporation. Profits and some losses are allowed to be passed through to the owners' income so that owners are only taxed one time. An S corp may have up to 100 shareholders.

Pros: All the benefits of a C corp without the double taxation. Higher number of possible shareholders means more potential capital from investors.

Cons: High legal and tax service costs just like C corps, not all states recognize S corp status, must file with the IRS for official status in addition to registering with their state.

Limited Liability Company (LLC) – An LLC combines the advantages of both the corporation and partnership business structures. This is a great choice for medium to higher-risk businesses. While LLCs pay no corporate taxes, owners are considered self-employed and must pay self-employment taxes in addition to personal taxes.

Pros: Excellent personal liability protection, zero corporate taxes, unlimited shareholders (unlike S corps which are limited to 100), and full participation for each LLC member (unlike limited partnerships).

Cons: LLCs have limited life spans in certain states (the LLC may be forced to dissolve and re-form after a certain number of years, or after the death or retirement of one of the owners).

Non-profit Corporation – A non-profit corporation is a business whose mission is to benefit the greater good of the public through charitable, educational, scientific, or other contributions. The organizational rules followed by a non-profit are similar to those of a C corp.

Pros: Non-profits are exempt from federal and state taxes.

Cons: Non-profits must file separately with the IRS for tax-exemption in addition to registering with their state. Profits may not be distributed to members or political campaigns.

It is crucial to note that there are also hybrid options when it comes to structuring your business. For example, Demond and I co-own our business and we structured it as an LLC, or limited liability company. For tax purposes, however, we file as an S corp under form 2553. We are essentially a cross between the two structures which allows us to reap the benefits of both. By filing as an S corporation, we avoid the double taxation experienced by normal C corporations. Please, do your research and perhaps even consult a state agent before making a final decision.

Once you've chosen a structure that works best for you, the registration process itself will depend entirely on that structure and your location. For instance, if you operate as a sole proprietorship and conduct business using your legal name, registration is not required at all. Even so, it is still a good idea to register so that you have full access to legal and tax benefits and protections. On the other hand, be absolutely sure that you are 100% committed to your business *before* registering. Once you register a company, there's no going back. You will now have quarterly and/or annual tax obligations depending on your business structure, and you will be held accountable to the government for reporting on any revenue earned. You will receive drop-by inspections and maybe even be audited by the IRS. Some people get a business idea and then dive right in. They haven't even mixed a product much less determined viability, and yet they've already registered with the government. This is a huge no-no. You can't simply register an entity and then abandon it – there is an official process you have to go through to actually close that business down. Once you register, you are on Big Brother's radar, and the government will be seeking whatever you owe. Before you even think about becoming a legal entity, make sure you know in your heart that you are serious.

STATE REGISTRATION

For most small businesses, registration will be complete as soon as you register your business name with your state and local government. It is mandatory for LLCs, corporations, partnerships, and non-profits to register with all states in which they conduct their business. If you have a physical location within a state, employees that work within that state, or you frequently conduct in-person meetings with clients within a state, you must register. Depending on the state in question, that process may either be done online, filed through the mail, or in-person documents, and most states will require you to register with a Business Bureau, agency, or the Secretary of State's office. If you have employees, you may also need to register in order to file payroll taxes.

For all entities excluding sole proprietorships, owners are also required to have a registered agent before filing. The registered agent has to be located in your state of registration and accepts legal documents on behalf of your business. When registering, you will need to provide the information of your agent as well as your business name, location, and management/team structure.

FEDERAL REGISTRATION / EIN

Federal government registration is typically unnecessary for most small businesses, with the exception of non-profits (who must file with the IRS for tax-exempt status), and S corps. You must also file with the federal government if you wish to trademark your business, brand, or product names, which, of course, is highly recommended. At the very least, most small businesses will need to file with the IRS for a federal tax ID, also known as your Employer Identification Number (EIN).

If your business is a corporation or partnership or has even one employee on payroll, you will need to register for an EIN. The process is actually free and quite simple! After registering your business, simply access the IRS website where you can find an EIN individual request application. The online assistance tool will ask you several questions like your name, social security number, address, and DBA (or "doing business as" name) and provide you with a nine-digit federal tax ID. You will use this unique number to do everything from hiring employees to opening a bank account, paying federal taxes, and applying for business licenses and permits. Think of it as a social security number just for your business. Should your business experience any changes such as a change of name, address, ownership, or tax status, you may need to have your EIN replaced. If you operate as a sole proprietorship without employees, you will simply use your own personal social security number in place of an EIN and no registration will be required.

REGISTERING YOUR BUSINESS NAME

Once you've chosen your business structure and landed on a name you love, it's time to protect it with an official name registration. This can happen in several ways.

ENTITY NAME

First, you can register an entity name. This is the legal name of your chosen business structure and is how the state identifies your business. Registration of an entity name prevents other businesses within the same state from operating under your name. This registration typically happens simultaneously with the registration of your entity. Filing your articles of incorporation or articles of organization registers the name with the state, however, each state has its own rules.

DBA or "DOING BUSINESS AS" NAME

If you wish to open another business under your existing entity but with a different name, you'll have to file what's known as a DBA. This is also known as a fictitious name. As I mentioned earlier, my husband and I chose to organize our business Black Onyx World as an LLC. Underneath that formal entity is our DBA, Alikay Naturals.

Depending on your structure, you may or may not have to use a DBA, but it's a good idea to file anyway. Like your EIN, your DBA will enable you to open a business bank account. Also, registering DBAs or fictitious names allows you to have multiple legal brands without the additional costs, bookkeeping, and tax responsibilities that come with opening as separate entities. The more separate legal structures you own, the more expenses and obligations. Instead, registering one parent entity and several DBA names will allow you to own and operate several brands with less hassle. I myself have several fictitious names because I have several brands: Black Onyx World LLC, DBA Alikay Naturals, Black Onyx World LLC, DBA Black-Onyx77, Black Onyx World LLC, DBA Fabulously Unique Expo, etc. Even though I have multiple brands through which I conduct business, when it comes to filing taxes at the end of the year, it's all done under Black Onyx World because that is my legal entity.

As for cost, DBA or fictitious name registrations can cost anywhere from $5 to $100 – it varies according to state. The method of filing also varies, as some states will require you to fill out specific paperwork with a local or country agency while others require state agencies. Finally, it's important to note that DBA registration does not provide legal protection, meaning that there can be multiple businesses within the same state with the same DBA. If you wish to have exclusive ownership over a name for your business, brand, product, or service, you'll need to check for its availability and have it trademarked.

TRADEMARKS

Trademarking your name is the best way to ensure it cannot be used by another business. It also ensures that you are not conducting your business under someone else's trademarked name, which could result in expensive trademark infringement lawsuits for you! To be sure your name is actually available *before* you register, search the official trademark database available through the United States Patent and Trademark Office. In addition to brand names, you can trademark the names of your products, services, methods, and any other intellectual property. If your desired name is available, lock it down within your company's first year of business.

I personally recommend trademarking definitely within the first three to four months of operation, or as soon as your business starts generating revenue. Why? Believe it or not, there are people out there who will see your business making money and trademark your company name for themselves just to be malicious! They will steal the name and then charge you triple the cost just to get it back. Unfortunately, this has happened to me. It took me four years to get the trademark for my L.O.C. Method because someone challenged me for the trademark. Do yourself a favor and get your trademarks as soon as your business starts making real money.

Getting a trademark can be pricey depending on how you go about it. I recommend using a resource called LegalZoom, especially for your first trademarking experience. LegalZoom does charge a fee, but it is relatively simple and allows you to learn what the process looks like so that you can duplicate it yourself for future trademarks down the line. You can also trademark your name on your own through the United States Patent and Trademark Office website, uspto.gov. This route is fairly simple once you do your research, but be warned – you have to be very attentive and respond very quickly when dealing with the USPTO. When they send you letters, you must respond as soon as possible or your case may be dismissed. If you don't have the bandwidth either yourself or within your team to keep up with the responses in a timely fashion, this is not the option for you. If you'd rather have assistance, you can of course hire an attorney. Keep in mind that this is the most costly route and an added expense for your new business; you may want to hold off on the attorney until your company has scaled to the point where you can fit it comfortably into your budget. Whichever method you choose, don't think about how much the trademark will cost as a deterrent. Rather than thinking about what it can cost to secure a trademark, think about what it can possibly cost you if you *don't* file. Trademarks are your intellectual property and securing them is a must. Save up towards the fee if you need to – it's more than worth it.

CHOOSING A BUSINESS LOCATION

So, you've got your name, you're all registered with the state, and you are now officially a real business owner. Your next step would be finding a company office, right? Well, not necessarily. I've seen many new entrepreneurs jump into lease agreements way before they were ready, and the truth is that choosing a business location should never be taken lightly. It's a huge commitment that should be done only at the right time. For startups, there is one question, in my opinion, that you should always be asking: *how can my business generate the most revenue at the lowest cost?* This is especially important when deciding to open a physical location for your business.

USE YOUR RESOURCES

Believe it or not, I actually believe that a physical office or workspace is a luxury and not a necessity when it comes to newly formed businesses. Many times, businessowners believe they need their name on a sign or a door to appear legitimate to prospective customers and clients, when that really just isn't the case. In the beginning stages, any costs that you are spending in your business have to be justifiable, and an office space just isn't a must-have expense. I highly suggest starting off your business online or working remotely. Save on expensive office leases by working from home, cafes, or coworking spaces. Especially if you own a service-based company, you can make your business mobile and bring your services to the clients. Think outside the box. I recently met with someone to do a consulting meeting in the downstairs section of her condo building. This woman was already paying for her condo and the condo association fee – she might as well utilize the communal space for meetings. It looked very professional, and not for one minute did I feel it was less than because it wasn't a traditional office. Think smart, use what you have or what's available to you, and keep your costs low.

If you run a product-based business, the same rationale applies. I turned my apartment kitchen into a lab to mix and make my products. I used my bathroom as a filming studio for my YouTube videos. If you can, create your products at home until your business has truly taken over your space. If you find yourself not being able to keep up with demand due to lack of space or resources, that is when you should consider finding another location. On the other hand, you should also look into alternate spaces if you cannot effectively manage both work and home life in the same place. If you're not getting rest because work has taken over your home, or you're not being productive with work because you're too comfortable in your home quarters, it's time to branch out and get a physical location.

If you do choose to run your business from your home, be sure that you conduct yourself accordingly – as a legitimate business. This means keeping track of your business expenses the same way you would if you worked in an office. For example, if you're driving to and from a coffee shop to conduct in-person meetings with clients, track your mileage and gas. If you're buying those clients coffee, track those purchases. Your pens, paper, etc. – all of these are business expenses you are making to keep your company up and running, and these things are deductible, come tax-time. You can even deduct a percentage of your rent as a business expense! Let's say you have a 1,500 sq. ft. apartment or townhome and you use one of the rooms exclusively as your home office. Figure out how many square feet make up that room and divide that number by 1,500 (or the total square footage of your specific apartment). This percentage will determine your home-based business deductions. If you meet IRS qualifications, deductible items will include utilities like electricity, phone, heat and internet expenses. This can add up to major savings for you – you just have to do your research and seize the opportunities! For a complete list of possible deductions for home-based businesses and more information on whether you qualify, visit the U.S. Chamber of Commerce website, uschamber.com.

RENTING AN OFFICE OR COMMERCIAL SPACE

Once your business has scaled beyond the confines of your home or a public workspace, you may want to find a place where your business can put down roots. There are many factors that go into selecting the right location. Firstly, you'll want to start off small. Unless you've been through two or three consistent years of business, you won't really be able to anticipate the fluctuations of your revenue. You'll have little conception of what your slow seasons are going to be, or how to prepare for them. What you don't want to do is start off renting a huge commercial location that you won't be able to afford when your business experiences a dip in revenue. Start with a smaller space until you can truly assess the consistency of your income.

The same goes for your lease-agreement. You'll want to find a short-term lease – if you can, one or two years, maximum. Most commercial spaces won't take one-year contracts – two years is usually the minimum. If you can find a landlord willing to lease on a short-term basis, explain that you ultimately plan to stay longer, but you first need to test it out and make sure that the space is conducive to your future growth. People tend to get too excited and allow commercial realtors to lock them into five or six-year term agreements. Then, if their businesses aren't as consistently profitable as anticipated, they get stuck buying themselves out of their leases or run the risk of costly lawsuits.

At this point, you might be wondering if starting small is playing it too safe. After all, if the plan is to grow and scale your business, wouldn't it make more sense to go slightly larger from the beginning? In my opinion, the answer is no. While the goal of a successful company is to scale, the goal of a *new* company is to reach a point of success. Don't rush yourself. You've got time. Your primary focus right now is not worrying about how many square feet you'll need five years down the line – it's simply making consistent sales and attracting more. Keep your eyes on *right now*. The most important thing when considering a building is whether or not the space aligns with your business. Make sure the building is set up to match your operational needs. Sometimes you'll find a space and fall in love, but love isn't enough. If what you require to make and store your products is warehouse space, but your desired location is mostly office space, that isn't the best fit for you. When you settle on a location, be sure that it is as functional as it is attractive.

The next thing to consider when renting space is accessibility. How accessible is this location for you and for your customers? Think about how long your commute will be before and after work. Is the building located within an area frequented or inhabited by your core customer base? Is it nearby where they like to shop? What about parking? If you're taking in-person meetings with clients, will they have ample parking options in a safe neighborhood? All of these are things that could attract or deter people from visiting your location and ultimately giving you their business. The right office space in the wrong location will do nothing for your company. Choose wisely.

NEGOTIATE, NEGOTIATE, NEGOTIATE!

Even once you find the perfect location, don't jump into signing any contracts. Take the time to review your lease and don't be afraid to negotiate or ask for changes. If anything you read doesn't sit well with you, make your adjustments and send it back to your landlord for review. Remember, they are not awarding you a prize. This is an exchange and just as the landlord expects to receive proper payment, you should expect to receive what you want as well.

Good negotiation comes from preparation. In other words, do your research! Many people don't know that there are a lot of deals and cost-reductions that you can get when renting, as long as you know what to ask for. No landlord is going to offer up a price cut – but if you're savvy enough to know the right questions to ask, you just might save yourself a lot of money. For instance, did you know that you can often negotiate free move-in and move-out? If you're moving into a building in the middle of a month, you can also ask for part of that month's rent to be waived as well. These things are fairly normal, but if you don't ask for them, you'll never know.

The first thing you should negotiate is the length of the lease. As we learned earlier, one-to-two-year agreements are favorable for new businesses, but you should also negotiate for an option to renew. This way you will have the option to stay in your building should the space prove to be fitting for your business. Next, you should also negotiate a cap for rent increases. Landlords typically like to boost up the rent every year. By establishing an increase cap at the beginning, you can ensure that your commercial space remains within your budget. You'll also want to ask for favorable clauses to be included in the agreement. These can include anything from permission to display your business' sign in or around the building, to a clause preventing your landlord from renting out to a similar or competing business.

Some things are not up for negotiation, but you can at least make yourself aware so that you don't sign anything that works against you. For instance, you always want to ask about the CAM, or common area maintenance fee. This is also known as a care and maintenance fee and is a charge paid by tenants to commercial landlords to cover the costs of maintaining common areas that will likely impact the tenants' businesses. These costs can include elevator, staircase, hallway, lobby, or parking lot maintenance among other things. In some commercial listings, the rent includes the CAM fee but in others, it does not. Many people will sign a lease thinking they're paying based only on the square footage, and then receive a higher charge to cover the additional CAM fee. For example, a friend of mine signed a lease for $1,200 a month. It wasn't until she had already gotten out of her previous lease and prepared to switch locations that she learned her rent did not include the $1.50 per square foot CAM fee. The additional charge ended up boosting her rent to between $2,000 and $2,500 a month – this was not something she could afford and so, I had to help her negotiate after the fact. Had she known to ask whether the CAM was included in the rent beforehand, she might never have signed the lease.

It all goes back to the importance of asking questions. When you rent a commercial space, there are certain responsibilities that you have as the tenant that you need to make yourself aware of. For instance, it is the tenant's responsibility – not the landlord's – to make sure that the fire extinguisher receives maintenance. If you don't, it is considered a violation of your building code and you are susceptible to a fine. Another example is lawn or garbage service. In some places, garbage bins come included with your rental. This is not always the case. In two out of the three commercial spaces that I've rented, garbage services were not included, and disposal became an additional cost to me and my husband. We had to pay the city a monthly fee to actually put a garbage and recycling bin outside and to have pick-up service on trash day. When we were starting out all bright-eyed and bushy-tailed, we didn't know any of this. When we finally found out, we couldn't afford the almost $200 a month for the city to dispose of our trash. My grandparents would actually volunteer to pack up our garbage every day and take it home with them to throw away. The moral of the story is that you must do your research and be your own biggest advocate.

PROTECT YOURSELF!

Finally, remember that renting can be a tricky business with some unsavory characters. You'll find landlords who will try to scam you out of money or blame you for damages that aren't even your fault. Always be proactive and make sure that you protect yourself from possible lawsuits and false claims. For starters, make sure that you document any and all agreements between yourself and your landlord, and always capture as many photos and videos of every inch of your rented space upon move-in and move-out.

This is a lesson that Demond and I had to learn the hard way. When we moved into our very first commercial space and the landlord gave us the tour, we noticed a lot of things that were less than ideal, to say the least. Dented warehouse doors, missing blinds, scratched paint – still, we were so young and hungry to grow our business that we didn't ask any questions. We figured the damages were negligible and that we could make it work – and we did! For months we manually opened and closed the warehouse door that was supposed to have been automatic. We bought paint and painted the walls ourselves, not knowing that commercial units are supposed to be painted every single time a new tenant moves in. We should have asked the landlord to paint, or to give us a paint credit in exchange for a discount on rent. Hindsight is always 20/20.

Anyway, two years later, when it was time for us to move out, the landlord claimed that there were a million things wrong with the space and that *we* had caused them. In reality, we had actually left the space in better condition than it was when we moved in, but because we took no photos or videos, we had zero proof. The landlord ended up suing us for damages! Not only did we end up paying to fix that broken warehouse door, but we also had to pay a huge fine to fix ceiling and wall issues. All of this was after being dragged through court for six months, and we also incurred legal fees from hiring our own attorney to defend us. All in all, we lost *a lot* of money.

All of this is to say, do your research, ask the right questions, and document *everything*. Do a walk-through when you move in and take a photo and video of every wall, closet, and corner. Also send any concerns that you have in an email (not a phone call or text message) to your landlord. Tell them that you've notated all concerns with the rented space, and that you want to give them the chance to document and address them as well. Store all photos, videos, and email exchange proof somewhere in your Google drive in a legal folder. This way, you'll have access to everything you need should any issues arise. If ever you are unsure of your obligations as a tenant or need assistance negotiating terms for a commercial lease, be sure to utilize resources like LegalZoom or consult a lawyer. We'll talk about finding the right legal team a little later on.

There is an old Jamaican proverb I love that speaks to the power of protecting yourself:

Di more monkey climb, di more im backside expose.

Translation: The higher the monkey climbs, the more he is exposed. As an entrepreneur – especially as you become more and more successful – there will be more eyes on you than you will even be aware of. Be sure to cover all your bases and put all the proper protections in place so that you won't be vulnerable or fall victim to those who envy or covet your success.

OBTAINING BUSINESS PERMITS and LICENSES

Landing an awesome space for your business also means keeping it up to code. Once you start a new business, you will need to file with your county, city, or state government for any necessary permits and licenses. The permits and licenses mandatory for your business will depend on your location as well as your industry, but the most important thing to know is that it is *your* responsibility to find out everything you need. Ignorance is not an excuse, and if you are found to be in non-compliance with any of the necessary regulations, you can end up receiving a crazy fine or worse, losing your business altogether!

Do your due diligence. You can go down to the offices of your city or state departments and find out everything you need to bring your building or office up to code. Another option is SCORE, a non-profit organization which provides tons of amazing resources to new and aspiring business owners. Search the location of your nearest SCORE office and speak to a representative who can get you started compiling the appropriate licensing information for your company. While you should conduct your own search for niche industry mandates, here are some of the most commonly required business permits and licenses:

Municipal or local licenses and permits - Whether you rent a commercial workspace or work from home, you will need to obtain a business license with your city. Business licenses must be renewed annually and typically range from $50 to several hundreds. To learn the exact requirements for your business, visit your city's website.

State licenses and permits – Some businesses may need a state license in addition to their local license. This usually applies to businesses that sell products or services which are regulated by state laws. Some such professions and businesses include attorneys, dentists, realtors, hairdressers, aestheticians, mechanics, and general contractors. Restaurants, food trucks, and businesses that sell alcohol will also require state licenses and permits. To view the specific licensing information for your state, visit the SBA website.

Federal business licenses – Federal licenses are only required for those small businesses whose industries are regulated by the federal government. Examples include the transportation, radio or television broadcasting, food and beverage manufacturing, agriculture, or firearms industries. Visit the SBA site for more details on federal licensing.

Regulations will also depend on the type of location. For instance, warehouses have different requirements than typical office spaces. Many times, businesses will scale and move into larger facilities or buy new pieces of equipment and forget that there are now extra permits that they have to secure. While it may seem like a hassle to constantly keep up with new laws, many of these permit regulations are put in place to protect the wellbeing of employees and everyone in the workplace. To ensure a safe work environment, every business must be in compliance with OSHA, the Occupational Safety and Health Administration. OSHA even provides an internet-accessible handbook for small business owners on the standard workplace requirements. This handbook will not only go over specific do's and don'ts, but it will inform business owners of information that they must prominently display within the workplace.

Keep in mind that state and federal regulations are constantly changing. You or someone within your operation need to stay up to date with the latest requirements, or you can hire someone to do it for you. Nowadays, you can hire consultants for a reasonable price to come and make sure your business is up to code. These consultants are typically people who used to work as government inspectors and have since retired. They will have the breadth of experience and knowledge to spot minor violations so that you can get everything up to proper operational standards.

FINANCING YOUR BUSINESS

At last, we've come to what some people consider the most daunting aspect of starting a new business: funding. There are multiple ways to finance your company, but all of these ways essentially fall into one of two categories – raising funds or self-funding. Many, if not most new entrepreneurs, take the first route; as collecting capital from one or more outside sources takes some of the financial burden off the shoulders of the founder. By accepting financial assistance, you can focus your efforts on company operations and creative development, thereby getting your business up on its legs and expediting the startup process. Now, let's discuss the most common methods of financing a new business.

BANK LOANS

Borrowing money from banks is one of the most traditional methods of raising large amounts of money. Like students taking out loans for school, entrepreneurs take out loans to start their businesses. The difference is that entrepreneurs must woo the bank with a solid business plan that shows a concrete plan of action. Many banks now offer funds specifically for small business lending, but securing a bank loan may still prove difficult depending on your idea, desired area of operation, credit history, and even demographics like race and gender.

SBA LOANS

Should your bank loan application be denied, you can apply for a loan from the U.S. Small Business Administration (SBA). SBA loans are available to any small business as long as you meet the qualifications. For one, you must have proof that you have applied for a bank loan and been unsuccessful. The SBA won't grant a loan to a company that has the ability to get the money on its own. Secondly, the SBA has to officially consider you a small business according to the criteria of your specific industry.

MICROLOANS

Banks and government institutions like the SBA often loan significant amounts of money, and as such, they need to be sure that their applicants are sound investments. This means that they look for those with a good credit history, or at least enough valuable collateral to put up should their businesses prove unsuccessful. If you have neither, you can instead apply for a microloan from a non-profit organization called a microlender. These small business loans are typically anywhere from $500 to $35,000, which is less than your typical big bank loan. As a result, microlenders generally demand less documentation and offer more flexible criteria for loan recipients. The downside? Microloans usually come with higher interest rates. This is a good option for those entrepreneurs who have proven success and revenue, but are maybe experiencing a period where they just need a little boost.

ANGEL INVESTORS and VENTURE CAPITALISTS

Angel investors and venture capitalists are both people who invest their own money into new business startups, but the two groups are slightly different. Angel investors or business angels are wealthy individuals who invest their personal money into companies in exchange for a percentage of ownership, or equity stake. An angel's main purpose is to provide financial contribution, not leadership. They usually have little involvement in the actual operations of a business, but involvement of course will depend on the angel-owner relationship in question.

Alternatively, venture capitalists usually work in a firm or a collection of wealthy individuals, corporations, foundations, etc. As there are more investors pooling their capital, venture capitalists typically invest larger sums of money than single business angels. In addition to more money, venture capitalists also have much more say or involvement. They actually become limited partners and can help a company grow through advice and recruitment of senior management. They make themselves available to the company's C.E.O to discuss ideas for strategy and development, and ultimately help steer the company to ensure the long-term success of their investment. Both angel investors and venture capitalists typically invest in innovative fields, often preferring tech and science companies.

CROWDFUNDING

Next up, we have crowdfunding – a means of raising and pooling small amounts of money from multiple people on the internet. Because crowdfunding websites pull their investors from the general public, this method is best for gathering smaller sums to fund projects or one-off ventures as opposed to the startup costs of a new business. Still, these funds can go a long way to things like permits, licenses, and registration fees, or the purchasing of materials for products. It's as simple as posting your crowdfunding link to your website or social media platforms. While your funders may not have thousands to contribute, the small contributions from a vastly larger audience of potential investors can really add up.

FRIEND and FAMILY LOANS

Finally, there is the option of borrowing money from friends and family. These are the people closest to you and so they likely see your potential. Loved ones likely won't make you jump through hoops like banks or investors, however, money can be a sensitive subject or even a source of turmoil. To avoid risking relationships, treat your family members as you would treat formal investors. Present a business plan and a timeline in which you plan to repay their funds. Also, apprise them of the risks so they have all the information upfront. You never want to take their generosity for granted and risk losing a meaningful relationship over miscommunication.

These are just the basics of some of the most common methods of fundraising. If you do choose to seek outside funding, understand that you are accountable to your investors. They've taken a chance on you and your vision, so do not take that lightly. Also, borrowing other people's money means higher stakes. Not only are your dreams and finances riding on the success of your company, but theirs are as well. While outside funding is an extremely popular route, it is not the only option. You can choose to self-fund through a number of ways.

CREDIT CARDS

First, you can finance your business with a credit card. Yes, this is as risky as it sounds, because if your business does not generate enough revenue and you miss payments, your credit score goes down the drain. Credit cards also come with ridiculous interest rates and penalties that can leave you with a mountain of debt. Still, credit cards are way more accessible to the average person than an angel investment or bank loan. You don't have to present a business plan or do a bunch of paperwork to get started making purchases for your business – the purchasing power is right in your pocket. In fact, according to a survey by the National Small Business Association, a whopping 50% of all small businesses choose credit cards to finance their startup or expansion costs, while only 6% used an SBA loan and 2% used venture capital funds. If you do choose to finance with a credit card, be sure to use separate cards for your business and personal expenses. The interest on things charged to your business card is deductible come tax time. Be smart. While you may not be accountable to a bank or a board of venture capitalists, you will have to own up to your spending sooner or later.

BOOTSTRAPPING

Finally, we've arrived at bootstrapping. This is the method that Demond and I used to finance our largest business, Alikay Naturals. Bootstrapping is a method of using one's own savings and/or profits generated by the company to fuel the company's operation and expansion. Bootstrapped companies receive no large sources of funding from outside investors, and so depend entirely on attracting regular customers and making consistent sales to sustain themselves.

To get off the ground floor, the C.E.Os of bootstrapped businesses have a few options:

Bootstrapping Option #1: Recycle your profits.

Starting with a small amount of revenue, you can take that money and put it into your business. That startup money can be from your savings, an extra shift, or perhaps an initial friends and family round of small-level borrowing. Once that money is spent to launch your operations, you will use the profits generated from your sales to feed your business. Basically, you are recycling your business' money back into itself over and over again.

This is how I started Alikay Naturals. With just $100 in tips from a shift at Olive Garden, it was that money – and only that money – that went into getting my business off the ground. Any income that Demond and I made from our multiple college jobs went toward paying the bills, paying for tuition, and feeding ourselves – not feeding the company. By the same token, neither of us took a salary or pocket money from the Alikay profits. We treated our company's income as its own entity; completely separate from our personal earnings.

Bootstrapping Option #2: Use your tax refund.

Another option is to use your full tax refund to fund your startup costs. Think about it. Your income tax refund is not typically money that you are absolutely counting on to maintain your everyday expenses or quality of life. Many people squander their refunds on a spur of the moment gift or a treat-yourself-purchase, when they could really set that money aside to launch their business. If you choose this option, however, make sure you have your business planned out in advance. Get everything ready so that you can hit the ground running when your tax refund arrives.

Bootstrapping Option #3: Make your "work" work for you.

Another very popular method of bootstrapping is to use your nine to five to fund your business. Whether you pick up overtime hours to generate extra money, or simply save a percentage of your income every month or every two weeks when you get paid, set that money aside for your business fund. By saving just 25% of each paycheck, you'll be amazed at how much money you can save up over time.

Bootstrapping Option #4: Start a side-hustle.

Lastly, consider starting and promoting a side-hustle to earn the money to fund your business. This hustle can be driving for Uber, selling home-cooked meals, cleaning, hairstyling, babysitting, or frankly, whatever it is that you are good enough at for people to pay you for. If no hobby or skill comes to mind, consider consulting or offering services for whatever you already do at your nine to five. For example, if you work as a copywriter, you can offer copywriting services on the side to make extra money.

Whichever way you go, bootstrapping is synonymous with hustle and must be done strategically. While there is nothing easy about starting a company from nothing, I wouldn't change my journey for anything in the world.

There are several benefits to bootstrapping that I believe make it one of the best options for financing a business. First, when you fund your business yourself, it gives you a great amount of clarity as to the viability of your business. There is no investor rescue fund coming to bail you out, so you can clearly see how much money is really coming in and going out. Use this opportunity to see if your idea or business model has legs before getting yourself in deeper. Second, bootstrapping forces an entrepreneur to be resourceful and learn how to truly budget. When you start with a large amount of outside funding, it's almost like being a rich kid with a hefty allowance. You don't learn how to truly stretch your dollar because it's not your own dollar being spent. You've gone from having next to nothing to having a pile of thousands or even millions of dollars in capital handed to you. Oftentimes, companies that start off with huge investments don't even have a proper structure, process, or flow. They've never known the struggle and so they don't build the same savvy for figuring things out as a bootstrapping entrepreneur. Sure, they still have to answer to their investors, but still, funding can sometimes be a cushion that makes C.E.Os lazy or at the least, prevents them from operating at their highest capacity.

With bootstrapping, that is simply not an option. You literally live or die by your own hustle. You figure out how to keep the lights on, put food on the table, and make payroll by the skin of your own teeth. Bootstrapping is not for the faint of heart and will show you what you're truly made of. Your competition might be doing things on a large scale because they have outside funding. Look at what they are doing and ask yourself, *how can I do the same thing, but on a smaller scale?* Bootstrapping weeds out the entrepreneurs that aren't fully committed to their visions, and those lacking the grit and guts to keep going. You can't be fazed by a slow season or all the scary statistics about failing new businesses. You have to put your blinders on and keep your eyes locked only on profits. You may be the last person in your company to take a paycheck, but you'll make sure that everyone else on board gets fed. You'll understand that profits are meant to scale your business, not your personal lifestyle. Your dream houses, designer labels, and first-class flights can wait. Everything you do, think, or breathe is about growing the business.

If you're starting a high-cost business, like in the tech industry, for example, it might not make sense to bootstrap. Tech software is very expensive to create and develop, and you might do better starting off with some kind of outside investment. If that's not the case, I highly recommend starting off bootstrapping on your own for as long as you can. At least one to three years of self-funding can make all the difference. When it's your own money on the line, you'll push and grind to make it work by any means necessary. Even so, it's impossible to bootstrap forever. After ten years of growth, Demond and I are finally beginning to consider outside investors. We've done what we could on our own, but if we want to scale, Alikay Naturals is going to need a major infusion of cash from the right investors. Still, we wouldn't have made it to this point without our bootstrapping experience.

MONEY MANAGEMENT

Just as important as acquiring money to finance your business is the actual management of your money. The average person is not as financially-literate as they should be, however for entrepreneurs, it's a must. Not only are you managing your personal finances, but you now have to also manage the income, expenses, and taxes of your business. Many entrepreneurs choose to open a business bank account. While not always immediately necessary, a business bank account offers many benefits and is highly recommended once your company starts making consistent money.

It actually took my husband and I quite some time to open a business bank account. For the first two years of our business, we operated out of PayPal. We had our debit card attached to the PayPal account so that we could make our purchases, but in the long run, it proved to be a pain. Not only did it make accounting and bookkeeping more complicated, but PayPal also carried unnecessarily high ecommerce processing fees. Once we opened a business bank account, we were exposed to a bunch of benefits that helped propel our business forward.

BUSINESS BANK ACCOUNTS

While online payment systems like PayPal are amazing resources, opening a business bank account is the best and most secure way to track and manage company finances. Business bank accounts allow you to physically separate your company funds from your personal funds, making it much easier to work with customers and vendors, as well as simplifying the tax filing process at the end of the year. You are eligible to open a business account as soon as you receive your federal tax ID or EIN (employer identification number). The process is fairly simple. All you have to do is visit your bank online or go to a local branch. In addition to your EIN, you'll typically need to present your business' license and formation documents. It is also important to note that business bank accounts are *mandatory* for any incorporated businesses. This means that if you structured your entity as a corporation, S corp, LLC, or incorporated sole proprietorship, you must have a separate account for your company by law.

I understand, the allure of mobile payment services like PayPal, Cash App, and Venmo is strong. They're quick, easy, and almost everyone uses them. One of the important things about having a business bank account, however, is that it ensures you are running your business the way you are supposed to. It's more professional, more stable, and more secure for both you and your customers. What if you build your business around Venmo and then the app falls into obscurity one day? These are the things you need to think about. I recently went to a clothing boutique to support a small business owner, but the owner did not even have a terminal set up to collect payment. She had no business bank account and was instead asking her customers to Cash App her the money for their purchases. These things reflect poorly upon you as a company and are also ineffective where it counts. Sure, you'll receive payments, but these apps can't break your business into the necessary accounts. They can't be synced to QuickBooks or other accounting software programs to track your records for taxes. Always think beyond the moment and prioritize the long-term structure of your business.

Benefits of a business bank account:

Security – Business accounts provide you with limited liability protection by separating your company and personal funds. They also protect your customers by keeping their personal information private and secure when they make a purchase.

IRS protection – Every business runs the chance of being audited by the IRS. While you of course hope that doesn't happen, business bank accounts provide excellent records of company spending in the case of an audit. The IRS also distinguishes between hobbies and businesses. Having a business account helps to prove that you are indeed a legitimate business. Keep track of all of your expense receipts and invoices and you should be okay.

Professional appearance – Having a business bank account lends you an air of professionalism that you can't fully get on your own. Customers and vendors will now be able to write checks addressed directly to your business instead of your personal name, which makes them feel more comfortable in your legitimacy. Furthermore, with a business account you will be able to hire employees to conduct business or make purchases on behalf of your company without giving your personal credit card information.

Purchasing power – Finally, you can open a line of credit or get a business credit card allowing you to handle emergencies or make larger purchases for your business, like new equipment.

There are several types of business accounts that you can open, the most common being checking accounts, credit card accounts, merchant accounts, and savings accounts. I personally recommend starting out with three: a merchant account (where all your money comes in – purchases from customers, vendors, and retailers), an operations account (from which you conduct all business spending), and a savings account (where you put aside money for taxes and/or a rainy day). As we discussed back in chapter six, "Top Nots," having different business accounts allows you to carefully track your money so that you have no doubt about where each dollar is going in and coming out. Not only is this great for records, but it's also helpful in detecting abnormalities. When you have all purchases tracked in a separate account from income, you can clearly see if unapproved purchases are being made, or worse, if money is being stolen from the company.

As for choosing a bank, consider whether you will be better off with a small local bank or a larger national chain. Both options have their pros and cons. For instance, not all local banks are available nationally. This can be a problem if you tend to travel for your business. The bank Demond and I started out with was a Florida-based bank, and while they carried amazing fees for small businesses, we didn't realize that they weren't nationally accessible. When we went to the Carolinas for a trade show, we could not go into a bank and take out money without an extra charge. Larger national chains won't usually have this issue, however, they may not offer the personalized service of a smaller bank. These are all things to consider.

Finally, banks often provide the option to be reimbursed for your overdraft fees. As a small business just finding its legs, there will likely be times when you get hit with an overdraft charge or two, and those can really add up! Don't be afraid to pick up your phone to call your bank and see if they might waive or reimburse your fees. I like to check in every six months or so. You never know! Don't let money just sit on the table because you were too proud or lazy to ask.

ACCOUNTING and BOOKKEEPING

Because the income and spending habits of a business are usually way more complex than those of an individual person, many entrepreneurs turn to the services of bookkeepers, accountants, and CPAs (certified public accountants) to help them track, understand, and improve their business finances. For bootstrapping businesses, however, there are several reputable accounting software services available online to help cash-strapped entrepreneurs manage their money themselves.

QuickBooks is an accounting software program designed specifically for small-to-medium sized businesses. Not only is it my number one recommendation, but it is also an industry standard. That is to say that once your business scales and you decide to outsource management to a professional, every accountant and bookkeeper out there will have a thorough understanding of QuickBooks and how it works. This will make the process that much easier to hand off in the future. With accounting software systems, you can do everything from tracking income and expenses to sending and accepting invoices; paying bills and employees to generating reports for tax-filing purposes. When handling your own books, be sure to stay on top of things. I recommend sitting down and looking at your expenses once a week, or at the very least, once a month.

If you'd rather outsource and you have the budget to do so, hire a bookkeeper and/or an accountant. While both professions deal with money management, they have slightly different responsibilities. A bookkeeper is someone who tracks and manages the daily financial operations within your business. They generally save all expense receipts and invoices and record transactions in programs such as QuickBooks (another alternative is FreshBooks). Accountants and CPAs, on the other hand, analyze data prepared by bookkeepers to provide broader advice and guidance on how to improve the overall financial health of your business. Accountants will handle income tax planning and prepare any financial reports and statements for banks and government review. When you need input on tax law, switching your business structure or entity, or other big money decisions, your accountant is your best friend.

In the early days of Alikay Naturals, Demond handled all of our bookkeeping so that we could keep our costs low. We then upgraded to our first CPA, who I privately studied for all her knowledge and expertise. The thing with money management is that even if you hand it over to a professional, you need to have your own baseline understanding. This will prevent shady people from misleading or stealing from you. It'll also improve your discernment when it comes to deciding how to spend money. When our CPA would file our taxes, I would be right there over her shoulder asking questions. If she put a certain number at a certain line, I needed to know why. When she sent in our paperwork, I asked to be included on the emails so that I would see the IRS response. Always make sure that you are part of the process, even if you're just peeking from the window.

TAXES

Having a CPA makes filing your small business taxes so much more manageable, but I will give you the basics. First, it's important to know that the type of taxes you will file depends on what business structure you have. Your legal structure or entity will determine what you pay, which forms you file, and when and how you submit. Remember, proper tax filing is a critical part of entrepreneurship. Fail to comply with state and federal tax laws and risk losing money, personal assets like your car or home, and possibly even your business altogether. Don't mess with the IRS and don't rely solely on the information provided in this or any other book. Do your due diligence, conduct thorough research, and consult with a professional. The IRS even provides a virtual workshop with video tutorials on small business taxes and tons of other educational articles on their website. For now, I will leave you with seven business tax terms you should be aware of: income tax, estimated tax, self-employment tax, employment tax, excise tax, sales and use tax, and unemployment tax.

Income tax: Just like individuals, businesses must also pay income tax. This is a yearly tax on your business' net income. Depending on your business entity, you may be able to report and pay business taxes on your personal income tax return. This is called pass-through tax. If you have employees, you are responsible for withholding income tax from their wages based on the W-4 form that they submit upon hire (and any subsequent changes to their filing status).

Estimated tax: You will be required to pay estimated taxes if you do not pay enough taxes throughout the year. As many new business owners don't take a salary from their companies, they don't get a paycheck, and so no money is withheld for income taxes. As a result, they must pay quarterly estimated taxes to make up for the money that would usually be withheld. Failure to pay sufficient estimated taxes can result in major penalties.

Self-employment tax: Business owners pay self-employment or SECA (Self-Employment Contributions Act) taxes to contribute to Social Security and Medicare. This tax is 15.3% of the net business income (12.4% for Social Security and 2.9% for Medicare), and so the amount owed will vary from year to year depending on profits.

Employment tax: Employment taxes include income taxes, FICA taxes, workers' compensation taxes, unemployment taxes, self-employment taxes and any and all other taxes that must be paid to federal, state, and local agencies. Some of these taxes will simply be withheld from employee wages (federal and state income withholding). Others will fall solely on the shoulders of the employer or business owner (like unemployment and workers' comp – more on these in chapter ten), while some others will be shared by the employer and the employee (like FICA, which goes toward Social Security and Medicare, similar to the self-employment tax).

Excise tax: Depending on your industry and the specific type of products your business sells, you might have to pay quarterly excise taxes. For example, cigarettes, liquor, and gasoline are all subject to excise taxes, and the taxes are usually built in to the price of the product itself. IRS Publication 510 will give you a comprehensive list of all products that are subject to excise tax.

Sales and use tax: Sales tax is a tax that gets added on top of the sales price of your product or service and is charged to the customer at the time of purchase. Different states have different regulations, so you must find out which products and services are taxable in your specific state. Most states do not tax the sale of food, digital downloads of music, games, and books, and prescribed medications. Most states also do not tax goods that are purchased for resale. If your business buys products to be resold or reused in any way – let's say you buy t-shirts from a vendor to resell to your customers – you must get a resale certificate to avoid double taxation on that product. In these instances, you would show your resale certificate to your vendors and they will not charge you a sales tax because they know you are already collecting sales tax on those items from your customers. As a business owner, it is your duty to calculate, collect, and send your collected sales taxes to the proper tax authorities. Use tax, on the other hand, is a tax that the buyer must pay only if no sales tax was collected when a taxable product or service was purchased. It is the buyer's responsibility to calculate, report, and turn over owed use taxes.

Unemployment tax: Employers must pay federal unemployment (FUTA) taxes to contribute towards benefits for workers who lose their jobs. Many states also have their own unemployment taxes, and both state and federal unemployment taxes must be paid solely by the employer (these are not withheld from employee paychecks). If you do not pay your unemployment tax, there can be big trouble if a terminated employee files a claim against your company.

As stated earlier, the information provided here is just the tip of the iceberg. Tax regulations are often subject to change and vary from state to state. It is your responsibility as a business owner to know and abide by all federal, state, and local tax law, which is why I highly recommend consulting an attorney or law professional for the most up-to-date information. You can pay several of these taxes through your payroll processor if they offer the service, but every C.E.O should still have a solid baseline understanding of the way his or her business taxes work for peace of mind and proper legal protection.

Taxes are of course simplest for sole proprietorships because they are owned and operated by an individual. For sole proprietors, business and personal income will both be reported on the personal income tax return at the same rate. There is no need to file business taxes separately. Additionally, sole proprietors pay a self-employment tax to contribute toward social security and Medicare. This is done through quarterly estimated taxes. Estimated taxes are how all businesses pay their Social Security, Medicare, and income taxes and are typically withheld from employee paychecks.

Partners or co-owners of a partnership must pay income taxes, self-employment taxes, and quarterly estimated taxes, but the business itself doesn't pay. These taxes are passed through to the owners themselves, so there is no corporate tax. Each owner of the partnership must report their individual share of the company's profits and losses on their personal tax returns.

C corporations work a bit differently. Remember that C corps are considered legally separate from their owners. As a result, C corporations experience double taxation. First, the corporation itself has a flat income tax rate. Then, the owners or shareholders get taxed on their personal tax returns after company profits are distributed as dividends. Shareholders who actively participate in work or operations are considered employees and must pay a self-employment tax. Dividends, on the other hand, receive a different tax rate. C corporations pay estimated taxes on a quarterly basis.

S corporations also experience pass-through taxation like sole proprietorships and partnerships. The S corp itself pays no corporate tax, however the business must file what is called an informational tax return. Unlike C corps, S corps are not double-taxed, but both structures pay quarterly estimated taxes. Also like a C corp, S corporations have the option to divide business income between salary, which is subject to self-employment taxes, and dividends, which are not.

Finally, the owners of LLCs or limited liability companies receive the benefits of both corporations and sole proprietorships or partnerships. LLC owners get liability protection like a corporation, but also come with more flexibility than other structures. While they can legally exist as an LLC, they also have the option to file taxes as an S-corp or C-corp. I personally choose to file my LLC as an S corp because that allows me to avoid the double-taxation.

To learn more in depth about the different types of taxes and which taxes in particular your business will have to file, contact a CPA or visit the IRS website for more detailed information.

OBTAINING BUSINESS INSURANCE

Another important aspect of starting a new business is obtaining the right type of insurance to protect your company and assets. Structures like LLCs or corporations do offer some protections, but these are usually limited to your personal property. In the case of lawsuits or unexpected occurrences like natural disasters, having business insurance will make sure your business assets are also protected.

COMMON TYPES OF BUSINESS INSURANCE

Certain types of insurance are required by law if your business has employees. These include workers compensation, disability, and unemployment insurance. For other types, it's up to you to decide what you need protected. Below are some of the most common types of insurance for businesses and what they cover:

General liability insurance – General liability insurance is for any entity and protects against financial loss due to property age, bodily harm or injury, slander, libel, medical expenses, and settlements.

Product liability insurance – This type of insurance is specifically for businesses that manufacture, wholesale, distribute, and retail a product or products. This covers financial loss that comes as a result of a defective product which causes injury.

Professional liability insurance – Professional liability insurance protects against financial losses due to negligence, malpractice, and other errors and is available to service-based businesses.

Commercial property insurance – Businesses that own and operate lots of property or physical assets will want to pursue commercial property insurance to cover damage or loss of property due to accidents like fires, severe weather conditions like hail and wind storms, and vandalism or civil disobedience.

Home-based business insurance – This insurance is only for those businesses which operate out of the owner's personal residence. Home-based business insurance gets added to homeowner's insurance.

Business owner's policies – Most small business owners and especially home-based owners qualify for a business owner's policy. This policy is an insurance package that groups all the above options into a bundle to save money and simplify the process.

Workers' compensation insurance – Workers' compensation provides proper medical benefits and wages in the event that an employee is injured on the job. This insurance is mandatory by law once you hire a certain number of employees. The number of employees varies depending on your state, and you must pay workers' compensation for each employee. In the state of Florida where my business is located, workers' compensation is mandatory once you have four or more employees.

Just like with taxes, it is critical that you do your research on business insurance. While some are optional, others are required by law and failure to comply can leave you susceptible to legal troubles and huge fines. For example, in the early days of my business, my husband and I were not adequately informed on insurance law. We thought that workers' comp was optional, and because we had eight employees at the time, we were in breach of Florida state protocol. We ended up receiving an insane fine of $13,000, which is a huge blow to any business, let alone a budding new company. We had to pay back pay for all the employees on staff for the duration of the time period we went without having proper insurance. It was a hard lesson to learn – one I want other business owners to avoid! Now, we use Automatic Data Processing, Inc. (ADP) to process our payroll, and they cover workers' compensation insurance for us in exchange for an additional fee every payroll processing period.

If you are unsure as to which type or types of insurance you need, visit the National Federation of Independent Business (NFIB) website to asses which risks your business is most likely to face. Next, search for a trustworthy commercial insurance agent. An agent will help you find and decide on a policy, but keep in mind that they work on commissions from insurance companies. Use your discernment and always get more than one opinion. Talk to different agents to compare rates, terms, and benefits for the best deal. Lastly, remember to update your insurance policy as your business scales. When you grow and acquire new, more expensive spaces and/or equipment, you will want to reevaluate your coverage.

BUILDING A LEGAL TEAM

With virtually all your time, money, energy, and resources on the line – not to mention that of your partners, employees, and investors – new business owners should always prioritize building a solid legal team. The thought of hiring lawyers or attorneys terrifies many fresh C.E.Os because all they see are dollar signs. Many people think that legal professionals have to be hired on a monthly retainer and they will have to pay exorbitant rates, and that's just not true. The truth is, when you're just starting out in your business, you can simply reach out and secure legal services as needed.

As budding entrepreneurs ten years ago, hiring a long-term lawyer just was not realistic for me and my husband. Instead, we received referrals from friends and entrepreneurial peers for independent attorneys. It's as simple as asking your network for reputable names. Referrals are usually not a conflict of interest as long as the people referring you are not your competitors. Additionally, be sure *never* to accept a referral from someone with whom you are doing business or signing contracts. You may think the suggestion is innocent and helpful, however, you never know the allegiances and loyalties that people have. You don't want to be referred to an attorney who will have you sign contracts that are not in your best interests.

Anyway, because we worked with smaller, independent attorneys rather than huge firms, we received personalized care and attention. Many times, larger firms have so many huge clients that the needs of their small business clientele fly quietly under the radar. Also, independent attorneys now offer all kinds of affordable templates for contracts. Rather than paying for a pricey consultation or ongoing monthly fee, you can simply pay an attorney one time to sit down and write you a really strong contract that you can then modify on your own. Many of your contractual needs will repeat themselves as you onboard employees or work with vendors and suppliers. Even if you only contact this lawyer every once in a while, at least you have gotten their information and established yourself as a client. This means that should you need their services in the future, you already have a name in your Rolodex to call and you know what rates to expect. This is extremely critical when you find yourself needing legal assistance in a pinch. If you wait to build a team until you're already being sued, you'll be searching for reputable options in a complete panic.

Another benefit to using independent attorneys is that a lot of the time, different attorneys have different specialties. In fact, Demond and I now have three or four separate lawyers for separate purposes within our company. We have a general business attorney, a contract attorney, an IP attorney (to handle all things pertaining to Alikay's intellectual properties – trademarks, patents, designs, etc.), and a legal registration and processes attorney (to handle all things related to the FDA). Even as a very successful business, we are not paying all of these attorneys simultaneously – remember, we are still a bootstrapped business and we don't spend on anything that's not absolutely vital.

NON-DISCLOSURE AGREEMENTS and NON-COMPETE CLAUSES

One area where a strong legal team is crucial is in the formation of NDAs, or non-disclosure agreements and non-compete clauses. NDAs and non-competes are business contracts written up to protect the trade secrets and tactics of the business, and the confidential information of both parties. Companies typically have all employees, consultants, and contractors sign both contracts upon initiation of the working relationship. With non-compete clauses, employees agree not to enter into competition with the company in any way, even after the employment period is over. Whether they resign or are let go, former employees that have signed a non-compete are not legally allowed to start or work for a competing business for a period of time designated within the contract. The terms may also prevent the employee from seeking conflicting employment within a certain geographic location. The employee is also not allowed to discuss any of their former employer's business dealings, relationships, or information pertaining to formulas, products, and operations.

An NDA – also known as a confidentiality agreement – is more mutual in nature. Non-disclosure agreements exist to protect the confidentiality of *both* parties. If two businesses enter into a negotiation – let's say, your company and a vendor, for instance – both parties will be protected under the NDA. Neither party is permitted to disclose the information shared between them. This is called a mutual non-disclosure. When employees sign NDAs, this is known as a non-mutual agreement as the employee is the only party signing.

While these are standard agreements for new employees, it's a little different with contractors or freelancers. While you can have them sign a non-disclosure to protect your company's private information, it's rarer that you'll get a contractor or independent worker to sign a non-compete. Typically, contractors are in an industry where they might technically also be working with your competitors. You can't prevent that, but you can at least prevent them from publicizing your specific trade secrets.

Never feel awkward or uncomfortable asking someone to sign a confidentiality agreement, or being asked to sign one yourself. It's all business – nothing personal. These kinds of contracts are vital to protecting your company's assets and making sure that there are no ulterior motives on your team. Think that sounds dramatic? Think again. I've actually had a former employee try to steal one of my products and sell it for herself. Employees have behind-the-scenes access to sensitive information that can make or break your company, or disrupt your place in the market. Envy, greed, and resentment can push people to do some nasty things, and should that ever happen, you want to be legally equipped to shut it down or seek proper compensation.

Even with legal protections in line, nothing is guaranteed. We were once in a position where we worked with an outside company on a project. Despite signed contracts, vital information got leaked and another competitor actually released a similar collection to the one that Alikay Naturals was working on at the time. The lesson we learned was that even when you legally protect yourself, you must also filter the information you give to outside workers. Contractors don't have nearly the same level of loyalty or respect for your company as staff members, and once something is leaked, there's no getting it back. Furthermore, to seek retribution, you need undeniable proof that they leaked it or violated the agreement with malicious intent – that's not easy to obtain. You're better off filtering your operation to only give pertinent information to key players. Now, all of my company's internal dealings are on a need-to-know basis. We don't share a lot of information with the contractors on a specific project. That way, we never put our business in jeopardy even if an NDA is breached.

TRADEMARKS, PATENTS, and COPYRIGHTS

Your legal team will also help you with securing trademarks, patents, and copyrights for your business. These are legal protections for your intellectual properties and ensure that no one else can duplicate or conduct business under your registered names or images. We already discussed trademarking your company name earlier in this chapter, but you can also trademark product names and logos. If your company is service-based, you can get something called a service-mark, which offers the same protections. Patents protect your inventions and copyrights protect your original artistic or literary works.

As I own a product-based business, I have the most experience with trademarks. The number one mistake I see entrepreneurs make is waiting way too long to register. Oftentimes, people think their business or business idea is too small or too insignificant to copy. Maybe they're still working from home or raising startup funds and figure they aren't large enough to be on anyone's radar. Don't underestimate the greatness of your ideas because of the size of your operation. You never ever know who has eyes on you! I actually recommend trademarking your names and logos *before* your official launch. File your trademarks as soon as you can so that no one else can take them. If you can't afford to do it before launching, try to wait no longer than three to six months into your business.

Before filing a trademark application, be sure to conduct a thorough search to see if your desired mark is actually available. If the U.S. Patent and Trademark Office determines that your mark conflicts with another registered entry, your submission will likely be denied, and your application fee will not be returned. Also, be aware that your marks can be rejected for

90 DAYS TO C.E.O

a number of reasons – it doesn't have to be an exact duplicate of someone else's mark to be turned down. If the USPTO thinks your mark is similar enough to another in spelling, appearance, design, or even phonetic pronunciation, they can reject your application. To increase your chances of a successful registration, conduct a free search on TESS, the Trademark Electronic Search System available 24/7 on the USPTO website. While TESS is a great start, also be advised that you could run into conflicting marks that are not federally registered. Some trademark owners opt to protect their marks using common law rights – these marks will not come up in TESS. To conduct a truly exhaustive search, you'll want to also search state trademark databases or get a trademark attorney who can do all of this for you. An attorney will also come in handy as defense should your application or registered mark be challenged or accused of infringement. To file an application or learn more about the registration process for trademarks, patents, and copyrights, visit the USPTO website.

SEEKING SUPPORT

Even with all the information in the world, I understand just how overwhelming it can be to start your very first business. Like I said before, entrepreneurship can be extremely isolating – if you allow it to be. Fortunately, there are so many amazing resources out there to lend help to new business owners. You're not in this alone and you don't have to feel lost. Do your research and take advantage of the wealth of support available to you.

285

JOIN LOCAL ENTREPRENEURIAL ORGANIZATIONS

Hindsight is 20/20 and knowledge is power. Looking back, I can only wish that I had been aware of all the amazing, free resources available out there when I was a budding entrepreneur. One of the reasons that I'm writing this book is to give you the leg up that I never had. With a decade under my belt, I've learned about some truly amazing offerings from local and national organizations that can give you a strong head start. Sure, success is possible without them, but I believe we go so much farther together than alone. The following entrepreneurial organizations will give you access to gems others take years to mine.

We already discussed how SCORE (Service Corps of Retired Executives) can help you with accessing information on securing permits and licenses, but that's just one of their resources. SCORE provides unmatched access to entrepreneurial education through live and pre recorded webinars, in-person events, small business courses, and mentorship programs. Go to the SCORE website or visit your local chapter and SCORE will literally use your zip code to pair you with the right small business mentor in your vicinity. You can even browse their mentor profiles to make sure you align with just the right person for your industry needs. The non-profit will also introduce you to free, local business networking events in your area so that you can meet, mix, and mingle with a like-minded crowd.

Aside from SCORE, you can find access to tons of free and paid events and conferences across the nation through the Small Business Administration. The SBA also offers help in everything from financing assistance to business planning and reconstruction after disaster. You can also use the SBA to help secure government grants and loans. Consider joining your local chamber through the U.S. Chamber of Commerce for access to more events, programs, and even discounts on vital services like FedEx. Finally, the business departments at local universities can also be an excellent resource for business advice.

Networking is important not only for finding mentors and consultants, but also for introducing yourself and your brand to new audiences. I was actually nominated by a local Floridian business organization for an entrepreneur award in my field. As a result of my informal membership with this organization, I was nominated for two years in a row and received amazing press interviews that really increased local visibility for my brand. Trust me, you never want to knock the power of your own community. There are so many amazing resources right in your own backyard that will boost your exposure and snowball into more sales, more customers, and more media eyes on your business. Even establishing a relationship with your local community college can put you in touch with a pool of qualified young talent for entry-level positions and internships within your company. Moral of the story – a closed mouth doesn't get fed! Seek support within your entrepreneurial community and you will find it. Don't forget to offer your support in return.

LAUNCH TIME!

Ladies and gentlemen, it's time for take-off! You've determined your business model, filled your mind with all the research and information it can handle, and structured and registered your business with the state and federal governments. The time has arrived for you to launch your business! Exciting, right? Of course it is. However, the launch of your business should be meticulously planned and handled with care. This is your baby we're talking about, after all, and you only get one chance to introduce it to the world.

PRE-LAUNCH

Before you can start throwing up ads and making sales, you've got to do a pre-launch. The pre-launch is a predetermined period of time (up to your discretion) of marketing and building anticipation for your official company launch. You've already decided on what products or services you're going to sell, but now you need to figure out how to bring your brand to life. Your pre-launch can include teaser videos or a day-by-day photo countdown leading up to your launch date. You can shoot a commercial and advertisements to get people excited for the big day. Consider creating a detailed social media plan of all the content you'll be posting until the launch. Send email blasts to your network to spread the news and build anticipation. You might even want to send your product out to a few influencers for reviews and feedback you can use for testimonials.

LAUNCH

Now that you've got the word out, it's time for business! Capitalize on all the attention and anticipation you've built up from followers and friends with an official launch party or event. A launch party not only helps you meet perspective customers or clients face-to-face, but it also aligns your brand with a memorable, tangible experience. Make that experience grand enough and it will keep your brand top of mind when your target audience is shopping. They'll remember how they felt at your launch, and be more inclined to make a purchase in hopes of reclaiming a bit of that feeling. Launch time is not the time to slow down – if anything, it is during your launch period that you want to release your most creative marketing and targeted strategy. Advertising will be heavy. If you're opening a brick-and-mortar storefront, for example, you'll have to do some groundwork. Hand out flyers, take out ads in your local newspaper, station brand ambassadors with product samples or service vouchers at locations frequented by your desired customers. Write compelling press releases and send them to magazine editors for media placement (more on press releases in the next chapter). Employ innovative guerilla marketing to generate buzz for your brand in unique ways. The more people are hearing about your brand, sharing it online, or recommending it to their friends, the more successful your launch.

POST-LAUNCH

Finally, your post-launch phase is simply an ongoing effort to maintain the positive momentum of your launch. You don't want the excitement to die down. This might mean an additional two to six weeks of marketing that is still strategic and thought-through, but perhaps not quite as heavy as it was during your actual launch period. Basically, your post-launch is really just the continuous marketing plan for your business over the next twelve months.

Remember those C.E.O checklists I told you about? You will use the bullets in the thirty, sixty, and ninety day checklists to help you launch your business. These basic fundamentals will get you off the ground floor. Refer back to these lists as you go and check off each item as it is accomplished. This process doesn't have to be overwhelming; I'm right here with you every step of the way! Next up, let's talk about running your new business.

Start Up

A newly established business.
Source: Oxford Dictionary

Capital

Wealth in the form of money or other assets owned by a
person or organization or available or contributed for a
particular purpose such as starting a company or investing.
Source: Oxford Dictionary

Revenue Channels

A source of revenue of a company or organization. In business,
a revenue stream is generally made up of either recurring
revenue, transaction-based revenue, project revenue,
or service revenue.
Source: Wikipedia

Cash Flow

The total amount of money being transferred into and out
of a business, especially as affecting liquidity.
Source: Oxford Dictionary

Value Proposition

(In marketing) an innovation, service, or feature intended
to make a company or product attractive to customers.
Source: Oxford Dictionary

B.2.B

Short for Business-to-Business service.
Source: Oxford Dictionary

B.2.C

Short for Business-to-Consumer.
Source: Oxford Dictionary

90 Days to C.E.O Plan

determining viability

- [ ] CREATE A BUSINESS MODEL
- [ ] VALUE PROPOSITION
- [ ] REVENUE MAP
- [ ] CHOOSE YOUR INDUSTRY
- [ ] WRITE A BUSINESS PLAN

registering your business

- [ ] DETERMINE A LEGAL BUSINESS STRUCTURE
- [ ] STATE REGISTRATION
- [ ] FEDERAL REGISTRATION / EIN
- [ ] OBTAIN BUSINESS LICENSES AND PERMITS
- [ ] LIST YOUR ONLINE BUSINESS

creating a product that sells

- [ ] SIMPLE
- [ ] INTERESTING
- [ ] MEANINGFUL
- [ ] PRODUCTIVE
- [ ] LONG-LASTING
- [ ] ENTERTAINING

registering your business name

- [ ] CHOOSE A BUSINESS NAME
- [ ] DBA OR "DOING BUSINESS AS" NAME
- [ ] ENTITY NAME
- [ ] TRADEMARKS
- [ ] SECURE DOMAIN NAME(S)
- [ ] REGISTER SOCIAL MEDIA PROFILES

naming your business

- [ ] TIMELESS VS TRENDY
- [ ] CONSIDER YOUR LEGACY

choosing a business location

- [ ] USE YOUR RESOURCES
- [ ] RENT AN OFFICE OR LEASE COMMERCIAL SPACE
- [ ] NEGOTIATE, NEGOTIATE, NEGOTIATE!
- [ ] REGISTER UTILITIES FOR YOUR BUSINESS

VISIT RGBUSINESSUNIVERSITY.COM/90DAYRESOURCES

90 Days to C.E.O Plan

financing your business

- [ ] BANK LOANS
- [ ] SBA LOANS
- [ ] MICROLOANS
- [ ] ANGEL INVESTORS AND VENTURE CAPITALISTS
- [ ] CROWDFUNDING
- [ ] FRIEND AND FAMILY LOANS
- [ ] CREDIT CARDS
- [ ] BOOTSTRAPPING
- [ ] LINE OF CREDIT

money management

- [ ] OPEN A BUSINESS BANK ACCOUNT
- [ ] SET UP AN ACCOUNTING SYSTEM
- [ ] SET UP A MERCHANT AND PAYMENT SYSTEM
- [ ] HIRE AN ACCOUNTANT AND BOOKKEEPER
- [ ] CREATE FINANCIAL STATEMENTS
- [ ] DETERMINE PRICING SYSTEMS AND SET SALES GOALS
- [ ] RESEARCH STATE AND LOCAL TAXES

taxes

- [ ] CREATE A TAX PLAN
- [ ] SET UP A QUICKBOOKS ONLINE ACCOUNT

building a legal team

- [ ] NON-DISCLOSURE AGREEMENTS AND NON-COMPETE CLAUSES
- [ ] FILE FOR TRADEMARKS, PATENTS, AND COPYRIGHTS
- [ ] DETERMINE THE LEGAL STRUCTURE OF YOUR BUSINESS
- [ ] HIRE AN ATTORNEY
- [ ] OBTAIN LIFE AND BUSINESS INSURANCE

seeking support

- [ ] PRACTICE ELEVATOR PITCH
- [ ] JOIN LOCAL SBA, SCORE
- [ ] ALUMNI ASSOCIATIONS
- [ ] MEETUP.COM
- [ ] LINKEDIN
- [ ] GET BUSINESS ASSISTANCE, A MENTOR OR COACH

VISIT RGBUSINESSUNIVERSITY.COM/90DAYRESOURCES

CHAPTER 10

L.O.C. and KEY

Once you've tackled the logistics of opening your business, keeping it up and running as a well-oiled machine is another beast. Not to worry! Successful operations are completely possible – the trick is to have the right systems, processes, and automations in place to keep the wheels spinning like clockwork. As C.E.O of a new company, you will definitely have your hand in every pot. The mark of a truly successful entrepreneur, however, is the ability to step away from the ground floor and lead from the top as your company grows. The more organized, decisive, and confident you are, the more your business will thrive. The L.O.C. Method™ was definitely one of the most wide-reaching and transformative elements of my journey as a creative and an entrepreneur. In this tenth and final chapter, we will cover everything you need to know to keep your business under L.O.C. and key.

L – Leadership

How will you lead your ship into waters unknown? Let's break down the mechanics of building a team, hiring and firing, and managing different personalities and work styles. Your leadership style will dictate the performance, quality, and excitement of everyone associated with your team.

O – Operations

What is happening within your company on a day-to-day basis? We'll identify all the moving parts in your machine from branding and marketing to filling orders and taking inventory. Efficiency is the name of the game to keep your operations running smoothly.

C – Change the game

As your company grows, things will change, and you might have a different vision for the future. How will you plan effectively for years to come? How will you innovate to stay in tune with and ahead of the trends? Let's get into preparing for paradigm shifts and maintaining flexibility for an entrepreneurial legacy that will stand the test of time.

Now, let's get into the good stuff and unpack your keys to success!

BRANDING

Before you begin conducting business, it's very important to establish a brand aesthetic. While general concepts and ideas will happen before an official launch, successful branding is woven into the fabric of your daily operations and informs almost all of the decisions you and your team will make. Branding is essentially how you represent your company to the world and can be categorized into three main parts: visuals, words, and intangibles.

Visuals – Your visuals will include everything from your company color schemes to fonts, marketing materials, website or blog design, product packaging, social media imagery, photography, graphics, business headshots, and of course, your logo.

Words – This category includes all website copy and social media messaging, the brand voice, tone, and style, slogans, taglines, and brand promises and mission statements.

Intangibles – Finally, intangibles are everything else that informs your brand identity: customer perception, customer or user experience, company culture, personality, and values.

Now that we have established the three main categories of business branding, let's dive into more detail on some of the most crucial branding elements.

LOGOS

Your logo is the core of your brand's identity. It's often the first thing that customers will remember about your company. Think about the Nike swoosh, Adidas stripes, McDonald's golden arches, or the NBC network peacock. These logos have become synonymous with the brands themselves. When designing a logo for your company, you want to ask yourself, *is this something I want to keep forever*? Of course, modifications can be made over time, but you want to start with a solid foundation that remains recognizable to loyal consumers.

If you are bootstrapping and want to design a logo yourself, there are websites like Canva or Picmonkey that allow you to create your own raw designs. There are also sites like Fiverr which offer affordable freelance services including graphic design. While these resources are super cost-effective, I personally think you should be very selective when it comes to designing a logo. Like I said, brand identity is of the utmost importance, and you want to make sure that you are getting a custom image that no other person or company in the world can duplicate. My first official logo was $250 – a lot of money for a broke college student at the time. I went to a friend of mine whose sister happened to be an artist with a sketch of my raw idea. I had laid out flowers on the ground, taken a photo, and sent the artist my image to convert to digital. Even though it was an investment, my logo has remained more or less grounded in that same original idea. Even though the image has evolved over time, I can still look back and see my brand vision represented loud and clear. Like your company name, your logo should be timeless and, of course, trademarked (refer back to chapter nine for information on trademarking).

Something else to keep in mind when it comes to creating logos is having multiple file types saved for your image. Different materials will often require different formats of your logo. For instance, the file you will use on your website or packaging is entirely different than the file used for merchandise like t-shirts or hats. You want to have your logo saved as a jpeg, a png, etc. When you work with an artist or graphic designer, be sure to request all variations of the vector file, or resizable, scalable images.

MOOD BOARDS

A mood board is like a tangible representation of your brand's personality; a collage of various different aspects of your brand vision from logos to company color palettes and fonts. Mood boards are helpful when you begin working with a graphic designer or marketing team – basically, anyone who needs to know how to visually represent your business. They're also helpful for laying out overall vision as well as visions for each individual product launch or campaign. By referring back to your mood board, you keep things consistent and establish brand loyalty with your customers. People like brands they can trust, and giving them symbols, typography, and colors they know and love over and over again creates a sense of comfort.

Like a logo, you can have your mood board designed by a graphic designer or do one yourself. Because a mood board is home to the most intimate, personalized aspects of your business, I recommend at least taking a crack at it yourself before handing it off. Again, Canva is a great beginning option to construct your mood board digitally. It offers tons of mood and storyboard template designs that you can then customize to your liking. You can also use sites like Pinterest to gather photos and words that inspire you.

I personally prefer to construct a physical board with printed images. Although I'm not a fan of vision board parties, I do use the vision board method to compile aspects of my mood board. I take a large piece of foam and I print and cut out my favorite inspo images and photographs that match my desired brand aesthetic. Then, I'll visit the Pantone website (pantone. com) to find and print colors that I like. On Pinterest, I can usually find pantone color wheels or blocks that actually have complementary colors to the ones I have already chosen, and I print those out as well. Having all of these things printed gives me an in-person, physical feel of my different elements and allows me to easily move things around on my board until I get it just right.

Here are some of the elements to include on your first brand mood board:

Thematic – Thematic elements include ideas or images that you might not explicitly use in a launch or campaign, but that may help you narrow in on branding direction. Thematic elements can include anything from quotes you love, images, or adjectives that call to mind feelings you want associated with your brand. You wouldn't necessarily run a promotion with the words "warm, comforting, reliable," but you might include these words on a mood board to give a nod to core brand sentiments.

Design – Design elements are ideas and images that you do actually plan on utilizing. Think logos, fonts and font sizes, and colors. If the mood board is for a particular product launch, think scents and textures. These elements will inform any illustrations or designs you make for ads, packaging, websites, etc.

Check out an example of my Rochelle Graham Business University™ mood board at rgbusinessuniversity.com/90dayresources.

BUSINESS CARDS and STATIONERY

Many new entrepreneurs may think business cards are outdated, but truth be told, they are a wonderful method for both branding and marketing your company. Business card designs should be in line with company colors and fonts, and should also include your company logo and a tagline or brief bullet point description of company products and services. Lastly, be sure to list your website address and business address, as well as your social media handles. You may even include a professional headshot on the back. While business cards should be on brand and carefully curated, you don't want to make them a huge expense. Keep in mind that many people will lose your card or simply throw it out – it's not personal, it happens. For this reason, try to order in bulk and keep your costs low. I recommend starting off with 100 cards and then increasing volume as your business expands. These low-cost business cards can be handed out during casual interactions or included in gift bags when you host events.

For higher-profile networking events and meetings, however, you always want to have nicer, more refined cards on hand. This may mean investing in high-quality, professional grade paper for a small percentage of your business cards. These are not to be handed out frivolously; they should be reserved for those people and places where you really need to make an impression. Remember, your business card has to speak for your brand. Make it count.

Your company stationery should also be branded. Any letters, contracts, or documents you send out to customers, clients, employees, or prospective partners should include a sleek and professional company letterhead in your brand's signature font. While VistaPrint is a great supplier for custom business cards, you can use 4allpromos and 4imprint to create branded stationery, merchandise, and marketing materials.

DOMAIN NAMES

A domain name is the unique part of a URL or web address that distinctly identifies your business or organization for users searching your company online. Like trademarking, I highly recommend securing a domain name for both your business and your personal brand as soon as possible! Your business brand is of course the name of your actual company, but I firmly believe that every C.E.O should also develop a strong personal brand as well. Your personal brand is tied to you as an individual, separate from your company. Branding yourself as an entrepreneur is crucial for building consumer interest and trust – everyone loves a good story, and sharing a bit of yourself with the world will gain you attention and dollars from people who want to support not only your business, but you as a human being. For instance, my business domain name matches the name of my company: alikaynaturals.com. My personal website, however, features my own name: rochellegraham.co. The former directs customers to pages where they can learn about and purchase my products; the latter educates my audience on Rochelle Graham-Campbell, the woman behind the brand.

For both your business and personal brands, secure those domain names as soon as possible. You don't want to launch a successful business, only to realize that your desired domain has already been taken. You also don't want potential customers to have to work harder than necessary to find your websites. Registering a domain name should ideally be one of your very first steps.

When choosing a domain, keep it simple. Most businesses simply go with their own names, ie: yourcompanyname.com. This increases your company's SEO, or search engine optimization, making you easy to find online. If your company's name is too long or cumbersome for a URL address, consider using an abbreviation. For example, the U.S. Small Business Administration can be found online simply at sba.gov.

As for purchasing your domain name, you can go through a registrar like GoDaddy or Namecheap. Before accepting your purchase, the registrar will search through a comprehensive database to ensure that your desired name is actually available and not being used somewhere else on the internet. It is also important to note that available domain names will be limited by suffixes. Common suffixes include .com, .org, .biz, and .net. Most companies will go for the first option, as .com specifies commercial websites. For this reason, it is also one of the first suffix options to go. When you conduct a search, you may find that "yourcompanyname.com" is taken, but "yourcompanyname.org" might be free for use. If possible, snatch up as many variations of your domain name as possible – the .com is not enough. Nowadays, you should also get the .co, .org, .biz and every other domain suffix variation you can get your hands on for your brands. This will prevent others from creating mock sites that will confuse or misdirect your customers. Also, be sure to mark your domain name expiration dates down in your calendar or set a reminder to renew them. If you fail to renew your domain on time, your website will become inaccessible. Once that happens, bots and business vultures out there can snatch up your names as soon as they expire, and charge you a hefty fee to get them back.

An alternative to buying your domain through a registrar is signing up with a website hosting platform that offers free domains upon registration. If you go this route, just remember that your domain won't usually remain free forever. After one or two years of use, you will typically be billed annually for the continued use of your domain. For our businesses, my husband and I love GoDaddy because they're reliable and cost-effective. They also have frequent discounts available if you keep an eye out!

WEBSITES

Another important element of branding is website design. In my opinion, every entrepreneur should have both a company website and a personal branding website (with a distinct domain name for each), and both should evolve over time. Like your business plan, your website should never be static – it should grow and change as your company offerings and accomplishments expand. There is nothing worse than wanting to do business with a brand and being directed to an outdated website. A quick tip is to actually keep a website update schedule on your yearly calendar, and set reminders to do a periodic website refresh. Updates will allow you to swap out old campaigns for new ones, and plug the most relevant ads into your website banners. Refresh your websites once a quarter, twice a year, or however often you choose, as long as you are consistently maintaining and updating to reflect your most up-to-date aesthetics and promotions.

Your company website should give all the information about your brand, mission, and products or services. Your personal website will inform customers and prospective customers about the person behind their soon-to-be-favorite brand, and help drive traffic to other potential streams of income, such as public speaking or coaching services. Your mood board will help you or your graphic designer come up with the look and layout of your webpages.

First, you must decide what kind of site you need and what functions you need your site to perform. For instance, you can have a blog, where you discuss popular or important industry topics. You can have a one-page website, which is essentially like a digital business card containing the most basic about and contact information. Many entrepreneurs, however, go with an ecommerce website, which gives you the ability to actually sell your products or services online. Even with an ecommerce site, you may want to include other features such as a blog to build engagement and establish yourself as an authority within your field.

Whatever type of site you choose, you must be selective about what payment processor you use, and consider how you might plan to use your website in the future. A payment processor is a third-party company that authorizes and processes payments made via your website – we'll discuss this more in depth in the "Payment Processing" section later in this chapter. For now, take note that if you're using your website for ecommerce, then you need to build it on an ecommerce platform. Even if you're not planning to start selling right away, it's easier to build your site on an ecomm platform from the start, rather than trying to convert a non-ecomm site at a later time. If you try to make the switch later, you will have to start from scratch. The moral of the story is that you must always plan ahead and think of the future of your business, even when first setting up your website.

Another important thing to consider when putting together your website is to make sure that your homepage is clean and uncluttered. Keep your page headers to a minimum – six or less is perfect – and ensure that each tab indicates a clear and distinct user function. Also, your homepage should get right to the point, clearly articulating to prospective customers whatever it is that you sell or do. Finally, there are certain legal claims and policies that are standard and legally required for websites. These include privacy policies, shipping policies, and more.

Next, you must choose a website builder and a hosting platform. A website builder is where you actually construct your website. You can use an online builder which allows you to put together your website from anywhere and at any time – all you need is a solid internet connection. Alternatively, you can use an offline builder which requires you to download website building software, save your own files, and then upload onto a server in order to launch the website. Offline options are more suited to professional web designers or entrepreneurs who are more technologically savvy. Many site builders come with tons of templates and tutorials that make building your website super approachable, affordable, and customizable.

A hosting platform is an online location you pay to rent space for your website to live. Hosts are not designed to actually build your site, but they give you access to a server which stores all your data and content so that it is accessible and operational for you and your customers. There are different types of hosting options available, from shared hosting to dedicated hosting and VPS hosting, and each type offers a different level of server storage, bandwidth, security, and price point. WordPress is one of the most popular options on the market and offers both website building (WordPress.org) and website hosting capabilities (WordPress.com).

For bootstrapping entrepreneurs, you can cut on costs by choosing free builders and hosts. Some of the best and most popular free and/or affordable options are WordPress.com, Wix, Weebly, Squarespace, and GoDaddy. While many free platforms have great capabilities, they also come with certain drawbacks. For instance, to make money, free hosting platforms will run ads on your website, and those ads may not necessarily align with or reflect well upon your business. Free builders and hosts also restrict your storage space and may even limit traffic to your site. In order to get rid of the ads, increase storage, or get access to a custom domain name, you may have to upgrade to a paid plan. Paid builders and hosts can come as inexpensive as $5 per month or even less, and offer benefits like 24/7 access to technical support, free emails, ecommerce functionality, and free domain names.

We'll dive even deeper into maximizing the functionality and user experience of your website later on in the chapter, but check out the website must-haves checklist below for some key aspects that every good website should have:

SOCIAL MEDIA INTEGRATION

PRIVACY POLICIES

EMAIL NEWSLETTER SIGN-UP

FREQUENTLY ASKED QUESTIONS (FAQ)

CONTACT FORMS

CALL-TO-ACTION BUTTONS

SEARCH ENGINE OPTIMIZATION

RESPONSIVE DESIGN

BRANDING STANDARDS MANUAL

Compile your mood board and all of your company's individual branding elements into a branding standards manual. A standards manual is like home base – it's a rulebook for anything having to do with designs for your brand. Your branding standards manual does include your mood board, but it is much bigger than that. This is where you will include the do's and don'ts of how to use your logo and represent your brand in any graphics-related way. For example, if you are sponsoring an event or working with another company, you need to be specific about how that other party will represent your business in any advertisements or promotions.

Have you ever seen a flyer where the logo is super blurry, miscolored, or stretched out? These are the types of things that may happen when you don't have a detailed branding manual in place. Don't be afraid to get specific! For Alikay Naturals, my manual specifies that our logo cannot be stretched beyond *these* dimensions, it must be *this* size, it cannot be covered or overlapped with any other image, it must feature *these* particular colors, and it has to be *this* many inches away from any other company's logos. Any time a new decision is being made about or within your company, you should refer back to your branding standards manual to see if that decision aligns with your branding vision. Having a standards manual establishes consistency and longevity, and it will also make it easier to represent yourself accurately when coordinating or collaborating with outside businesses or graphic designers. From advertisers and retailers to outside hires, a branding standards manual presents everyone with access to the same rules for who your company is and how it should be represented.

REBRANDING

Finally, sometimes it is necessary to refresh your brand's image with an update or to completely rebrand altogether. A refresh is any simple tweak or addition that breathes new life into your company image. This can be through introducing a new tagline, launching a new product line, or switching to a secondary color palette from your mood board. I recommend refreshing your brand just about once a year to give customers something new and exciting to hold their interest.

A rebranding is a more drastic switch-up to your look. Perhaps you no longer feel that your brand colors are flowing well. Maybe your logos are not prominent enough or they've become outdated. If your company has been running for a long time, you may possibly want to introduce a new theme every year so that your brand doesn't become bland or boring. My company recently rebranded to completely restructure our packaging. We redid all of our labels to enlarge our logos, copy, and label sizes themselves. We also switched out the headshot photo of me that was being used on packaging and updated our copyright for 2019-2020. A few years ago, we also bolded the font within our logo to be more prominent. A rebrand should maintain the integrity of your mood board while enhancing implementation.

Always remember, the goal is to be constantly improving your brand. Your brand may look a certain way when you first launch, but you may change your mind and decide to go in a different direction down the line. That is okay! It's only natural that your tastes will evolve as you grow as an entrepreneur. Trust those instincts. It's all about starting where you are but getting better over time.

MARKETING, PUBLIC RELATIONS, and ADVERTISING

Even with all the branding in the world, a business is only as successful as its marketing. Marketing refers to all company efforts to promote products and/or services with the specific goal of increasing sales. Underneath the marketing umbrella, we have public relations (PR) and advertising. PR is the process of cultivating key relationships in order to promote and manage a positive company image in the media and among company audiences. Finally, advertising is a tactic of marketing that refers specifically to the strategic imaging and placing of advertisements to draw attention to a specific company offering. The effects of marketing and advertisements can be measured in dollar amounts or visible increases in revenue. Public relations success is measured in brand exposure or media placements in magazines, publications, or radio and television segments.

CONTENT MARKETING

Content marketing is the creation of original, high-value content to attract audiences and ultimately encourage more sales. Ask yourself, *what does my customer want from me? What do they need? What are the pain points they're struggling with, and what can I provide to make it easier, quicker, or more convenient for them to use my product or service?* Answering these questions will help you determine the kind of content that you want to create. You want to show people how your product or service is used, and provide them with positive and transparent testimonials. This may mean actually asking a customer to come in and be recorded using your product and talking about their experience.

The types of content you create will depend on preference, but popular options include videos, blogs and articles, and podcasts. While these forms of content are not the main focus of your business, they will generate interest among potential customers by providing them with just enough value to keep them wanting more. Your content should plug your products and/or services as a unique solution to consumer problems or pain points, thus driving audiences from your content to your website or store. For example, I upload videos on both of my YouTube Channels (Alikay Naturals and BlackOnyx77) to provide valuable content on natural hair care and styling. Viewers who click on these tutorials to learn a new hair styling or maintenance technique may then be urged to visit my website and purchase the products featured in my videos.

The most important thing with content marketing is consistency. You have to have a schedule for content creation just like you do with your social media. Without strong content, you cannot have a strong social media marketing strategy, so it is important to plan everything out and put yourself on a schedule. If your graphic design happens in-house, you might pick one day of the week to do all of your ads. If you choose to shoot your own stock photos, decide what days you will shoot and what days you will edit – maybe once or twice a month. You can also use websites like BigStock to get royalty free stock images. If you have an outside graphics team, you might submit to the graphic designer for new ads every two weeks. Maybe you get templates created in advance of your posting schedule so you can simply drop in new images or copy as needed. Whatever content you come up with, create a calendar for when you will post each of these content deliverables.

Once posted, it is also crucial to track and analyze the performance of each content item. Pay attention to the clicks, views, likes, and shares that your content receives. Also keep track of the days and times that your posts perform at their best. Start off by posting different days and times and then check your analytics to see your peak hours, or when your audience is most engaged. We will dive into more specifics on analytics later on in this chapter, but the most important thing to know is that analytics will help streamline your content creation. If the numbers show that a specific post is getting great engagement from followers and prospective customers, you will want to figure out a way to repost that content. Don't be afraid to share the same content twice! Of course, space out your duplicate posts enough so that your social media feeds don't become repetitive, but there's nothing wrong with sharing a photo or video again in a couple of weeks or months if it performs exceptionally well. You can also repost content from other pages. If you come across a great post or quote that you can relate back to your brand or your industry, use one of your brand stock quote templates, recreate the post in your brand colors, and repost it on your own platform. When reposting from others, however, always be sure to give credit to the original creator and tag them in your post and caption!

You should also ask yourself how you can repurpose old content for other platforms. Let's say you created a video that did exceptionally well. Can you then take that video and run it as a social media advertisement? Can you turn it into some sort of webinar? Can you post it on your website as a response to a frequently asked question? Think smart. Of course, not all of the content on your social media pages should be repurposed or reposted. Make sure that you're also creating unique, quality, original content featuring your brand logo. Especially when you're on a budget, however, repurposing and reposting your content are excellent ways to save both time and money.

SOCIAL MEDIA MARKETING

Social media is home to the creations and conversations that are driving social culture at large – so much so, that many people now head to Instagram and other platforms first for their entertainment, education, and social awareness. These platforms are also being used more and more as search engines for customers looking for specific products and services. For this reason, your social platforms will be home to much of the content that you create to attract and drive sales. With all this opportunity at your hands, you must use it wisely. The first step of successful social media marketing is understanding that your platforms must be used strategically.

If social media is not your thing as an individual, that's fine. However, if you have a business, it is no longer an option not to have a social presence. First thing's first, you should secure a consistent business username across all major or relevant platforms. Even if you do not plan on having a presence on a certain social channel, still secure the name so that it cannot be stolen by a competitor or disgruntled individual with malintent against your business. For instance, Alikay Naturals focuses its main social media marketing efforts on Instagram, Facebook, and YouTube. We also have a Twitter and Pinterest page, but those are used less frequently and considered our second-tier platforms. We don't use Snapchat at all, however we still have a registered account under our name.

It's also important to stay up-to-date with new apps. Social media is ever-changing, and when new platforms launch, you need to jump on them. For instance, TikTok has recently become very popular. I'm not sure if Alikay Naturals will ever use it, but we've already gone ahead and made an account. When navigating the social media world, think about the demographic of your target audience. Will your customer use this new app? How can you create new content to engage with them on this platform? These are the types of things you need to think about.

When it comes to choosing your usernames, keep it nice and simple. If possible, stick to the name of your brand. If you can, avoid things like underscores and numbers in your username, unless your company name was already taken on that social platform. In that case, you may have to add a symbol or character to make your name unique, but remember that the goal here is to be easily searchable by customers. Simplicity is key – not only is it great for brand recognition, but it's also the most professional way to represent yourself and your business online. This applies to both your business pages and your personal social media accounts as well. Remember, unless you keep your personal page private, this page is simply another reflection of your business. Babygirl88 might feel cute and nostalgic, but it's not a good look for your brand.

On that note, let's discuss the differences between your business and personal social media pages. Many C.E.Os make the mistake of mixing the two when they should really be kept separate. On your business page, the focus should be on your product or service and your customers. You can post yourself once in a while, but make sure that your face isn't popping up on your business feed every day. Save those posts for your personal page. By the same token, having a personal page is not free reign to share whatever you want – not for C.E.Os, at least. Remember that your personal page tells customers who you are as the core representative of your brand. They should get to know you, yes, but they don't have to see every intimate detail of your social life. If you are someone who lives a super wild and outrageous life, you may want to consider making yet another personal page solely for friends and family that you keep private. If you're inclined to oversharing selfies, or photos of your kids and the new puppy, the same suggestion applies.

After securing your username, it's time to decide what content your business will post. This is when all that content we discussed will come into play. Come up with a comprehensive list of content ideas and keep it on hand or easily accessible. This way, you can jot down new ideas as they come to you – I use the "notes" section on my phone. Content can include everything from product promotions and brand announcements to how-to tutorials, pictorials, relevant news clips, quotes, or facts, and reposted user-generated content. Keep in mind that video content performs especially well and should feature heavily in your social marketing. While much of your content will be branded with your company color schemes, fonts, and logos, you may also want to leave room to be spontaneous. If a fun social conversation is trending, it is totally okay to create a funny meme that relates back to your business. Also pay attention to fun and silly holidays that relate to your industry. For instance, World Afro Day is a big one for Alikay Naturals. You can find a comprehensive list of quirky and obscure national holidays with a simple online search. Getting in on these relevant conversations keeps your brand top of mind, however, recognizable brand-consistent images and videos will be your social media bread and butter. Use sites like Canva and Picmonkey to create branded templates that can be recycled for different purposes from campaign launches to product features and quick user-friendly tips.

Now that you have your usernames and content variations, it's time to compile it all into an organized posting schedule, or social media calendar. Just like with all aspects of your business, social media content should be planned out in advance so that you can stay ahead of the curve. At Alikay, we're planning out posts at least two weeks in advance of posting or more. Make use of social media scheduling apps to preload completed photos, text graphics, and videos into their designated platforms. Popular scheduling apps include TweetDeck, Hootsuite, Buffer, and Later.com. These apps typically come with a limited free-trial period, and then offer more expansive features – including social media analytics reporting – when you upgrade to paid plans. When you preschedule, your posting will go off without a hitch should you or your social media manager be unable to post in real-time. Scheduling also allows you to easily plan multiple posts a day without getting overwhelmed. Remember, the goal of social media marketing is to make sales. This means that you need to work within social media algorithms to stay consistently visible on customer timelines and newsfeeds. Decide how many times per day you want to post on each platform and load the respective posts into each app. Unlike a personal page, it is not unlikely for your business accounts to post three, four, or five times a day – or more!

Down below, I have included an example of a social media marketing calendar. Feel free to use this example as a reference for your own calendar, and change the times and platforms as you see fit.

At Alikay, we have a social calendar running on a quarterly basis. All the content that we create and share aligns with whatever campaigns and promotions we have at the time. Our social media marketing manager knows exactly what photo, video, ad, or campaign we have to post on what day, and she updates the calendar accordingly. This way, if she's ever sick or out of the office, our graphics department can still take a look at the calendar, see what needs to be created by when, and submit all deliverables on time. Don't just post for the sake of posting – there should always be a method to your madness. Post on purpose! Everything you share needs to be intentional and align with your business goals.

Once your posts go live, be sure to make use of hashtags. Hashtags are an important part of social media marketing, particularly on Instagram and Twitter. Industry or niche-specific hashtags drive more traffic to your posts by allowing your content to be easily searchable by platform users. While hashtags are important, don't get carried away with using too many in your captions. Instead, try listing your hashtags in the first comment underneath your post. This way, you'll still pop up in searches, but you won't clutter the look of your post. In addition to hashtags, every post should include a clear and concise CTA, or call to action. A call to action is any directive that tells consumers the specific action you want them to take after viewing your social media post. Great CTAs include visit my website, click here, comment below, click the link in bio, swipe up, and learn more. A call to action will often get the sales process started by prompting potential customers to visit your website where they can make a purchase.

INFLUENCER MARKETING

Influencer marketing is working with bloggers or content creators to help increase sales by leveraging their social audiences. In the last few years influencer marketing has sky-rocketed, giving traditional advertising avenues a run for their money in terms of brand dollars. Businesses still spend tons to market their products in magazines and digital publications, however it has grown increasingly common for companies to allocate funds specifically for influencer collaborations and partnerships.

Important things to consider before working with an influencer:

1. Does their audience align with your core customer base?

If you sell shoes and apparel, it makes no sense to partner with a comedy vlogger – even if they have a ton of followers. Their primary audience might not overlap with the customers you're seeking to target.

2. How good is their engagement?

Follower count doesn't always equate to engagement. If you see that a popular Instagram creator has tons of likes but strikingly few comments, their audience may not be engaged. Without engagement, that influencer may not help you make many sales.

3. Is that influencer actually a businessperson?

Some people are simply ultra-popular because they take pretty photos. They may have a great following but very little interest or understanding of how to leverage that power. They may not post consistently or conduct themselves in a professional manner. They may be unresponsive to your emails, prove difficult to work with, or be late with deliverables. Proceed with caution.

4. You run the show.

Many entrepreneurs get blinded by big numbers and end up giving in to every whim of the influencer. Understand that this is a business exchange and money that your company is spending for a service. Operate from a place of strength and hold influencers accountable.

Once you find a compatible influencer, establish ground rules. Is this an ongoing collaboration or a one-time deal? Are there any specific product claims you need them to include verbatim in their content? What are the deliverables and scope of work? How long after the agreement do they have to submit their deliverables for approval? Be very clear in your expectations and the do's and don'ts of how the influencer should represent your brand. Also, don't be afraid to negotiate on the rate. If the influencer has a rate that is way out of your budget, it's not a good fit. However, if they respond with a fee that's a few hundred bucks out of your range, negotiate and see if you can get them to come down.

Another huge tip is to look into working with smaller influencers. Many C.E.Os think their influencer marketing dollars are best spent on the bloggers with the largest followings; that may not always be the case. There is a huge market with nano and micro influencers as well. While the actual numbers are debated, nano influencers are typically accepted to be those with less than 1,000 social media followers, while micro influencers have between 1,000 and 100,000. Bloggers with followings of 100K to 1 million tip into the macro and mega-influencer categories, and while their reach is impressive, their engagement is often the opposite. The bigger and more famous an influencer gets, the more distant the relationship between them and their followers tends to be. They may have difficulty convincing their followers to actually go out and buy a product because their motives are being questioned.

With nano and micro influencers, on the other hand, the smaller, more manageable numbers mean more tightly-knit communities. Their followers tend to be more actively engaged and invested in their posts because the influencers can actually take the time to respond to individual comments and direct messages. This builds up trust, and followers become supporters who truly feel that they are online friends with the influencer. This makes it easier for the influencer to encourage sales for your business with sponsored posts and discount codes. Not to mention, nano and micro influencers typically offer way more affordable rates than those with hundreds of thousands of followers. For the best bang for your influencer marketing buck, consider partnering with smaller content creators.

AFFILIATE MARKETING

Affiliate marketing is very similar to influencer marketing – the only difference is that affiliates do not receive a flat rate. When you work with affiliates, they will market your product or service in exchange for a commission percentage which results in a monthly check. You can do this one of two ways. First, you can conduct manual affiliate marketing, where you present the influencer with a unique code or link that will give their viewers or followers a discount on your product or service. You can then use that unique code or link to track revenue generated by that specific influencer and cut them a percentage of profits. For instance, many companies work off a 15/10 split. The influencer gets a 15% commission of sales and customers (who purchased from your company via the unique influencer code) receive a 10% discount off their purchase. Alternatively, the affiliate may receive a 15% commission and the customers may get free shipping on their order.

Second, you can set up automated affiliate marketing through a third-party company. This company will act as a middleman between you and influencers looking to serve as affiliates for brands. These companies have huge databases of influencers and will pair you with an affiliate for a small percentage fee. Then, once the influencer has completed the scope of work, the third-party company will send them a check on your behalf.

Whether you're working with influencers on a short-term basis or as ongoing affiliates, the important thing to remember is that you only want to work with professionals who respect your company. Regardless of followers or engagement, ask yourself, *has this person actually tried my product or service? Do they like it? Are they likely to reflect positively upon my brand?* Before sending any official contracts, I will often send a prospective influencer a care package of products to try both as a gesture of good faith and to hear their honest opinion. Asking these questions will help you determine if you're making a sound investment of your valuable marketing dollars.

BRAND PLAYBOOK

Every year at the beginning of quarter three, my team and I sit down for our annual strategy planning meetings: finance, sales, and marketing. In these meetings, we define everything from our sales targets and marketing budget to our new campaigns and product launches. All of the modes of marketing we discussed above – content, social media, influencers, affiliates, etc – must be consolidated into a comprehensive game plan, broken down by quarter. I call this my brand playbook.

The brand playbook is your marketing plan; a detailed roadmap you'll be following for the next twelve months. For Alikay Naturals, our brand playbook includes a collection of Excel spreadsheets which lists each and every aspect of this overall marketing strategy, grouped by month and allocated funds. Having these meetings at the beginning of Q3 allows us to plan marketing for the upcoming year. After the big annual meetings, we conduct smaller meetings each quarter to track progress and redirect our marketing plan as needed. This brand playbook or marketing plan is broken down into four core components: a social media plan, a sales and promotional plan, an advertising plan, and an email marketing plan.

We have already discussed social media marketing at length, but to recap, your social media plan should reflect the marketing goals identified during your Q3 meeting. All social content should be planned in advance, adhere to a posting schedule, and run alongside any current campaigns to maximize sales.

Next is your sales and promotional plan which should detail exactly what promotions your company will have, and align them with specific dates. What national or industry-specific holidays will your company observe with a special sale? Perhaps you want to offer a discount for your company anniversary or birthday. A golden rule is to limit the number of promotions and sales your company offers. You never want to become that company that has discounts year-round, so plan ahead, be selective and creative in your offerings, and lay out all sales in a calendar schedule.

Next up, we have your advertising plan. By now you get the picture – just like content, social media posts, and sales and promotions, your advertisements should also be planned ahead on a schedule. Even if you don't have tons of money for fancy billboards, there is still so much that you can do for quality advertising. For example, you can run social media ads on Facebook and Instagram, or partner with influencers or popular social media pages in your niche for sponsored content. Another option is to run a Google Ads campaign. Finally, we've come to email marketing. We will discuss email marketing services more in depth towards the end of this chapter, but as with everything else, you want to create a schedule for all of your emails and align them with any running campaigns and promotions to prompt customers back to your website. With detailed social media, sales and promotions, advertising, and email marketing plans in place, your brand playbook begins to take form.

The next step is to identify your top three goals. At Alikay naturals, the question is always: how do we want to grow, specifically? When you identify what your top three goals are for the year, it makes it easier to then work backwards and ensure that any move – any campaign, product launch, service, or event decision matches up with those goals. Next, we conduct a S.W.O.T analysis (strengths, weaknesses, opportunities, threats) to reassess where our business currently stands (refer back to chapter seven). We also reassess our core customer. Who are they and what has changed for them over the past year? These analyses help us determine what needs to be improved upon based on results from the previous year. Then, we take an industry-wide look as to where our product prices fall. We compare our prices to those of our top five or six competitors to see whether we should be charging more or less. The same can be done for service-based businesses. For more information on how to effectively price your products, visit rgbusinessuniversity.com for my Rochelle Graham Business University™ course on "Pricing & Costing: How to price your products to be profitable for customers and retail."™

Next, we discuss new product or service launches as well as any upcoming events. What new offerings will our company introduce in the coming year? What trade shows or events do we want to attend to network or sell products? When are those events happening? Once we have those in mind, we pinpoint on the calendar exactly when we will start the planning of each launch, the dates of the official launches, and the dates of our chosen events and trade shows. From here, we look at our marketing mix – marketing tools we're currently using and new approaches we want to take for the next year. For Alikay, our marketing mix includes trade shows and events, strategic curated brand events, consumer print advertisements, promotional materials, digital marketing, video or content production, photoshoot production, social media or brand ambassadors and influencers, and PR agencies.

Now that you have your marketing plan, it's time to discuss your overall marketing budget. Every single item in the marketing mix mentioned above must fit neatly within your budget. Remember, as a new business, you don't have money to waste. Especially if you are self-funded, you have to allocate your marketing dollars strategically to make sure you're only spending money on the most effective things. So how exactly do you determine your marketing budget? Common practice for many companies is to look at their revenue from the previous year and calculate out 10-20% – that percentage will be the total marketing budget for the coming year. Some companies may even go as high as 30%, but those are typically larger companies, or those with the extra funding to go all out on advertising. At Alikay, we typically go with 20%.

Once you determine your spending cap, you can then distribute those funds across your marketing mix. In other words, take that 10-20% of your previous year's revenue and divide that number amongst your social media, trade shows and events, digital marketing, video and photoshoot production, influencers, PR agencies, etc. Now that you have your magic number, you can prioritize which items in your marketing mix are most important. For example, maybe you determine that you'd rather spend money on video production than a bunch of events. This will help you narrow down your list to only those events that are most pressing for your company to attend. I also make sure to include a miscellaneous and reserve marketing fund specifically for unforeseen expenses.

Let's review. First, you will have your big three – your annual strategy meetings for finance, sales, and marketing. As the year progresses, you will also have smaller meetings every quarter to check progress and pivot strategy, if necessary. These meetings will help you to compose a comprehensive marketing plan, or brand playbook, which is comprised of a social media plan, sales and promotional plans, advertising plan, and email marketing plan with corresponding calendars and budgets. While the brand playbook determines your game plan for the year, you must consistently track analytics and sales to ensure proper productivity and success.

ANALYTICS

Finally, every solid business has a system in place to measure analytics. From social media campaigns to advertisements and influencer collaborations, you need to see whether your marketing dollars were well-spent. Analytics allow you to gain insight into the success or failure of a strategy based on data. Did that ad get a ton of clicks over to your website? Did that influencer's sponsored post result in more sales? You can also receive analytics for your website performance itself. How frequently are customers adding to cart and actually purchasing once they do visit your site? Analytics will give you your answers.

Nowadays, there are many systems and analytic tools available to measure performance. You can track data through social media platforms such as Instagram by upgrading from a personal to a business account. This provides insights such as the number of times a post was viewed, shared, or saved by followers, as well as the number of new followers earned after a specific post. You can use Google Analytics (GA) to track insights on your own webpages. Simply create a GA login and username and link it to your website. Your analytics dashboard will show you vital information such as your highest and lowest-performing webpages, duration of time on site, abandoned carts, geographic location of customers, and more. You can also see how people are accessing your site (through a computer, tablet, or smartphone) and set your site up to work on each option. If you have a web developer or SEO manager, you can also add them to your Google Analytics account so they have access to everything. I also advise setting up Google alerts for your brand name and personal name. These alerts will notify you any time these names or terms are mentioned online, helping you to effectively track media press placements as well as conversations involving you or your brand. You can even set up alerts for your competitors' names to track how they are performing, as well.

I highly recommend taking a course or hiring someone for your marketing team with lots of experience interpreting data. Data analysis is a specific skill set, and while you can learn the basics, it is advisable to surround yourself with expertise to ensure your marketing strategies and campaigns are as efficient as possible. Marketing specialists will measure things like ROIs or returns on investment to determine how much profit or revenue can be attributed to each specific marketing channel (and if that return is worth the money spent). If you hire a professional for analytics, they can present you with an analytics report for all your marketing channels on at least a quarterly basis – I personally like to hear something from my marketing team every month, or even more frequently during a huge campaign. While each piece is crucial, no one element of a marketing strategy works alone. It's important to examine the overall picture of your brand playbook when assessing performance.

PUBLIC RELATIONS – IN-HOUSE vs. PR FIRMS

Now, let's talk about public relations. As we established earlier, publicity is key in boosting the public image and perception of your company as well as your personal brand. You can choose to handle PR in-house, or within your own operations, or you can opt to hire a publicist or PR and marketing firm. Many entrepreneurs choose to work with outside PR firms for their connections and unique ability to bring in results – or so you would think.

When you bring in an outside PR specialist, it goes one of two ways. One, your publicist is awesome and needs very little oversight. You won't even feel the need to be cc'd on emails or ask where you're being pitched because you'll see your company securing valuable media placements left and right. This is the result of a publicist who lives and breathes your brand. Take Yvette Noel-Schure, for example – publicist to *the* Beyoncé Knowles Carter. Yvette is a personal shero of mine, both as an inspiring female entrepreneur and a kick-ass publicist. These days, Beyoncé barely does press, and yet she has a better public image than anyone. You can tell how hard Yvette rides for her client, and how fiercely she protects and admires her. This is the model of an ideal publicist.

On the other hand, you could end up with the publicist from hell. In my experience, this has been more common. I've trusted publicists to promote my brand only to see zero results. Either I realize they're prioritizing other clients, or I notice that every placement I do get has been as a result of my own network and outreach. I've also had to fire a publicist after three years because I realized she didn't believe in my brand. I would ask to be pitched to large publications and she would always have an excuse. According to her, Alikay was always too small, too lacking, too *something* to dream of landing that feature. Ultimately, I had to stand up and be an advocate for my own company. At the end of the day, it's very difficult to find someone who believes in your brand as much as you do. If that's the case, I say, save your money. If it's not Yvette, I don't want it! You're better off being your own publicist if you can spare the bandwidth.

In my honest opinion, a publicist is not a necessity, but a luxury. Especially in the early days of your company, you should be going hard to market yourself. The truth is that you *can* do it in-house. All you need is a pitching deck, a media kit, press release skills, and some hustle.

Sales pitch deck – Your sales pitch deck is a presentation that outlines the unique selling points of your business. Focused on facts, figures, analytics, and growth, your sales pitch deck is what you present when pitching your products or services to potential clients, retailers, or investors.

Media kit – A media kit is a presentation you present to pitch yourself for speaking engagements or press features. A media kit will often contain your primary keynote speaking points as well as the ins and outs of your brand – how you started, top products or services, points of difference, etc. You will also include your social reach as well as a rate card for booking purposes.

Press release - Finally, when you handle your own PR you will need to learn how to write a killer press release. Press releases inform the media of key details and selling points of your flagship products, services, and new launches. Furthermore, a good press release will show editors or journalists why their specific audience will benefit from reading about your brand. Press releases should be tailored to the publication you are pitching to increase your chances of securing an awesome feature. Once you've written your press release, you can use

PR Newswire to send them out. PR Newswire is a distributor which will send your press releases out to a huge network of major and minor publications so that your business can get the exposure it deserves.

Today, Alikay Naturals does in fact work with an outside PR firm, but I make sure to have a system of checks and balances in place to ensure that I am getting my money's worth. For one, I receive detailed PR recap reports on a monthly basis. This includes all information from where my company has been pitched that month, to what direction we are taking moving forward. If we land any media placements – small or large – I need to know which ones and receive specific links. Furthermore, I don't let the fact that I have a PR team absolve me of my duties as C.E.O! I am still the number one ambassador to my own brand. This means that I keep my eye out for any media calls or placements I want. Oftentimes big publications will post inquiries or feature opportunities for small business owners on their social media platforms. There is also a site called HARO – Help A Reporter Out – where journalists can connect with niche industry experts for credited quotations in their articles. Whenever I see something I think could be a good fit for Alikay, I simply screenshot it and send it over to my PR firm. Remember, at the end of the day how your company is marketed is under your control. Take the reins.

90 Days to C.E.O Plan

branding

- ☐ DESIGN YOUR LOGO
- ☐ COMPLETE A BRAND MOOD BOARD
- ☐ BUSINESS CARDS AND STATIONARY
- ☐ SET UP YOUR WEBSITE
- ☐ BRANDING STANDARDS MANUAL

marketing, public relations & advertising

- ☐ CONTENT MARKETING
- ☐ SOCIAL MEDIA MARKETING
- ☐ INFLUENCER MARKETING
- ☐ AFFILIATE MARKETING
- ☐ CREATE A BRAND PLAYBOOK
- ☐ ANALYTICS
- ☐ PUBLIC RELATIONS – IN HOUSE V. PR FIRMS
- ☐ CREATE A LAUNCH PLAN
- ☐ GUERRILLA MARKETING
- ☐ CREATE A SALES PITCH DECK
- ☐ CREATE A MARKETING PLAN AND BUDGET
- ☐ REGISTER FOR GOOGLE ANALYTICS

VISIT RGBUSINESSUNIVERSITY.COM/90DAYRESOURCES

SUPPLIERS and VENDORS

Suppliers and vendors provide businesses with the raw materials and components they need to actually create and sell their finished products. In Alikay Naturals, for instance, we could not create our hair and skin products without the natural oils that we purchase in bulk. Typically, your company operates as a vendor when you vend or sell your products to customers. In business-to-business commerce, however, the supplier is the vendor and your company is the customer. As key players in the production process of your goods, you will want to build solid long-term relationships with cost-effective, timely, and reliable vendors and suppliers.

FINDING VENDORS

The first step to finding the right vendor or supplier is determining what items you need to create your final products. Once you have an idea, you can ask for vendor referrals from peers and even competitors, as long as your questions are non-proprietary. Large vendors will commonly sell to competing businesses within the same industry. Another option is to simply conduct a Google search. Identify what you're looking for and search key words accordingly – wholesale, custom, bulk. After compiling several options, do a price comparison.

LEAD TIMES, PRICE BREAKS, and PAYMENT TERMS

One thing to consider is domestic versus overseas suppliers – each have their pros and cons. For example, you might find better deals and prices from foreign suppliers, but you risk obstacles such as communication issues due to time zone differences and language barriers, unexpected holidays, potentially poorer quality, and longer lead time. Lead time is the amount of time that passes between placing your order and your goods actually being shipped. You want to avoid long lead times that could interfere with your ability to fulfill orders to customers or retailers. Your customers won't care why their shipments are delayed – they just want their goods on time. Domestic vendors are closer to home and will generally have shorter lead times, however they may also come with higher pricing. When considering lead times, also factor in the time it will take to process and actually make your order before transporting it from their warehouse to your door.

When you're first courting a vendor, ask them for the pricing of different quantities. If you know you typically need to order a lot of something, request pricing info for quantities of 100, 250, 500, 1,000, 2,500, and 5,000 units of that item. This will help you gain clarity on potential price breaks or discounts that you can receive for purchasing at a higher volume. Many suppliers may have an MOQ or minimum order quantity, in order to accept your business. If the MOQ is ridiculously high and you have no way to store that large of an order, that may not be the right supplier for you.

Payment terms can be tricky and will often determine which vendors you're able to work with. Never hesitate to negotiate, especially if you've been working with a vendor for a long period of time. My rule is to negotiate prices annually, or even every six months. This includes big companies that you work with, such as freight companies. Alikay ships with FedEx Freight and we are consistently negotiating better terms with our increase in volume. Remember, as your company grows, your relationship with that vendor's business is also growing. They will generally want to retain your business and will often be willing to come down on price for long-term customers. Don't underestimate the power of your order! Additionally, make sure that you are as forthcoming as possible with your payment term expectations from the very start. Vendors may have you start off with payment upfront, but later on they may give you a credit application that you can fill out. Payment terms are typically thirty or sixty days, on average. This gives you that flexibility when your business is low on cash and you need a little bit of wiggle room. Whatever your payment terms are, be sure to pay your vendor bills on time! Even if you start out with a term of thirty days, the vendor may extend your agreement to sixty or even ninety days after order once they see that you consistently pay on time.

BUILDING RELATIONSHIPS

Finally, build relationships with the sales reps that work for your vendors and suppliers. These sales reps are your main points of contact and will help you out with deals and troubleshooting in the case of missed deliveries or damaged shipments – it's best to be on their good side. If you've been working with the same rep for a while, figure out when their birthday is or keep track of your anniversary for that account. You'll be surprised how much of a difference it makes when you take that small effort to wish them a happy birthday. Your sales rep may help you out when you're in a tight position. Perhaps you need to order something, but you don't have the cash up front, or maybe you need an extended time to pay an invoice because you're waiting on a payment from a retailer. Suppliers are more likely to be flexible with you when you've built up a rapport with them.

Finally, it is always a good idea to have a backup vendor so you never put all of your eggs in one basket. Your primary vendor will fill regular orders and a secondary vendor will be there for emergencies in case a component is missing, or something goes wrong with your primary supplier. For more detailed information and resources on where to go to get quality vendors, visit rgbusinessuniversity.com/90dayresources and check out the Rochelle Graham Business University™.

TRANSPORTATION OF GOODS – SHIPPERS and FREIGHT COMPANIES

Now that you've got materials from your suppliers and completed products in-house, you need to figure out how you will transport those goods first, from the supplier to you, and second, from you to your customers. If you are a service-based business or you're selling a digital product, good news. Your transportation is easier because you can simply e-deliver those items. However, shipping and general transportation is a very important aspect of logistics for physical product-based businesses.

SHIPPERS

Personally, I always recommend that companies work with at least one to two shippers. Different shippers have different rates for moving different sized packages, and the rates may change year to year. Make sure you are doing your research on the price offerings of different shippers on an annual basis, or even more frequently. Even if you don't plan on leaving your current shipper, know the prices out there on the market so you can work with your shipper to possibly match those better prices. Keep in mind, the higher the volume of orders that you are doing, the less you should have to pay. The main logistics companies for shipping are FedEx, UPS, USPS, and DHL. When my company was first starting out, we used USPS, and now we use FedEx.

Another important step is to find a shipper that is compatible with your e-commerce platform. For instance, my company uses Shopify for our e-commerce, and this platform actually integrates with FedEx and USPS using an integration tool called ShipStation. This means that we don't have to manually type in addresses that we want to ship to. Once a customer has placed an order, the information automatically syncs with our shippers so that everything is easily automated. While ShipStation is what I use for my company, you should look into various ecommerce integration tools to compare rates and find the option best suited to your business' needs. Things like this are important for cutting down the number of steps you and your team have to take from point A to Z.

FREIGHT TRUCKS

You are also going to need a freight or trucking logistics company – this is entirely different to your shippers. Freight logistics companies refer to companies that pick up pallets or truckloads of products, and this is typically necessary for larger companies or companies doing extremely high-volume orders. For instance, at Alikay Naturals we sometimes ship twenty-five, thirty, or forty pallets to a single retailer. These orders are much too large to fit on a FedEx or USPS truck, so we have to use a freight truck to transfer. For trucking, you can either use an independent freight company, or check if your shipper actually offers freight services. FedEx actually offers FedEx Freight, which is what we use at Alikay. Just like with shippers, make sure you are negotiating for competitive pricing with your freight company. We talk with a representative every 3-6 months to review the volume of our shipments and talk about better discounts. At this point, we have bartered down our costs to almost nothing!

INTERNATIONAL SHIPPING

The next thing is to decide whether you will be shipping your products internationally or domestically (within your company's home country). International shipping comes with several considerations. First, you must look into the fees that you will have to pay to your merchant services company in order to accept international payments - more on this in the "Accepting Payment" section, later on. You'll also have to consider the fees you'll pay to your shippers to ship overseas. You have to negotiate a different rate for international shipping as opposed to domestic. Second, you must consider the specific laws of other countries. When you ship internationally, different countries will have different laws and regulations for the types of products they do and do not accept. For instance, maybe your product contains a certain type of plastic or ingredient that is banned somewhere else. You'll need to look into these rules for any foreign countries where you plan to conduct your business.

Third, familiarize yourself with the customs processes. If you are consistently shipping to a certain country, you'll have to have the appropriate customs forms and documents filled out and accessible in your office. There will also be special packaging slips that must be filled out in a certain way so that all your packages can pass through foreign customs with no problem or interruption. Finally, think about the climate of the country you are shipping to. If you have a temperature-sensitive product, ask yourself if there are any significant climate changes that your product will have to go through to get to a certain destination. If so, you need to know how to prepare for that so your products aren't affected. These considerations also apply for importing products or materials from overseas. If you have an international supplier sending you components, research to find out whether there are any specific licenses that you need to have in order to be able to import or accept those shipments.

CARGO ACCOUNTS

Cargo accounts are one of my biggest business hacks when it comes to shipping and receiving goods for my business. Many people – even my entrepreneur friends – don't realize that you can open a cargo account with an airline in your city to help you ship and receive products overnight. Cargo accounts are clutch for B2B (business to business) transactions where you need to urgently ship a package, or you're waiting to receive a component, material, or product to be sent to your company from a vendor. Overnight shipment is typically very, very rare, especially when it comes to large orders. Shipping with your normal shippers – even on a rush order – will take two business days (two-day priority). If it's an overseas order, that will take even longer. When you work with freight companies, they also have their own trucking schedule. Unless you have your own truck that you can send out to pick something up, you'll generally have to wait the standard two business days here as well. Cargo airline accounts allow you to forgo the wait and send and receive your shipments overnight, or sooner.

First, set up a cargo account with an airline that travels to and from your city. Every airline has a cargo dock or station where you can drop off a package to be sent from your business. Simply check for available flights to your desired city, drop your package to an airline dock, and it goes right onto a plane to wherever you need it to go. These are the same flights that carry passengers; we just never think about the cargo that's also onboard! If you need a package to arrive in another state by 9pm, same-day, there is most likely no shipper that is going to be able to make that happen. With a cargo airline account, however, you can literally ship something at 5pm and have it delivered to another state by 9pm that night, just by putting it on a plane. If you have a great relationship with your vendor, you can possibly have them pack up and drop your package to an airline on your behalf, and it will get billed to your cargo account.

This has come in handy for me several times. One time in particular, Alikay Naturals was vending products at a two-day tradeshow. Our sales were doing well – so well, in fact, that we completely sold out of products on day one and had nothing else on hand to sell for the second day! Because we had a cargo account, we simply called one of our employees back in Ft. Myers, Florida who had a key to the office. The employee packed up a couple of boxes of product and dropped them to our local airline cargo dock. We received our products the very next day in time for the show.

When it comes to business, everything is time sensitive. Cargo shipping has been a life-saving hack; Alikay actually has three different cargo accounts. I recommend having accounts with more than one airline because you never know which one is going to have the flight you need. Visit my website for Rochelle Graham Business University™. My course "How To Vend and Sell Successfully at Small Events and Large Trade Shows"™ will teach you more useful business hacks like this one.

PACKING SLIPS and INVOICES

Packing slips and invoices are important documents when filling customer orders, but it's important to note the difference and treat each document accordingly. Packing slips are simply an itemized list showing what products are going into a certain package. Invoices show the monetary value of each purchase and the sum total amount made on each order. In my opinion, you should never have your employees see the actual invoices for company orders – this is a matter of privacy protocol. Invoices show how much customers are paying you; they show how much money is flowing in and out of your business. This should be privileged, private information for the sake of confidentiality. The only person on your team that needs to see the invoices and dollar amounts is the employee that is actually printing out the orders. Privacy is everything when it comes to safety and security; certain information – like your sales proceeds – does not need to be disclosed to all employees. When it comes to your packaging team, all they need to see is the packaging slips, so they know how the right quantity to pack of each item.

CUTTING YOUR COSTS

Finally, as an e-commerce business you must always be searching for ways to cut down your shipping costs. Perhaps my biggest savior in this area has been investing in a thermal printer. Typically, I see lots of businesses using traditional paper printers to print out all their shipping labels. Not only are the printers themselves expensive, but the constant cost of restocking on ink and toner is a killer. As an alternative, you can buy a thermal printer which uses heat instead of toner to print your shipping label! All you have to do is make the one-time investment of the thermal printer, the thermal or heat-transfer printer rolls, and the alcohol strips used to clean your printer. The printer rolls and cleansing strips are a vastly insignificant investment compared to traditional printer paper and toner. With a thermal printer, your shipping labels are printed as adhesives that you simply stick onto your packages. This is a huge save on costs for your business' domestic shipping. For recommendations on my favorite thermal printers and shipping resources, visit rgbusinessuniversity.com/90dayresources.

It is important to note, however, that printed shipping labels are actually required for international shipments. When shipping overseas, you will need to use waybill pouches, or clear, adhesive shipping sleeves that stick onto your packages. You'll have to print out your shipping labels and slide them inside the pouches for easy access for customs officials, who need to remove, examine, stamp, and reinsert your shipping labels. If, however, you only ship domestically, traditional paper printing is an unnecessary expense.

Another vital means of cutting down your shipping costs is bulk-purchasing. Buying in bulk simply means buying wholesale, or buying a lot of a specific item. Your tissue paper, crinkle paper, tape, bubble wrap, and boxes – all of these things can be purchased in bulk to save money. You can also order wholesale poly mailers (or clear, elastic bags to protect products from weather conditions), and bubble mailers (which contain padding for safe transport of fragile items). As my company also functions as a manufacturing facility, I buy my hair nets, gloves, and foot and floor covers in bulk, as well. One of my favorite websites for bulk-purchasing is Uline. Uline offers bulk options for your shipping and office materials, as well as thirty day payment terms that can really help your cash-flow.

You can even find some materials for free, if you look in the right places! For instance, USPS actually offers those waybill pouches or clear shipping sleeves, free of charge. They usually come in a pack of 100 and you can order them right off the website. FedEx and UPS also offer free envelopes and boxes for order. For larger boxes of a certain size or custom dimensions, you will have to pay, but many of your standard-sized boxes can be found for free. These are the types of things you should be looking for to save money as you scale and grow your business.

While saving money is always a goal, it should never come at the expense of your customer experience. Shipments and packages are a part of that experience. When a customer opens your package or box, they should be greeted by that same high-quality, satisfying brand experience that they had while exploring your social media and shopping on your website. Be sure to put real effort into the presentation and preparation of your packaging, but remember not to go so crazy that you hike up the costs. The key is to find a way to make your packages beautiful while maintaining cost control. For instance, a simple, hand-written thank you card is a sentimental, yet inexpensive way to show customers that their package was prepared with care. You don't have to start off with customized boxes, tape, and labels – you can add all those fancy things as you grow and your company actually has the revenue to afford them. At the start, simply focus on creating a customer experience of maximum magic at a minimal expense.

INVENTORY MANAGEMENT

Now that you've got reputable vendors on board, put a system in place for how you will store and track all of your inventory. Your inventory will include office supplies, raw materials from your suppliers, as well as finished products manufactured by your company. You can track inventory manually or electronically. Manual tracking is helpful for smaller-scale purposes, such as tracking the products brought to and sold at trade shows, however, it can also be done on a larger scale with the necessary systems in place. Alikay Naturals actually did all our inventory tracking manually for our first seven years of operation until we scaled to afford an electronic system. Electronic inventory software is useful for large-scale purposes like counting all the products and product components stored in your entire warehouse. Even when you work with a digital system, it's important to keep a watchful eye for proper tracking.

Assigning one person to make all product or component purchases for your business makes inventory tracking much easier and more organized. For Alikay Naturals, that person is Demond. Of course, I and the rest of the staff also have access to the inventory counts, however, it starts with Demond. Next, be sure to have clear restock thresholds so you know at what point you have to restock a certain product or item. This ensures that you don't fall behind and maintain enough numbers of each product to fill customer orders on time. Finally, it's also important to conduct damage reports so you know what products need to be remixed, repackaged, or relabeled. Our electronic inventory software allows for quick and easy scanning of products that need to be fixed or replaced.

My staff typically conducts inventory checks every Monday and turns in numbers to Demond so he knows how much to purchase at the start of each week. You should take inventory – at minimum – every month. Knowing how much stock you have will allow you to take on and fill realistic orders from customers and bigger clients like retailers. When you start selling to places like Target and Rite Aid, you have to know exactly how much you have, so you know what you can promise. Inventory management is also crucial to ensure that no one can steal products or materials from your workplace unnoticed. Last but not least, inventory management helps you with business forecasting. This is basically just having a clear understanding of what is going to happen in your business in the next thirty, sixty, or ninety days up to six months out, so that you can order and adjust your inventory accordingly.

PAYMENT PROCESSING

You've built your brand, come up with a marketing plan, and put suppliers, shippers, freight trucks, and an inventory system in place. Now you're finally ready to start selling! Before you get down to business, you have to set up your ecommerce company for payment processing. This is basically just a means

90 DAYS TO C.E.O

for accepting your customers' money through your website, and securely storing their financial and personal information (credit card numbers, addresses, etc.). To get started processing your payments, you'll need to set up the following: payment gateways, a payment processor, and a merchant account.

GATEWAYS, PROCESSORS, and MERCHANT ACCOUNTS

The good news is we've already learned all about merchant accounts (refer back to the "Money Management" section of chapter nine). To reiterate, a merchant account is a bank account that accepts all your incoming funds. After a successful transaction with an individual customer or retailer, the money will be deposited to your merchant account. Before you can receive money, however, you need a way for your website to recognize an incoming transaction request. This is done by what's called a payment gateway. A payment gateway then sends the request to a payment processor, which accepts and executes that transaction request. Before accepting a transaction, the payment processor checks for all necessary payment information, verifies that the customer's entered information is accurate, and makes sure that the required funds are actually available. Once everything checks out, the processor then takes the money from your customer and sends it to your merchant account. Payment gateway to payment processor to merchant account. This three-way process is how you receive your funds.

Unlike with cash transactions, you, as an online merchant, never actually receive money directly from your customer. You receive it from your payment processor, which receives

349

it from the customer. The transaction itself actually happens off-site. The customer uses your site to browse, shop, and add to cart, but once the actual order has been placed, all financial processing and verification happens through the payment gateway and processor. This all happens within seconds! When it comes to finding the right gateway for you, you can opt for a third-party gateway, which comes with set-up and monthly costs, or simply choose an ecommerce platform that already has an integrated gateway built in, like Shopify. In my company, for instance, customers shop at alikaynaturals.com, however, it's Shopify that actually accepts the money and stores customer financial info. Your ecommerce platform is what turns your website into an actual online store. Because Shopify is the one accepting and storing my customers' valuable financial details, it takes the pressure of ensuring safe and secure transactions off of me. This is a big reason why it is so important to choose a reliable ecommerce platform to partner with your website. More on partnering with ecommerce platforms later in the chapter. Below are some of the best and most common payment gateways and processors.

Payment gateways: PayPal, Payline, Stripe, Authorize.net
Payment processors: PayPal, Payline, Stripe, Square, Google Checkout

As you can see, several companies offer both payment gateway and payment processing services. It is also important to note that some gateways will offer you the opportunity to make in-person POS (point of sale) sales through free card readers.

These come in handy for in-person sales at brick-and-mortar stores, trade shows, and events, however, they often carry additional rates. When you manually punch in a customer's credit card number, there is no way to verify that the customer actually presented you with their card. As a result, you will be charged at a higher rate and fee.

ADDITIONAL FEES and PAYMENT THRESHOLDS

Certain processors also command higher percentage fees for accepting international payments. When choosing your gateway and processing provider, be sure to do a thorough comparison of flat and additional fees to make the best choice. Additionally, as your business grows and brings in larger sums of money, you should consider implementing a payment threshold for credit cards. Keep in mind that processing fees are higher for credit cards or PayPal payments. It's one thing to process a $500 payment, but when you're taking $50,000 or $100,000 at a time from a larger customer, you don't want to lose 3.5% of that to a processing fee! Instead, set a payment threshold, or an amount of money after which credit cards and PayPal payments will not be accepted. Request larger payment amounts via wire or manual check instead, and avoid the high processing fees.

FINANCIAL STATEMENTS

With your company in business and your payment processing in place, you'll also want to track the ongoing status of your finances. Financial statements help you to monitor your business' fiscal health and are often presented as status reports from your accountant or financial advisor. Even if you do your own bookkeeping, you should be preparing and reviewing financial statements on a regular basis. Three of the most important financial reports within a business' financial statement are: balance sheets, income statements, and cash-flow statements.

Balance sheet – A balance sheet gives you a picture of your company's financial position as of a specific date and time. This report will include your company assets on the left-hand side of the sheet, and company liabilities and equity on the right-hand side. Assets are cash or valuable properties owned by your company. Liabilities are your company's debts, and equity is the difference between the two (or the amount of money remaining if your company sells all of its assets and pays back all of its debts).

Income statement – An income statement is also known as a profit and loss statement. This report shows the amount of revenue your company earned over a specific time in addition to your losses. Basically, it shows your company's profitability and can be used to show investors your growth over a certain period.

Cash-flow statement – A cash-flow statement actually shows you all the cash that flows in and out of your company during a specific time period.

For more information on the different types of financial statements and overall financial management for your business, consider hiring an attorney or financial advisor.

BUILDING YOUR TEAM

When people ask me the hardest part of running a business, they are always shocked when I say, managing employees. It's one of the toughest challenges that any company – large or small – can face. Before we can talk about effective team management, however, we need to get into the nitty-gritty of finding, interviewing, and hiring staff. While you can start off doing things on your own, a staff will be necessary as you begin to grow and scale. Not only will you need more hands on deck as the customer orders roll in, but you will also need to delegate simply so that you can focus on steering the ship.

CREATING A JOB DESCRIPTION

Before you can scout or hire applicants, you must first create detailed job descriptions. Before you write a job description, you should decide exactly what positions you need to hire for. I typically do this by identifying the gaps in my company operations. I ask myself, what are the tasks that need to be done within my company, and what type of position would execute those tasks? The more specific you can be regarding those tasks or daily responsibilities, work hours, and skill and education requirements of every position within your company, the better job descriptions you will write. The better your job descriptions, the richer the pool of applicants you will receive and the more you can hold employees accountable once hired. Once you finally hire a new employee, make sure you present them with a copy of their official job description and send one to HR, too.

LISTING AVAILABLE POSITIONS

The next step is listing your available positions online. Job listings should include a brief description of your company and company mission, the job description, instructions for application submission, and of course, salary information. We will discuss strategy for deciding salary and payroll budget in the "Payroll & Payroll Taxes" section of this chapter later on. As for listings, there is a plethora of platforms where entrepreneurs can list available jobs. Some of the most popular are Indeed, Simply Hired, ZipRecruiter, Monster, Craigslist, and LinkedIn. Keep in mind that most of these sites allow you to post listings for free, but your job won't get seen by many candidates unless you pay to have it boosted. Some platforms charge a fee of, say, $25 or so; others are ridiculously expensive and not worth your time. As a new entrepreneur, job board listings are a cost you should be working into your budget.

Another option to supplement your job board postings is to create a we're hiring graphic that existing employees or family and friends can share within their networks. This graphic will of course include information about the job, your company, and a link leading people back to your formal website. Also consider posting on physical job boards in the student centers of local universities and community colleges. These are great places to find a wide breadth of eager, educated, entry-level applicants. Finally, don't underestimate the value of good, old word-of-mouth. Send out an email blast to your professional circle letting them know that you're looking to hire. Friends and family can also be a great source for referrals.

Now let's talk about interns. We'll get into actually structuring your company's internships and managing interns a little later on, but for now, take note that you can list internships on job boards just like you would for regular, full-time positions. Another great idea is to meet with the intern coordinators at local colleges, universities, and trade schools that specialize in the skill sets you're looking for. If you build a relationship with these intern coordinators, they can actually help you list your available internships on the college or university job boards so that they reach a ton of students. Be mindful that if you choose to list on school job boards, you'll have to stay on top of yearly university schedules. You may have to list every single semester, which means being aware of when the semester is starting. If it starts in August, for example, I would say that you should be listing your internships no later than June to give students ample time to find your listing and apply. Appoint someone on your team to keep up with this responsibility and relist open internships.

INTERVIEW and RESUME REVIEWING TIPS

At Alikay Naturals, the interviewing process can be pretty extensive. Number one, this helps us screen out all the people who've expressed interest in a position and narrow it down to our favorite, most qualified candidates. The first step is an online assessment. When we list a position on Indeed, we typically include a few assessment questions filter out prospects. If the people applying don't match these criteria, their resumes will be filtered out and they won't even be considered. For instance, if the job is location-specific at our headquarters in Florida but the applicant lives in California, there's no point in bringing them in for an interview. Once they pass the online assessment, it's on to a phone interview with my general manager. If the general manager approves, the applicant comes in for their first in-person interview with me.

If the job requires a very specific skill set, like graphic design, for instance, I might have them complete an assigned task before our meeting. It could be as simple as giving them a few pictures of Alikay Naturals products and asking them to create an advertisement. We keep the instructions clear but vague, so as to determine whether the applicant can read between the lines and think outside of the box. If they come in with the assignment not done or incomplete, we won't hire. If they come in missing critical components, we won't hire. Only if the applicant has managed to impress us with their ability to achieve the task and surpass the bare minimum instructions do they become a seriously viable candidate. At this point, we begin the official in-person interview.

Once you've attracted a number of applicants, it's time to start the interviewing process. You'll first narrow down prospects by evaluating their resumes. First, you want to look for formatting. Did they provide all necessary information? Education, work experience, special skills, and contact info? Does the resume contain only pertinent details and fit neatly onto one page? Finally, be sure to read closely for any typos or grammatical errors. At worst, typos are an indication of an unqualified applicant. At best, they show an inattention to detail. Other things to look out for are huge, unexplained job gaps or frequent job-hopping. This can show an inability to commit or workplace instability. Lastly, an unprofessional email address is always a no.

When it comes to the actual interview, you should come as prepared as the applicant. Have your questions formed in advance and tailored to extract specific information. Scenario-based questions are great for learning how an applicant thinks, problem-solves, or adapts on the spot. You want to develop questions that are a good mix of traditional interview questions – think back to things you've been asked during the course of your employment history – and questions that are specific to your niche, industry, or company. Once you ask a question, try not to do so much of the talking. You're not the one in the hot seat. Lead the conversation but let the applicant give a detailed answer.

Pay attention to body language and vague answers as they may be an indication of confidence. Of course, look for professional attire and eye contact, and always give the applicant the opportunity to identify their perceived strengths and weaknesses. After the interview, confirm this assessment with the applicant's references. People can look great on paper but prove to be headaches or underperformers when you speak to past employers. Avoid hiring applicants who speak negatively of past jobs or avoid direct answers. Finally, go in with a mindset of *not* wanting to give them the job. I know this sounds harsh, but I've found that this mindset helps you to be more discerning in hiring out of quality rather than desperation or need. Too often small business owners are so strapped for staff that they end up looking at possible applicants with rose-colored glasses. It's almost as if they are the savior, come to save your company! Wrong. Always operate from a place of strength. You are the one offering a job that they want! Make them sell themselves to you. To conclude, always ask for their minimum salary requirements.

HIRING

Never give someone a job if something about them feels off in your gut. Hiring an employee should feel like gaining an asset; you should be excited. If you see major potential, but still aren't quite sure, call them back for a second or even third interview. Also, not everyone you hire has to be full-time. If you like an applicant but feel that they're a little wet behind the ears, bring them on as a paid intern, a part-time employee, or hire them under the condition of a training period at a length of your discretion.

When deciding to officially make someone a job offer, I like to refer to the 7 C's of hiring, a concept developed by entrepreneur and author, Alan Hall. The 7 C's of hiring great employees are:

Competent – Does this applicant have the required skill set and job experience I need?

Capable – Is this applicant capable of growing beyond their current responsibilities?

Compatible – Does he or she have a likable personality? Will they get along with coworkers, clients, or partners?

Commitment – Does this person's job history indicate that they are serious about long-term employment?

Character – What are this person's values and how do they represent themselves in person and online or on social media?

Culture – Does this person fit in well with the established company culture?

Compensation – Has the applicant agreed to the offered compensation or presented a reasonable counter-offer?

If your applicants meet all of the above, congratulations! You've got yourself a new hire.

EMPLOYEE MANAGEMENT

It's one thing to hire new individual employees and it's another to manage a staff. Running a successful staff of team members means handling multiple personalities, implementing conflict resolution, and creating a general atmosphere of cohesion and productivity. While you can hire an office manager as you scale, in the beginning, all management responsibilities will be yours. My management style is a mixture between uplifting and firm. My staff understands that I believe in them, but they also know that we are not friends. This is a business and my company is my bottom line.

My company offers training to ensure that our employees remain at their best. We have an actual budget allocated for training our staff that includes online educational courses and local workshops and training sessions. When you invest in your team, it boosts performance, efficiency, and overall satisfaction. Another key element of management is providing opportunities for your employees to advance. Hopefully you have hired ambitious workers who seek upward mobility. There will come a time when they will express a desire to move up in the ranks and take on a new title and responsibilities. It is your job as the leader to assess their readiness for professional development with regular performance reviews.

Most businesses conduct employee performance reviews every six months. This gives you an ample amount of time to observe the employee in question and take note of their productivity, attention to detail, teamwork skills, and work ethic. This will also be a great time to receive feedback on management. Your employees may voice a concern or have a suggestion for optimizing company operations. Listen to them. You should also conduct year-end reviews that are more detailed. This is when you evaluate any raises or performance-based bonuses. The standard is generally a one to three percent raise, but you can offer a little more if you think it's fair and you can swing it in the budget. While every employee deserves a chance to rise in ranks, never feel pressured to give a raise or a new title simply because you were asked. These are privileges that must be earned.

WORKING WITH FAMILY

It is not unlikely that some of your first hires may actually be family members or friends. This can be a helpful solution for creating easy team chemistry or keeping trade secrets close at hand among people you trust. However, working with family comes with its own unique set of challenges and things to look out for. First, you cannot give special treatment. I personally employ many family members from my grandparents to my father-in-law and brother-in-law. All are subject to the same non-disclosure and non-compete agreements and held to the same standards of excellence as everyone else. I tell my management specifically, *I know that's my granddad, but if he messes up, make sure to speak to him and get it corrected.* It is important for regular staff members to know that they are no less valuable because they aren't related to you. Don't be lenient on family – that bond will always be there. Set boundaries and demand that they show up on time, ready to work. If a family member isn't fitting the bill, you have to be willing to let them go. By the same token, make sure you're treating your family members fairly. Just like you wouldn't talk down to your normal employees, make sure you don't belittle your family members. Furthermore, relatives must receive the same opportunity for employee reviews and raises as the rest of the staff.

INTERNS

Some people think of interns as less valuable employees, but this is not true. Interns can be a great addition to your business, especially when you're first starting out and you don't have a large budget to pay people. They can also be a wonderful asset even when your business is established. Keep in mind that interns are young, eager, and itching to get out into the workforce and flex their skills. They may be looking to receive credits at their college or university, or they may be looking to actually find a home at a company they love in the hopes of moving up to a full-time job. Find the right intern and you will find yourself a hard-working, enthusiastic team player. Also, as a C.E.O, you should appreciate the unique opportunity that interns give you. Interns are brand new workers; they haven't yet bounced around from job to job and picked up poor work habits like indifference and laziness along the way. They're still malleable enough for you to have a hand in shaping a truly excellent worker. Sure, they provide extra assistance for your operations, but it is also a privilege to have a chance to advance someone in their professional development. Therefore, think of your company internships as an opportunity for both you and your interns.

The next thing is deciding whether you're going to offer paid or unpaid internships. If you have an unpaid internship, remember to be fair – you don't want to use people. If you're not paying, you then need to make sure your company is offering some other kind of extreme value, education, or training to this person. Many companies offer college credit, but you should also be honing your intern by teaching them valuable hard and soft skills that they can bring with them after the internship ends. You can either allow your intern to work with you as executive assistant to the C.E.O, or you can offer them an internship in one of your company departments to gain focused experience in a specific area (ie: graphic design, marketing, sales, production, etc.). Don't just plug them in anywhere you want. During the interview process, be sure to ask prospective interns exactly what it is that they want to learn. What do they have an interest in? What are they looking to gain from the experience of working within your company? Upon conclusion of the internship, revisit these questions in an exit interview to determine how successful your internship actually was. Did they enjoy their time with your company? Did they learn whatever it was they wanted to learn? How can you improve your internship program for the future? These are all questions that can provide a wealth of information to you and your company.

You'll also need to decide on an internship term. How long will it last? A semester? One month? An entire year? This information should be included in the listing and reiterated during the interview process. As for payment, figure out the going pay rate for internships in your industry. Again, you can speak to the intern coordinators at universities and colleges to get a good idea – it doesn't have to be high. Remember that even paid interns should not be paid as much as full-time employees. You want to pay them a low entry-level amount, pretty much enough to make sure it's worth the time that they spend working with you, and to make sure they have enough gas money or public transportation fare to get to and from the workplace. Whether they're unpaid or paid, always give your interns a letter of recommendation for their good work at the conclusion of the internship. You may also include a nice little token like a gift card and a thank you note – a small token of appreciation. Finally, consider allowing them to use some of the work they've done for your business in their professional portfolios.

LABOR LAWS

As an employer you will have to understand and comply with labor laws. Many of these laws have to do with having the right legal protections and adequate pay rates in place for employees. More on determining salary in the "Payroll & Payroll Taxes" section of this chapter. Larger companies or those with great funding can afford to hire lots of HR specialists or legal counsel to keep them apprised of the changing legal standards for employment regulations – small businesses cannot. Still, it is your responsibility to adhere to the laws and treat employees fairly. Some of the most recognizable labor laws include minimum wage, overtime pay, misclassification, workers' compensation, and wrongful discharge or termination laws.

Minimum wage – minimum wage indicates the lowest possible hourly pay that you are permitted to pay employees according to the law. The specific hourly rate varies based on state, and many states are in the process of issuing minimum wage-hikes based on cost-of-living. To determine the minimum wage for your specific state, visit your state's labor office (you can find a directory at the U.S. Department of Labor website, dol.gov).

Overtime pay – Any hourly wage employee who works more than forty clockable hours a week must receive overtime pay at a rate of at least one and one-half times the regular pay rate, according to the Fair Labor Standards Act. There are some exceptions which you can check at the U.S. DOL website. Salaried employees do not receive overtime pay.

Misclassification – Misclassification is when you say a worker is an independent contractor, but the law identifies them as an official employee. Failure to accurately classify your workers will result in tax issues for both parties. More on employees vs. contractors in a bit.

Workers' compensation – Workers' compensation protects employees who get injured on the job or who fall sick because of unregulated conditions. Employers pay workers' compensation insurance so that those employees may receive payment for lost wages or medical care. Once you reach a certain number of employees (dictated by your state of business), workers' compensation is mandatory, and failure to provide this insurance will result in hefty fines. In Florida where my business operates, workers' compensation is mandatory once you hire four or more employees.

Wrongful termination – If you are accused of wrongfully discharging or terminating an employee, you may be sued. Visit your state labor office to learn about your state's specific wrongful termination laws and see which termination reasons are justified under state or federal law.

For a comprehensive list of labor laws, visit the United States Government Services and Information website (usa.gov).

EMPLOYEES vs. CONTRACTORS

Employees are just one type of worker you may be hiring to work within your business. You will likely also work with many contractors, freelancers, and independent workers on either an ongoing basis or special, one-off projects, as needed. For example, security or IT services are commonly outsourced to contractors. You may not require their work on a daily basis, but you will definitely benefit from their expertise for maintenance or emergency purposes (like in the event that your website crashes during a major sale). You can find contractors and independent workers through peer referrals, or through sites like Amazon Mechanical Turk (MTurk), Upwork, and Fiverr.

Below, find some of the main differences between employees and contractors:

Training – Employees work within the internal structure of your business and as such, must be thoroughly trained in procedures, company culture, as well as job requirements. Contractors, on the other hand, are appealing because they offer their own skills and expertise. Aside from the details of the project at hand, you won't generally have to provide any extra training.

Communication – As employees work with you every day, they are more readily accessible than contractors who split their time between numerous clients. You may not always be the priority.

Contract term and scope of work – The duration of an employee's employment is unpredictable. You never know when someone will quit or move out of state. With contractors, on the other hand, there is a stable contract term outlined at the beginning. You and your contractor will also have to agree on a clearly defined scope of work. The scope of work will detail every item, project, or deliverable that is to be completed by the contractor within the contract term. With employees, there may be some flexibility surrounding job responsibilities – your staff may occasionally take on additional tasks as needed, especially during crunch-time when there is a huge company project or deadline. With contractors, however, you must adhere to the limits of the scope of work. You cannot simply ask independent workers to add more to their plate without negotiating an extra pay amount for that new work.

Schedule – As the C.E.O, you set working hours for everyone on your staff. By contrast, contractors set their own schedules, and you cannot legally create a shift or control the hours that they work for you. If you do set a contractor's schedule, they are now classified as an employee by law, and all payroll and tax filing must reflect that status. If not, you can get into major legal trouble. At the onset of the working agreement, you and your contractor may agree on a work schedule along with the scope of work. For instance, you may say that you need a contractor to work with you four hours per day, twenty hours per week, but you cannot force the contractor to agree. If they do agree, you cannot add any extra hours on top of that agreed upon schedule.

Loyalty – As employees of your company, your team members are not legally allowed to work with your competitors. Contractors, however, often refuse to sign non-competes. They may be working with one or several of your competitors and there is little you can do outside of having them sign a non-disclosure agreement.

Payroll taxes – Unlike with employees, you do not have to pay payroll taxes for independent workers. They simply work for a fixed rate dictated and agreed upon between both parties upon drafting of the contract.

Chemistry – Employees are people who you have vetted. You've conducted multiple interviews, trained them according to your likes and dislikes, and gotten to know them. Many times they fit right into the fabric of your company and can even grow to feel like family. Contractors are strangers. Even if they are pleasant, they only have a limited exposure to company culture and the chemistry may not always feel natural.

As you can see, there are pros and cons to each group, but both contractors and company employees are essential to seamless operations within your business.

EMPLOYER/EMPLOYEE IMPORTANT DOCUMENTS and REGISTRATIONS

New employees will require a number of crucial documents both for their personal records and your company files. These documents include the job application form (including signed reference and background check authorization), Form I-9 (for employment eligibility verification), and Form W4 (for federal income tax withholding). Other pertinent documents include the employment contract, signed non-disclosure agreement, signed non-compete agreement, pay schedule, holiday calendar, benefits plan (if applicable), job description, payroll or direct deposit set up, access points list, and of course, an employee manual. Contractors also require a Form I-9, but they receive a W9 in place of the W4. For contractors paid over $600 a year, you will issue a 1099. Having all of these documents securely stored away will protect you should your employee records ever be audited by a federal, state, or local agency.

In addition to these documents, there are also several registrations that you must complete as the employer. Of course, we've already discussed registering with the IRS for your EIN or federal tax ID (refer to chapter nine). Your EIN is connected to payroll tax reports and payments and must be acquired before you hire anyone. Next, you must also join the IRS Electronic Federal Tax Payment System (EFTPS) so that you can withhold taxes from employee paychecks. After you make your hires, you must register all new employees with your state's new hire notification system. This allows for the government to collect child support payments from employees. Visit the U.S. Department of Health and Human Services website for more information on registering new hires with your state system. You will also have to contact your state's taxing agency and register as an employer within your state. Finally, you'll have to register with the labor department in order to pay unemployment taxes, and register for worker's compensation with your state's worker's compensation agency.

In addition to employee records and employer registrations, federal law also mandates that you visibly display certain documents within your place of business. These documents include a Family and Medical Leave Act poster (if you employ fifty or more employees), an Occupational Safety and Health Act (OSHA) poster, a Fair Labor Standards Act poster, a Notices to Workers with Disabilities Act/Special Minimum Wage poster, and an Employee Polygraph Protection Act poster. All of these posters may be ordered from the Department of Labor and should be displayed in a common area frequented by employees, such as a break room or lobby.

EMPLOYEE HANDBOOK

Finally, it is critical that you create an employee handbook for each new employee that joins your operation to read and sign. Not only is this a legally binding document between you and your new hire, but it also facilitates the training process by providing detailed information on company policies, procedures, workflow systems, and benefits. The more thorough and comprehensive the information in your employee handbook, the less hands-on you yourself may need to be in the training or onboarding process. After interviews are conducted and hires are introduced to the company, you can delegate the onboarding process to a company manager or executive assistant who will use the handbook to apprise your hires of the way things work.

PAYROLL and PAYROLL TAXES

Every employee you hire must be paid a fair wage for reasonable hours as mandated by law. For a new business, especially one that is self-funded, it can be tricky determining exactly what that wage should be. People will often make you feel like you're not paying them enough. Even if your wages are fair and in line with industry standards, you will sometimes feel pressured to offer larger and larger salaries. Take it from me – don't allow yourself to be bullied or guilted into high salaries that you simply cannot afford. Someone once told me, *you are not paying your employees to live a lifestyle that they want to live. You are paying your employees to do the job that they are providing for your company*. In other words, it is not your responsibility to pay for the fancy houses and extravagant vacations your employees wish to have. As a C.E.O, your only responsibility when it comes to payroll is making sure that employees are paid fairly, on time, and within your company budget. If someone wants to be paid more, they have to prove that they can do more. Whether that means stepping up in workplace responsibilities, or taking advantage of extra training or education to improve their skill set, employees must do more to earn more. Never create salaries out of obligation.

Now that we've cleared that up, your first step is deciding on salary versus hourly pay.

SALARY VS. HOURLY PAY

Salaried employees – Salaried employees get paid a flat rate for their service. This is typically an annual salary that is paid on a biweekly basis. For instance, a salaried employee might make $40,000 a year, and each paycheck will reflect the same amount regardless of how many hours the employee actually works (unless salary is renegotiated due to promotion).

Hourly employees – Hourly employees are paid per hour for their work. If they work more hours, they are paid for that extra time. When you pay by the hour, employees must work a minimum of forty clockable hours before they are entitled to receive overtime pay, which is fifty percent higher than their normal pay rate.

There are pros and cons to both options. With salaried employees, for instance, you will never have to pay overtime pay, even if the employee works over forty hours in a week. As long as the work that they're doing is still within the reasonable limits of their job description, their pay will remain the same. For hourly employees, on the other hand, you cannot require extra hours without issuing overtime wages. If your business is experiencing tough times, however, and you need to make cutbacks, it is much easier to simply reduce employee hours rather than eliminating an entire salaried position. Be sure to have a concrete overtime policy built into your company contracts so that all wage expectations are clear upon hire. Determine whether salary or hourly pay is the best option for your business before coming up with actual pay figures.

DETERMINING STARTING SALARY

A good start for determining starting salary for your staff is to do some research on salaries across your industry. Job board sites like Glassdoor give insight into the average pay ranges for titled positions within your city. This will help you figure out the industry standard for particular positions, and it will also help you to beef up your job descriptions as you come across additional job responsibilities that you hadn't thought of. On many of these sites, you can type in your city, state, and the type of job, and they will tell you the average pay for small, medium, and large sized corporations. Use these as a starting point for creating a competitive wage, but remember to adjust based on factors like the employee's level of education and/or experience. When listing your available positions online, you can either post the starting salary or a range, but be sure to include compensation commensurate with experience. If you find yourself in an ultimate pinch where you simply cannot match competitive rates, consider turning to family or interns for your first employees.

Once you have an understanding of industry pay standards, you need to come up with a payroll budget. How much can you actually afford to pay in salary or wages for each individual position? When answering this question, do not forget to calculate in the employment taxes for your state. For example, you may decide upon a weekly salary of $700, but you will actually end up paying $850 for that employee in total – $700 going to the employee and $150 going to the state for taxes. Figure these expenses in so that you create realistic salaries for each position and remain within your overall payroll budget.

Once you settle on what you consider to be a reasonable starting salary, hold off on the offer until you ask the applicant for their minimum range. If they quote a figure lower than the one you came up with, great! If their figure is higher than your budget, don't promise anything you can't deliver. Any good hire will try to negotiate, as they should. The fact remains that you still have to be smart and reasonable about what you can match and how you allocate your funds. Keep in mind, you have other employees to pay, as well! In the event you can't go higher on salary, it's always fair to let an applicant know that there will be room for bonuses as tenure and responsibilities grow.

OVERTIME

While you want employees that will go the extra mile, try as best as you can to limit the amount of overtime worked within your team. For one, overtime is time and a half pay – if everyone on your team is staying late or working weekends, that money adds up and payroll time can become even tighter. Oftentimes employees will cite unreasonable workloads or insufficient resources for needing to work overtime. This may be an indication of one of two things. First, the employees in question may be being dishonest or oblivious to the mismanagement of their own workday. To rectify any dishonesty, make sure you have a system or person in place to make sure employees are clocking in and out on time. This ensures that workers are only paid for hours they've actually worked. Second, it's also possible that the all-hands-on-deck nature of your small business has caused insurmountable workloads. Your employees are being honest and it's simply just too much work for the workday. In that case, you may need to examine your operations and consolidate responsibilities so your employees can breathe. You also don't want your staff giving their whole lives to work. Limiting overtime requests keeps the workplace culture light and allows employees to go home to their families on time. Make sure your overtime policy is stated clearly in all contracts for new hires.

PAYROLL TAXES

As an employer, it is your legal responsibility to pay federal payroll taxes. To do this, you will withhold a portion of your employees' paychecks to send to the IRS. The amounts you withhold will depend on each individual employee's income and tax filing status. This money goes toward programs like Social Security and Medicare.

There are three components to your payroll taxes: Federal Income Tax, Federal Insurance Contributions Act (FICA) for SS and Medicare, and Federal Unemployment Tax Act (FUTA) for government unemployment taxes. For Federal Income and FICA taxes, you will either send payments to the IRS on a monthly or semi-weekly basis; it depends on how many employees you have on payroll. FUTA taxes are reported annually and paid every quarter. For more information or to learn the specifics of your company's payroll taxes, visit the IRS website.

TERMINATION PROCESS and LOSING EMPLOYEES

While you may not want to think about it, the time will come for every C.E.O or business where an employee quits or must be let go. Sometimes this will be a blessing, and sometimes it will feel like a major blow, if the person was a valuable and dedicated member of your team. Whether you're firing someone, or they decide to resign, you must have processes in place to facilitate a smooth transition.

FIRING AN EMPLOYEE

There's a saying I love that goes, "slow to hire, quick to fire." As we've already discussed, hiring a new employee should be done with care. You want to really take your time in the vetting and interviewing process, sometimes conducting two or three interviews before extending an official offer. Firing is a different situation. You cost your business more stress, money, and detriment by holding on to an employee that is no longer a good fit for the position. If an employee is consistently messing up – whether that be by coming in late, slacking on responsibilities, or clashing with their coworkers or the company culture – you have to make the swift decision to let that person go. Quick to fire means, don't drag out the process; fire that person as soon as you realize he or she is just not working out.

Sometimes, you may be hesitant to let a bad employee go because you don't think you're in a position to lose them. You might think it's better to hold on to them rather than have the position vacant and end up with those responsibilities falling back onto your team or your own plate. Yes, it's true that vacant positions can pose a problem, especially as your business grows. However, lazy or underperforming employees are like a toxin to your business operations, and their poisonous effects tend to spread and infect the rest of your good employees. Get them out as soon as possible, or if necessary, keep them on board until you find a new hire. You can always go ahead and relist that specific position online to attract new prospects while you wait for the right new hire. If that bad employee gets his or her act together, simply dissolve the listing. If not, fire them and then you'll at least already have some options on the table for replacements.

DISCIPLINARY DOCUMENTATION and TERMINATION LETTERS

Before you even make the decision to let someone go, make sure that you are keeping proper documentation of all employee mishaps, mistakes, and issues in your HR employee files. Florida, where my company operates, has what is called at-will employment. This means Florida employers may fire employees at will, or as we see fit without warning or having to provide just-cause. As long as the motivations are legal (meaning, the employee is not being fired due to discriminatory reasons such as race or religion), we can fire as we please. This is not true for many states. As a C.E.O, it is critical that you do your research and learn the HR hire and fire policies for your area. If you do not have at-will employment, you will need to have adequate reasoning on file whenever you let someone go. This will protect you legally in case your company is ever audited, or that employee brings up legal action after termination.

Documentation must be in written form – verbal warnings are not sufficient. If you do issue a verbal warning to an employee, make a written note and provide a copy to the employee as well as your HR department for records. Make sure your language is clear as to the violation at hand. For instance: *Hi, Randy. You just missed an important deadline for xyz. I know we've talked about it in person, but I need to have it documented so that you and I are both on the same page that this cannot happen again.* Whatever your warning statement says, sign it, have the employee in question sign, and then put it in their HR file and give them a copy.

Once you feel that you've issued enough warnings, the time has come to begin the termination process. It is important to write up a formal termination letter; this should be done on the same company letterhead you used to write them their job offer. Make sure to include a bullet point recap of all the specific incidences and reasons for termination (with their dates). Request a signature (though they may not sign it), sign it yourself, give them a copy, and file a copy with HR, as well. Letting someone go is never a comfortable process, but it's important that you build the skill set to fire swiftly and appropriately for the health of your business.

DEALING WITH RESIGNATIONS

Like terminations, resignations are also inevitable. Sometimes your company is just not the right fit for the personality, work style, timing, or circumstances of an employee's life. If the employee that resigns was a lackluster team member, good. That only means less paperwork on your end while you avoid termination. However, you will come across times when you have to accept the resignation of a stellar staff member who leaves what feels like a void in their wake.

As hard as it may be, don't take it personal when an employee quits. This is a lesson that took me some time to learn. Sometimes we may have developed a fondness for that person. Other times, we may simply appreciate their unique skill set or work ethic. You may also have poured a lot of training dollars, resources, and energy into that worker. When they choose to leave, it's easy to feel resentful toward their decision. This is completely unproductive. That employee's reasons for leaving may not have anything to do with you. Maybe they're looking for a career change or going back to school. Perhaps they're moving to another state. It's also possible that they love you as a boss, but just don't vibe well with the job itself, or their coworkers. Lastly, yes – some people just will not like you. No matter the reasoning, remember that employees are human beings with their own preferences and their own agency. They don't owe the same allegiance to your company as you do. One thing my husband Demond always says is this: when people leave, thank them so much for helping the ship to get this far.

Just know that when they hop off, the ship is going to keep sailing forward! Remind yourself that you are the captain; the crew may come and go but the destination remains.

Some employees leave and go on to find bigger and better opportunities for their unique personal and professional paths. Be happy for them! Other times, employees will leave and you will know in your gut that it is not a good decision. Your intuition may be telling you that this is the wrong move for their family or career, but remember, that is only your opinion – keep it to yourself. In times like these, I lean on one of my favorite Bible quotes and the inspiration behind my daughter, Serenity's, name: *God, grant me the serenity to accept the things I cannot change, the courage to change the things I can, and the wisdom to know the difference.*

Finally, if a truly valuable employee decides to resign, there is nothing wrong with asking for clarity about what brought them to that decision. This is what's known as an exit interview. You can prepare a brief survey to ask why the employee is leaving, how they perceived their relationship with management and other staff, and what they liked and disliked most about their position, among other things. If they can share something that you can tweak or fix, that only improves the operations of your company. Perhaps it will even convince them to stay.

As a matter of fact, don't be afraid to ask someone if they can give you more time. If an employee has given you a two-week notice and you really need four weeks to be able to properly transition the position, feel free to ask them for those two extra weeks. Also, when you hire new employees, build a resignation clause into their contracts. This is especially important for high-level positions like managers. These are critical positions that your company operations truly depend on, and a sudden loss of a manager or executive can be potentially crippling. At the time of hire, ask for a thirty, forty-five, or sixty day notice before resignation and get it in writing. This will help make your transitions much smoother down the line.

If the employee still chooses to leave, however, let it be. The quicker you can accept the loss of a strong employee, the quicker you can pivot your focus back to the rest of your team. Appreciate those who remain and turn your eyes forward to finding a new replacement.

HUMAN RESOURCES

Now that you have a staff, how will you manage them? Even if you are a three-person operation just starting out, it is always important to have a human resources system in place. Of course, your HR department will house all important employee documents. Make sure that each employee and contractor has a detailed HR file including everything from their applications and agreements, to job terms, descriptions, and of course, warnings and disciplinary reports. It is also important to do your research on state and federal labor laws to see how long certain documents must be kept on file. Some things you are legally required to have on file for four to seven years!

HR is also essential to creating a positive, uplifting, and effective workplace culture. As C.E.O, that culture trickles down from you to all other employees. The most important thing is to establish yourself as a leader, not a boss. Back in chapter four, we popped the boss babe balloon, or shattered the lazy, socially trending perceptions of what it actually means to be a boss. While there's nothing wrong with the term itself, I personally prefer to think of myself as a leader. Leadership invokes the feelings and energies I want associated with my business. In the words of business author and speaker Tom Peters, "Leaders don't create followers, they create more leaders." Let's take a look at some of the key differences between bosses and leaders.

A Boss	A Leader
Scolds and talks down to employees	Gives constructive criticism to make employees better
Expects staff to work hard but not themselves	Works hard and leads by example
Me me me mentality; brags and is cocky	Is proud of themself and team accomplishments
Dismissive of employee concerns	Listens with intention to find resolutions
Treats employees like a number	Treats employees like human beings
Demands respect but doesn't give it	Expects and gives respect
Doesn't care how the work is done as long as it's done	Holds staff accountable for doing excellent work
Yells at employees	Speaks to staff in calm intentional tone
Focuses on the now and doesn't plan ahead	Plans and prepares staff for long-term company and career goals

As you begin the process of expanding your team, show them that you are on their side. Yes, you are their boss, but you are all partners working together to shape the company vision. Value your team members' opinions and give feedback and room for growth. Uplift and empower your team with your words and attitude. Never forget – a captain is only as good as his or her crew.

CUSTOMER/USER EXPERIENCE

We've already discussed the basics of setting up your website and social media pages, but now let's get into the details of user experience. User experience refers to the way potential and returning customers navigate and perceive your brand in everything from products and services to customer service. It's not enough to have an online presence – you should constantly be evaluating how you can better interface with your consumers to enhance their overall experience, as well as your brand reputation.

WEBSITE FUNCTIONALITY

Yes, your websites should be aesthetically-pleasing, but they've also got to work. Put systems in place to check on the functionality of your webpages, as well as to periodically update your images and banners to keep things fresh. Make sure all webpages are easy to navigate and search engine-optimized. Search Engine Optimization (SEO) is the process of using keywords relevant to your specific industry to increase traffic to your website and individual webpages. By using buzzwords, you will boost your ranking in potential customers' online search results, thereby boosting your chances of landing new sales.

Moving on, the most relevant web pages every site should have are a homepage, a shop page, an about us page (about the company, about you as C.E.O, or both), and a contact page.

Be sure to include clickable icons for all of your social media platforms, as well as a home page pop-up prompting visitors to sign up for your company email newsletter. All websites should also have mobile functionality so people can navigate from their phones and tablets without error.

To avoid website failure or malfunction, choose a host that offers a high bandwidth. The higher the bandwidth, the greater the speed and connectivity of your site. For any image needs, use BigStock Photo. BigStock is a website where you can source affordable, royalty-free high-resolution stock photos, images, and vector graphics. Anything you find on BigStock can be used on your website without you running the risk of being hit with a lawsuit.

Another important thing is to partner your website with an ecommerce platform. I cannot stress this enough. Ecommerce platform partnering allows you to make sales on your website – it's what turns your site into an actual online store. Like I mentioned earlier, Demond and I have been using Shopify for at least three years. I like Shopify because it's reliable; it keeps up with the trends and is constantly innovating and updating for a better user experience. It also offers safe and secure storing of my customers' financial details, so I run less risk of exposing my tribe to dangerous cyber-attacks. I also like the ease of their analytics and reports. I can see my money at all times, what's working and what's not working, and bounce rates (the percentage of visitors who visit my site and then leave). Through Shopify, we can make any webpage on our site shoppable simply by adding a buy button. We can embed products, collections, and shopping carts for a mobile-friendly and secure checkout experience, and integrate with shipping systems like FedEx and USPS. If you have a brick-and-mortar retail location or need to sell at in-person events like trade shows, the Shopify POS (point of sale) App allows you to accept purchases through your smartphone and pocket-sized card readers. While this platform works for me, it is important to do your own research and choose an ecommerce platform with the right capabilities for your business. Other popular options include BigCommerce, Magento, Big Cartel, Etsy, Ebay, and Square.

Finally, research effective plug-ins for your website. Plug-ins are separate software components that add additional capabilities or functions to your site. These functions will often enhance user experience, or prompt potential consumers to keep shopping. For instance, you can create a plug-in that pops up when a shopper clicks on a certain product. The pop-up may say something like, If you liked this item, you may also like these. Other plug-in options may prompt users to sign up for company emails or help you add quick contact and FAQ pages. Plug-ins are a great way to increase the time that customers spend surfing and shopping your website.

SOCIAL MEDIA ENGAGEMENT

User experience is highly important on social media as your social platforms will often be the first point of contact for prospective customers. Many customers take to Instagram, Facebook, and Twitter to voice their concerns, ask questions, offer praise and feedback, or lodge fiery accusations. It is your job as a brand to field and respond to comments and direct messages in a professional and timely manner.

First things first, separate your business page from your personal page. While I suggest that C.E.Os build up their personal brands to capture consumer interest and loyalty, it is still important to make the distinction between your brand and yourself. First of all, it saves you the headache of having to manage more than one page on each platform. You can manage your own accounts while your social media team will handle the company pages. Secondly, it encourages customers to voice their concerns and opinions in the right place – your business platforms. If you are not building a personal brand but still maintain an Instagram, Twitter, or Facebook account, be sure to make your pages private. Business accounts, on the other hand, should always be open to the public.

The next thing is engagement. It's not enough to post pretty graphics and scour social media for influencers to partner with – you have to actually engage with the people commenting on your pages. This means liking and responding to comments, answering questions and direct messages, and reposting user-generated content. People love to see real humans using your product or service, so be sure to work customer testimonials, tutorial videos, and reviews into your marketing mix. Just be careful of low-quality content. Only repost an image or video that has good lighting, and of course, that features your brand in a positive way that is also in keeping with the overall aesthetic of your page. Finally, you can also engage by going live or conducting polls on Facebook, Instagram, or Periscope, tagging customers, commenting under posts on relevant industry profiles, and commenting on profiles of loyal customers. As a developing brand, you should use social media to seek out customer feedback and opinions as a way to improve.

When it comes to engagement, there are also some hard no's. For one, my company never responds to trolls or nasty commenters. This is a waste of your time and energy. Most social platforms allow you to flag nasty or inappropriate comments as spam, and you can also choose to block a repeat offender. We also don't respond publicly to individual customer service complaints. If we receive a directed question about a product or order issue in a comment or direct message, we will respond to point the commenter towards the proper communication channels. When this happens, be sure to use a pleasant but firm tone: *Hi there. Thank you so much for your comment. We are unable to discuss individual orders publicly, but would be happy to talk in private. Shoot us a DM or email and we will get back to you within the next forty-eight hours.* A simple response like this takes the attention on your post away from the inquiry and also makes the commenter feel heard.

Finally, don't forget to create a LinkedIn profile for your business. LinkedIn is the professional hero of social media, and is wonderful for networking, building your company's reputation, and even sourcing qualified applicants for open positions. You can also write and share LinkedIn blog posts on topics related to entrepreneurship or your specific industry in order to establish yourself as a professional authority, or simply increase content marketing.

IN-PERSON EVENTS

Engagement is also critical for in-person events like meet and greets and trade shows. Not only are these events opportunities for you to make sales, they are also the first introduction your customers will have to the face behind the brand. Always be professional and approachable, and offer service with a smile. You want customers to walk away with a good taste in their mouths about you and your brand. Always have samples and business cards to distribute and accurate shelf-to-self representation. Essentially, this just means to make sure that who you are on the shelves comes across in your in-person persona. If your brand is known for being cool and edgy, represent yourself as such in person. People should get what they expect from your brand.

In-person events should never be thrown together. It takes dedicated hard work and detailed training to prepare for and put on successful events. I myself have vended and sold at in-person events with my company all over the world, including Italy, Paris, and all over the United States. I have learned many invaluable lessons, many of which are included in my Rochelle Graham Business University™ course, "How to Vend and Sell Successfully at Small Events and Large Trade Shows."™ To learn my secrets, be sure to check out the course at rgbusinessuniversity.com.

CUSTOMER SERVICE

No matter how small your company, customer service is a mandatory part of your operations. For one, strong customer service will help you retain the customers you already have as well as attract new ones. When customers and clients are satisfied, they spread the news to their friends, leading to new business for your brand. Secondly, having a customer service system – whether that be through a dedicated phone line or email address – grounds your business as a real-life, human-run company. People appreciate calling and being able to ask questions to real humans instead of robots and automated voices. Customer service makes it clear that you care about your customers' brand experience.

BUSINESS PHONE NUMBERS

Rule number one is to have a customer service line or phone number available right from the beginning. This number should be separate from your personal cell phone number! Never give out your own phone number to clients or customers – that should be reserved for only the people you know and trust the most. Instead, you can opt for a virtual phone system that will add a unique business number to your personal phone. One option is Grasshopper. Grasshopper provides multiple business phone number options from toll-free 800, 877, 888, 866, and 855 numbers, to vanity numbers that make your company phone number easily memorable to customers – think, 1-800-FLOWERS. Alternatively, Grasshopper also lets you choose a phone number with a city or state-specific area code. This is a great option for building trust and comfort with your local community as a small business. Virtual phone systems like Grasshopper offer affordable monthly subscription rates.

For bootstrappers, there are several free options for securing business phone numbers as well. If you have a Gmail account, you can sign up for Google Voice to make free calls and texts from your Android, Apple phone, or computer. Other options include FreedomPop and eVoice. For free plans, you may be limited in the minutes, texts, and data you can use per month, however these are wonderful cost-saving alternatives if you don't have the cash flow for a more extensive subscription. I highly recommend FreeConferencecCall.com, where you can host and record free phone and video conference calls. VoIP or Voice over Internet Protocol allows you to make calls with just a computer, internet access, and a headset. If you opt for a traditional landline business phone system, RingCentral and Ooma Office are among the most noteworthy options.

When it comes to actually operating your new business phone line, you can either do it yourself, assign the responsibility to a staff member, or outsource to another company. Yes, that's right – there are companies you can actually pay to take on your customer service operations if your team doesn't have the bandwidth. If that's not an option or you'd rather handle customer service in-house, you can even create a fake customer service or assistant email address to field customer inquiries, or change your voice and take calls as your own customer service rep. When you're just starting out, it's all about thinking outside of the box. Get creative!

POLICIES, PROCEDURES, and FAQs

Just as an employee handbook details policies and procedures for internal relations, you should create a customer service handbook to set up policies for common customer complaints. Things to consider include your company's return policy. Will your business accept product returns or exchanges? Will you offer a money-back guarantee for an unsatisfactory service experience? How many days after an order will customers have to file a complaint or ask for a return? Will your product come with a warranty? These are all crucial questions to ask yourself before you start selling to the public. Create a Frequently Asked Questions section within your website to provide these answers and come up with a system for adding and responding to new FAQs as they come in.

Your customer service handbook should also include phone and email scripts. Whether you have someone on staff fielding inquiries or you've outsourced to a virtual customer service provider, your company policies should always be communicated in a clear and consistent manner. Scripts will tell your employees or service providers exactly what to say, and how to say it. Be sure to emphasize the importance of an even, friendly tone and solution-oriented, non-emotional responses to disgruntled customer calls. This is just another way for you to remove the guesswork by creating automated systems within your business.

EMAIL SYSTEMS, ETIQUETTE, and MARKETING

In today's day and age, you'd be hard-pressed to find anyone who doesn't conduct some form of business through email. Not only is email a common and professional form of communication both within your internal team and between your team and outside actors, but it is also a key element of a solid marketing plan for your business. Before we get into anything else, the first step is to find yourself a great email service provider.

All email systems or service providers are not created equal. When choosing a provider, here are some of the most important things to look for: easy email-building, subscription forms or email captures, analytics and reporting services, mobile app compatibility, 24/7 customer support, affordable or free plans. Some of the best free email service providers are Gmail, Outlook, and Yahoo Mail, but do your research to find a provider that is most compatible with your needs.

PROPER EMAIL ETIQUETTE

Email etiquette is of the utmost importance as a business owner. Every documentable form of communication is an immediate reflection on your brand and on you as a C.E.O. When communicating internally, you can sometimes be more relaxed. I frequently use shorthand, abbreviations, and incomplete subject headings when I'm emailing my own staff because we have developed a unique communication style that works for us.

When it comes to emailing anyone outside of your direct team, however, there are certain rules you must adhere to.

The first thing is to always be professional. This starts with your email address itself. Be sure to use an email handle that includes your company name – yourname@yourcompanyname.com is a fool-proof option and is much more professional than a random gmail address. Every hired employee should receive their own company email address as well, or you can simply create department addresses – support@yourcompanyname.com, hr@yourcompanyname.com, etc. Next, always have a proper email signature including your name, title, contact phone number, and workplace address, if you have a physical location.

When it comes to the body of your emails, address people by their full names – not a nickname – and please, be sure to spell them correctly! A misspelled name in an email shows a lack of attention to detail and is often a slap in the face to the recipient. Secondly, proofread all of your emails for typos and grammatical errors. There are even programs you can install on your computer to automatically do a check for you before any emails are sent. Next, have a proper email signature. Your signature should include your name, title, business phone number, and business address. You may also want to include your business tagline or logo for brand consistency.

Another important aspect of strong email etiquette is brevity. Emails should be informative, not entertaining – especially when they're addressed to partners, retailers, or other

ROCHELLE GRAHAM-CAMPBELL

professional parties. No one wants to open their inbox to find a novel. Condense your email content as much as possible while maintaining your main points, and be sure to include paragraph breaks or bullet points for easy digestion. A quick and clear email shows that you respect the recipient's time. Finally, make sure all emails include a clear and concise subject line. Your email subject should make the purpose of your email very clear, and should also indicate whether the contents are of urgent priority.

EMAIL MARKETING

More old-fashioned than its millennial cousin, social media marketing, email marketing is too often overlooked or under-prioritized by budding entrepreneurs. The truth is that while great for generating buzz and building community, social media is not the most reliable marketing tool. We've all experienced the dreaded social media blackouts where our favorite apps just stop working for hours. Not only is this annoying, it's a hindrance to your revenue stream. Think about it, if you've only bothered to build your marketing through social media, you're losing out on money every time apps malfunction or there's a change in the algorithm that may not work in your favor. Furthermore, we have to be smart and consider the possibility that these apps won't be around forever. Remember MySpace or Vine? If a social platform shuts down, you want to have an ongoing way to market to existing customers and attract more business. This is where email marketing comes in.

394

When people visit your website, there should be a pop-up of some kind that asks people to sign up for your email newsletter. You can also add an auto-opt in option, which will automatically sign shoppers up for your email listserv upon checkout. Keep in mind that by law, you must get permission to add someone to your email listserv. If your site uses an auto-opt in feature, make sure that your emails clearly state the option to manually opt out or unsubscribe from unwanted emails. Even so, you should always encourage people to sign up. When customers make a purchase, your purchase confirmation email should also include the option to subscribe for more emails on upcoming launches, deals, and sales. The more often prospective customers are prompted, the more likely they are to actually sign up. The moment someone signs up for your email list, they should automatically receive some sort of initial email that welcomes them into your community and then sends them into a funnel of two or three other emails which will be sent to them over a set time period. These emails are crucial for setting the tone of your company-customer relationship, and helping customers to get to know your brand beyond their first purchase. You may even include some sort of welcome offer like a "thank you" discount for their next purchase. Then, as your carefully crafted emails come in, they may be prompted to click through to your website and continue shopping. Email marketing equals more money in your pocket. Take advantage!

Once you've accrued a strong listserv, don't waste it! Some people go through all the effort of getting people on their email list, only to let them sit there collecting cobwebs from lack of use. You always want to make sure that you are actually managing and using your lists by coming up with an email marketing calendar or schedule. Like with your content and social media marketing, email marketing should be planned out to align with current promotions and campaigns. Next, schedule in a time to periodically scrub your email listserv. This is when you go through your list and have your email server remove all of the bounced and rejected emails. This is important for controlling costs, as many servers will charge you based on the number of people you have in your listserv. To avoid unnecessary costs, you want to ensure that you only include actively engaged email addresses. Your server can check for faulty email addresses or unopened emails. If someone hasn't opened your emails in a year, they're probably not interested. You should scrub them off of your listserv to make room for other people who actually want to engage with your brand and read your emails. Finally, some people are so eager for sales that they fall into the trap of buying email lists. You never ever want to do that. Not only is it illegal to add people to your email listserv without their permission, but it's plain old bad for business. You want to come by your audience organically and ethically – that's how you make sure you're building a loyal consumer base.

As for email marketing services, some of the most popular and effective options are Mailchimp, Constant Contact, and Sendgrid. If you are trying to get more specific with your email marketing, then look into something like Klaviyo or ActiveCampaign. My company uses Klaviyo, a new type of email marketing system that offers marketing automation and segmentation. This will actually help you to segment or group your customers by likes and dislikes, needs, interests, etc., helping you to send more targeted, effective emails. The right email marketing service will help you do everything from creating beautiful, branded emails, to designing landing pages with clear CTAs, and building digital ads. Choose wisely!

BUSINESS APPS

In keeping with the theme of organization, business apps will also help you save time and energy while boosting the efficiency of your operations. I've already introduced you to Asana back in chapter six – the online project management tool that saves my life on a daily basis. Another app I love is TurboScan, which allows you to turn any physical paper into a digital document accessible from your phone or tablet! Expensify is great for receipt tracking and expense management. OfferUp is a mobile app that lets you buy and sell merchandise from local users at the click of a button. Business Card Reader (BCR) Pro allows you to import contact information from a business card directly into your phone contacts – great for easy networking! Finally, Google Calendar is one of my tried-and-true, favorite business apps for time and schedule management. There are a million and one awesome apps out there designed specifically to make life easier for entrepreneurs. Do your research and see which apps can help you and your company. Remember, the name of the game is efficiency and ease. We want to automate our systems and cut out as many steps as possible.

TRACKING RENEWALS

Your company's operations will only be as successful as your organization. A major pro-tip is to keep running documents containing all of your renewal information. For even more precision, you may find it helpful to have separate tracking documents for each department (managed by the department head). These documents can be built out as simple Excel sheets, and will include everything from your business permits and licenses and their expiration dates, to your contract agreements with dates of termination. Certifications, subscriptions, inventory units, registrations, etc. This should all be carefully monitored so that you don't have any unplanned cancelations or expirations sneaking up on you. For example, imagine you're in the middle of a huge sale season, and your website domain expires because no one knew it was time to renew! A simple oversight like this could be death to a new business just getting off the ground. Renewal documents will save you these unimaginable headaches. For Alikay Naturals, our excel document lists all of our accounts and subscriptions, the credit card information, password, and username that was used to make the account, and the dates of renewal. Of course, these documents should only be shared with trusted employees on a need-to-know basis.

DON'T BE A WANTPRENEUR!

Don't live your entire life being a wantpreneur. A wantpreneur is someone who talks constantly about what they want to do… one day. They want to have this, they want to do that, they want to create that product, they want to offer that service, they want to open that business, but sadly, they never do. The difference between a wantpreneur and an entrepreneur is action. An entrepreneur is the person who went for it – fail or fly!

I know I've just left you with a lifetime's worth of information and it's very easy to get overwhelmed. I totally understand. I want you to read my next words and then read them again: *you can do this.* As long as you keep taking action, as long as you keep putting one uncertain, unsteady foot in front of the other, you will make it. It won't happen overnight. It won't happen when you want it to. It won't happen just because you've read this book. It will happen because you won't stop until you *make* it happen. And if you should ever doubt yourself, open this book. Call on your Fairy Godmother. Now, go out there and make magic.

definitions
every C.E.O should know

Know. Like. Trust

KLT factor. The foundation necessary to establish a rapport with a potential business partner.

Production Capacity

Volume of products that can be generated by a production plant or enterprise in a given period by using current resources.
Source: Oxford Dictionary

Systems

A set of principles or procedures according to which something is done; an organized scheme or method.
Source: Wikipedia

Prototype

A first, typical or preliminary model of something, especially a machine, from which other forms are developed or copied.
Source: Oxford Dictionary

Lead Time

The time between the initiation and completion of a production process.
Source: Oxford Dictionary

Bandwidth

The energy or mental capacity required to deal with a situation.
Source: Oxford Dictionary

Perpetuity

A bond or other security with no fixed maturity date.
Source: Oxford Dictionary

90 Days to C.E.O Plan

suppliers & vendors

- ☐ FIND VENDORS
- ☐ LEAD TIMES, PRICE BREAKS, & PAYMENT TERMS
- ☐ BUILD RELATIONSHIPS
- ☐ TRUCK & FREIGHT SHIPPERS

building your team

- ☐ CREATING A JOB DESCRIPTION
- ☐ LISTING AVAILABLE POSITIONS
- ☐ INTERVIEWING & RESUME REVIEWING TIPS
- ☐ HIRING
- ☐ EMPLOYEE MANAGEMENT
- ☐ WORKING WITH FAMILY
- ☐ LABOR LAWS
- ☐ EMPLOYEES VS. CONTRACTORS
- ☐ EMPLOYER/EMPLOYEE IMPORTANT DOCUMENTS & REGISTRATIONS
- ☐ EMPLOYEE HANDBOOK
- ☐ PAYMENT & PAYROLL TAXES
- ☐ FIRING & TERMINATION PROCESS

inventory management

- ☐ LINE UP SUPPLIERS AND SERVICE PROVIDERS

user experience

- ☐ WEBSITE FUNCTIONALITY
- ☐ SOCIAL MEDIA MANAGEMENT
- ☐ IN-PERSON EVENTS

customer service

- ☐ REGISTER A DEDICATED BUSINESS PHONE LINE
- ☐ POLICIES, PROCEDURE, & FAQS
- ☐ ACCEPTING PAYMENT
- ☐ EMAIL SYSTEMS
- ☐ BUSINESS APPS & TOOLS
- ☐ TRACK RENEWALS
- ☐ CREATE EMAIL SYSTEMS

VISIT RGBUSINESSUNIVERSITY.COM/90DAYRESOURCES

401

90 Days to C.E.O Plan

human resources

- [ ] CREATE JOB DESCRIPTIONS
- [ ] LIST AVAILABLE POSITIONS
- [ ] CREATE AN EMPLOYEE HANDBOOK
- [ ] REVIEW EMPLOYER RESPONSIBILITIES
- [ ] GET WORKERS COMPENSATION
- [ ] UNDERSTAND LABOR LAWS
- [ ] CHOOSE PAYROLL SERVICE
- [ ] HIRE OR SECURE IT (TECH SUPPORT)

VISIT RGBUSINESSUNIVERSITY.COM/90DAYRESOURCES

THANK YOU

"This book is dedicated to everyone who may not have come from much but who has the ambition to make a better life for themselves."

- Rochelle Graham-Campbell

I dedicate this book to my family, who are my rock, my support system, and my biggest cheerleaders in life. Thank you to my mother, Marlene Moulton, for being such a strong, intelligent, and fabulous woman, and for teaching me how to be the same. Thank you to Richard Moulton, my stepfather, for choosing me as your daughter and for teaching me that I am a light. Thank you to both of you for instilling in me as a child that I can be anything in this world as long as I work for it and do my best. That advice has gotten me far.

Thank you to my grandparents, Veda and Roy Smith, for being my biggest cheerleaders from the day that I was born, and for the sacrifices that you have made in your lives for me to have the life that I have today. I will always love you in this life and the next. Thank you for always believing in me and loving me.

To my grandparents, Elsa "Yaya" Gordon and Ralstan Gordon — thank you for always being there for me and showing up for me when I need you; loving me, now and always. I am so grateful to you both — I love you.

To my amazing husband, Demond Campbell — you see in me parts that the world never sees, so thank you for loving me through it all and being by my side through this journey called life. Thanks for always protecting me and having my back. I love you so much. Growing up and growing old with you is one of the best decisions of my life. We got this baby!

Thanks to my wonderful handsome son, Landon Levi. I see so much of myself in you and that brings me joy. You are so creative, expressive, outspoken, thoughtful, loving, and talented. You truly are an amazing human being and don't ever let the world tell you otherwise. You aren't extra or too much. Always be yourself, the world will have to adjust. I am so honored to be your mother. I already see glimpses of entrepreneurship in you at the age of seven. I can't wait to see what you do in this world. Thank you for always being so understanding when mommy has to take business trips because you know the goals that we have. We sit and talk about our big dreams together and you know everything that I do is for you and our family. I love you so very much, you are my heart.

You and your sister are my legacy and mommy is going to make you proud.

Thank you to my little spark of joy, Serenity Sapphire. You are so very special and although you are not even two yet, I see so much potential in your eyes and independence in your personality. Watching you grow has really taught me to cherish every single day of life, and your hugs, smiles, and cute giggles after a long hard day make all of it totally worth it. You are going to rule the world, baby girl, and I'm going to be there to cheer you on just like you're always randomly clapping and singing to cheer me on too. Remember that you are more than enough and don't ever let the world tell you otherwise. I love you very much.

A final thank you to all of my supporters. You all are so amazing; you're my online or distant family in my head. No matter where on my journey you started with me — whether in the bathroom at age twenty-one recording YouTube videos, buying my handmade ringleader earrings from Nyamani Chic, buying my Alikay Naturals products for yourself and family, coming to the events that I host, purchasing courses from Rochelle Graham Business University™, giving me hugs when you meet me for the first time, crying tears of joy, expressing words of gratitude and love in person or on social media, supporting me by telling your friends and family about my company, taking photos of yourself with Alikay Naturals products when you spot them in a store and sending them to me — It all makes me so proud because you know that a win for me is a win for all of us! So, for everything you do, I just want to say thank you. I am so appreciative of you for supporting my dreams all of these years and thank you for being on this ride with me for the next chapter of life to come.

God bless you all!

-Rochelle Alikay Graham-Campbell

CPSIA information can be obtained
at www.ICGtesting.com
Printed in the USA
LVHW080330260720
661549LV00009B/430